SEA FEVER

SEA FEVER

A BRITISH MARITIME MISCELLANY

MEG CLOTHIER AND CHRIS CLOTHIER

P

PROFILE BOOKS

First published in Great Britain in 2021 by
PROFILE BOOKS LTD
29 Cloth Fair
London EC1A 7JQ
www.profilebooks.com

The author and publisher wish to thank the following for permission
to reproduce: 'Basking Shark' by Norman MacCaig. Reproduced
with permission of Birlinn Limited through PLSclear; and 'Sea
Fever' by John Masefield. With permission of The Society of Authors
as the Literary Representative of the Estate of John Masefield.

1 3 5 7 9 10 8 6 4 2

Designed in Gill Sans & Garamond Premier Pro
by James Alexander at Jade Design
Printed and bound in Great Britain by Clays Ltd, Elcograf S.p.A.

A CIP catalogue record for this book is available from the British Library.

ISBN 978 1 78816 1619
eISBN 978 1 78283 4977

FSC
www.fsc.org
MIX
Paper from
responsible sources
FSC® C018072

For

Rowan
Bruno
Eira
Seren

INTRODUCTION

*Whenever I find myself growing grim about the mouth; whenever
it is a damp, drizzly November in my soul; whenever I find myself
involuntarily pausing before coffin warehouses, and bringing up the
rear of every funeral I meet ... then, I account it high time to get to sea
as soon as I can.*
Herman Melville, *Moby-Dick*

The sea. A place to live and work, a place to see and be seen.
A place to run risks, a place to run away from it all. The sea
is Rule Britannia – and two fingers up to authority. The sea
is our bulwark, our barricade. Our playground, our larder.
It is the songs and poems that drum deep in our collective consciousness. It is our island's joint inheritance, made
as much from stories as sediment and saltwater. The sea is
where we can breathe deep, fling our arms wide and look
outwards to friendship, opportunity and adventure.

Sea Fever tries – personally, partially – to capture a
little of this sundry spirit, hoping to divert you whenever
southwesterly 5 to 6, rain or showers, moderate becoming poor
disrupts your better-laid plans. But once the cold front
passes and the barometer rises, please jettison us without
a backwards glance.

The sea will be calling.

THE SHIPPING FORECAST

There is no more quintessentially British sound than the shipping forecast. For some, it's a lullaby at the end of a long day. For others, it's more important than the news. For sailors stuck on shore it elicits varied emotions. Pity (*Irish Sea, northeasterly 6, wintry showers, poor*), jealousy (*Portland, Plymouth, west 3 or 4, mainly fair, good*) or outright fear (*Rockall, southwesterly gale 8, becoming northwesterly storm 10 later, rain and showers, poor, occasionally very poor*). It even stars in its very own Britpop classic.*

At sea aboard a small boat, once you've lost phone signal, it takes on a quasi-religious quality: disembodied words, handed down to a (furiously scribbling) skipper, and woe betide the lowly crew member who interrupts with a query about the course.

However you listen to it, the shipping forecast is a sober reminder that we are all islanders perched on a scrap of land in the North Atlantic, at the mercy of whatever sea and sky may throw at us.

It is issued by the Met Office four times a day at roughly 11 p.m., 5 a.m., 11 a.m. and 5 p.m., and transmitted on BBC Radio 4 at 0048, 0520, 1201 and 1754. Each forecast covers the twenty-four hours from midnight, 6 a.m., noon and 6 p.m. respectively.

About four minutes and 350 words long, it follows a strict format familiar to loyal listeners. First come gale warnings, if there are any, followed by a general synopsis

....

* Thank you, Blur: who doesn't want to go around the Bay of Biscay and be back in time for tea?

giving a rough overview of what's going on weather-wise, including the position of areas of *high and low pressure,* measured in *millibars (mb).* For example:

> Now the shipping forecast issued by the Met Office on behalf of the Maritime and Coastguard Agency at 0015 on Thursday the 19th of April. There are warnings of gales in Trafalgar, Hebrides, Fair Isle, Faeroes and Southeast Iceland. The general synopsis at 1800: high, Germany, 1032, slow moving with little change, new low moving rather quickly north, expected 300 miles east of Iceland 995 by 1800 Thursday.

Next the forecast tackles each of the thirty-one forecast areas surrounding the British Isles, starting with the coast of Norway, working clockwise south through the North Sea, west along the Channel, followed by an excursion to northern Spain, and then back up to finish off in Iceland.

The exact order is: Viking, North Utsire, South Utsire, Forties, Cromarty, Forth, Tyne, Dogger, Fisher, German Bight, Humber, Thames, Dover, Wight, Portland, Plymouth, Biscay, Trafalgar,* FitzRoy,** Sole, Lundy, Fastnet, Irish Sea, Shannon, Rockall, Malin, Hebrides, Bailey, Fair Isle, Faeroes, Southeast Iceland.

Each area forecast is broken down into three parts: wind speed and direction (if the wind is expected to be force 8 or above on the Beaufort scale, it is given its full title: *gale 8,*

....

* Trafalgar features only in the 0048 version of the forecast.
** FitzRoy, named after Vice-Admiral Robert FitzRoy, captain of HMS *Beagle,* and founder of what became the Met Office, only came into being in 2002. Previously it was called Finisterre (Latin for *the end of the earth*) after a cape in northwest Spain, but the name was changed to avoid confusion with a Spanish forecast area.

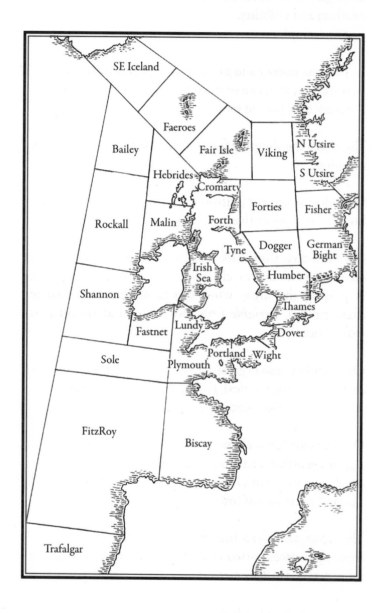

severe gale 9, storm 10, violent storm 11, hurricane force 12);
weather; and visibility.

For example:

> Trafalgar, easterly 6 to gale 8 in far southeast otherwise
> northerly 5 to 7; rain or showers in west; moderate or good,
> occasionally poor in west

The words the shipping forecast uses all have a very specific
meaning:

On gales: *imminent* (within six hours), *soon* (six to twelve
hours), *later* (more than twelve hours away)

On wind direction: *backing* (wind moves anti-clockwise),
veering (wind moves clockwise), *cyclonic* (a depression
is passing the area; wind direction likely to change
dramatically), *variable* ('no idea really, but nothing to
worry about')

On visibility: *good* (greater than 5 nautical miles), *moderate* (2 to 5 nautical miles), *poor* (1,000 m to 2 nautical miles,
very poor (less than 1,000 m)

On sea state: * *smooth* (waves less than 0.5 m), *slight* (0.5 to
1.25 m), *moderate* (1.25 to 2.5 m), *rough* (2.5 to 4.0 m), *very
rough* (4.0 to 6.0 m), high (6.0 to 9.0 m), *very high* (9.0 to
14.0 m), *phenomenal* (more than 14.0 m)

The 0048 and 0520 broadcasts are followed by reports
from up to twenty-two coastal stations (as well as by the
more detailed *inshore waters forecast*), which give you actual

....

* Available if you're reading the shipping forecast online.

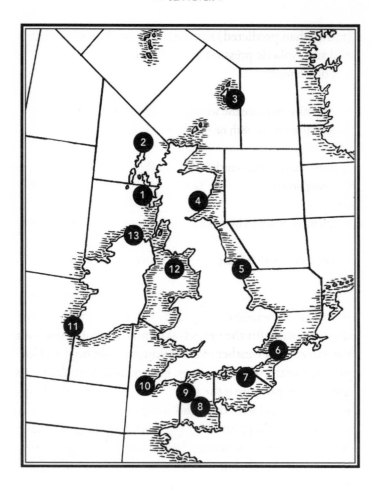

1. Tiree
2. Stornaway
3. Lerwick
4. Leuchars
5. Bridlington
6. Sandettie Light Vessel
7. Greenwich Light Vessel
8. Jersey
9. Channel Light Vessel
10. Scilly
11. Valentia
12. Ronaldsway
13. Malin Head

(rather than predicted) information about wind, visibility and atmospheric pressure around Britain.

For example:

And now here are the weather reports from coastal stations for 2300 on the 18th of April.

Tiree Automatic, southeast by south 6, haze, 4 miles, 1013, rising slowly

Stornoway, south by west 6, 7 miles, 1011, falling more slowly

Lerwick, south by east 4, recent fog, 2 miles, 1020, falling slowly

If you are a meteorological aficionado, you can combine these reports with the general synopsis to create your own *synoptic chart*, a weather map marking areas of high and low pressure, with concentric lines, known as *isobars*, drawn to show where pressure is the same. This (given practice) helps you understand why the wind has got up so dramatically – or why it's disappeared altogether. Of course, nowadays you can summon a synoptic chart to your phone with a few jabs of your thumb, but sometimes it's nice to do things the hard way.

ORIGINS OF SHIPPING FORECAST AREA NAMES

Towns	Islands or near islands	Estuaries	Fishing banks	Seas, bays and bights	Rocky islets	Capes and headlands	People
Cromarty	North Utsire	Forth	Viking	German Bight	Fastnet	Trafalgar	FitzRoy
Dover	South Utsire	Tyne	Forties	Biscay	Rockall	Malin	
Plymouth	Wight	Humber	Dogger	Irish Sea			
	Portland	Thames	Fisher				
	Lundy	Shannon	Sole				
	Hebrides		Bailey				
	Fair Isle						
	Faeroes						
	Southeast Iceland						

SEASICKNESS

Seasickness – so tightly enmeshed with seafaring that the ancient Greek word for ship, *naus*, huddles inside our word *nausea* – is capricious. Treat it with bravado, and it will haunt you. Show it respect, and it might spare you. The following advice should work just as well whether you're mackerel fishing, whale-spotting or grimacing on a lumpy cross-Channel ferry.

LAND AHOY

'Homesickness is a bit like seasickness.' Roald Dahl is spot on. 'You don't know how awful it is till you get it, and when you do, it hits you right in the top of the stomach and you want to die. The only comfort is that both homesickness and seasickness are instantly curable. The first goes away the moment you walk out of the school grounds and the second is forgotten as soon as the ship enters port.'

In other words, however horrible seasickness feels at the time, it *will* end.

APPEARANCES CAN BE DECEIVING

The forecast might promise *variable 1 to 3*. From the dock-side the sea might look sedate. But beware: out past the harbour-mouth, out past the headland, the swell from a faraway storm may be doing uneasy battle with the chop whipped up by a sea breeze.

DON'T EAT

For an hour before you put to sea, shun coffee, Marmite and battered fish. Do not give seasickness ammunition. If you're likely to be away from land long enough that you can't avoid eating, turn first to the sacred quintet: Ginger Nuts, salt & vinegar crisps, Ritz crackers (accept no alternatives), lemon sherbets and Coke.

DON'T DRINK (ALCOHOL)

And never *ever* put to sea on a hangover. Seasickness shares the morning-after's creeping existential dread, and nobody wants to double down on that.

DON'T SMOKE

In Rudyard Kipling's *Captains Courageous*, poor-little-rich-boy Harvey is so keen to prove he doesn't get sick that he *accepts a cigar*. He staggers on deck: 'There he doubled up in limp agony, for the Wheeling "stogie" joined with the surge and jar of the screw to sieve out his soul.' In fact, he's so sick that he *falls overboard*, which is a cautionary tale if ever there was one.

MAYBE TAKE DRUGS

Magic cordial, originally deployed on the battlefield in *The Lion, the Witch and the Wardrobe*, is the only medication that quells seasickness instantly. Away from Narnia, people swear by various pills, but they can make you very drowsy. A cinnarizine haze is admittedly quite pleasant, but not if you have to look after anyone other than yourself.

KEEP THE WIND ON YOUR FACE

Swaddle yourself in as many layers as possible (seasickness often rides on cold's coat-tails) and stay on deck. If you're travelling overnight, only go down below once you're so tired and wind-blasted that you'll fall asleep the moment you lie down. Better still, pass out on deck. While you're asleep, you often seem to synch with the sea, meaning you may awake the proud owner of a pair of sea legs.

MAKE LIKE NELSON

The vice-admiral wrote: 'I am ill every time it blows hard and nothing but my enthusiastic love for the profession keeps me one hour at sea.'

That's the real secret. Technically, seasickness is an imbalance of the inner ear, but this physical upset is compounded by helplessness. To combat this, and thereby recover control of your stomach, assume as much responsibility as your skills allow: ask to keep watch, to hold a rod, even better to steer. *Moby-Dick*'s narrator, in fact, tells us he never goes to sea as a passenger, because *passengers get seasick.*

This might seem hard to apply on a ferry, but make-believe works almost as well: stand near the bow, stand tall, look forwards, scan the horizon for enemy ships, breathe deeply and (under your breath) issue the command to *beat to quarters.*

WHEN ALL ELSE FAILS

Be sick to *leeward.*

AND FINALLY

If you ever find yourself pregnant, morning sickness* will have a pleasing familiarity to it. It's just like seasickness, but without the fresh air and lovely views.

....
* *Mal de mère?*

SEASIDE RESORTS

The seaside has always existed as a *place*, but it wasn't until 250 years ago that we began to go there for *pleasure*. Until then, the beach was where you launched a fishing boat; the coast was where you mustered an army. The sea might be fruitful, but it was never your friend. What changed? To begin with, it was a health fad: Richard Russell, an eighteenth-century physician, was one of the chief evangelists of *sea bathing*, which, when combined with *sea drinking*, was touted as a radical cure for pretty much everything. His masterwork, *A Dissertation on the Use of Sea Water in the Diseases of the Glands*, gave proof after proof of its efficacy:

> A girl from London, about twelve years of age, had her eyelids, nose and upper lip infested with a swelling and redness. Besides the glands of her neck, between her ears and clavicles, were swelled and hard. She had taken many medicines according to the advice of the London physicians, and at length was brought down to Southampton. I directed her to leave off all remedies and to stick to bathing in the sea water, to drinking it and to hot embrocations.

As with many miracle cures, Russell's method was suspiciously comprehensive, applicable to: head pains, gonorrhoea, excoriated breasts, fever (of the hectic variety), spasms and convulsions, wet *and* dry leprosy, immoderate flux of the menses *and* obstruction of the menses. Perhaps he'd simply lit upon the abiding truth that everyone feels a lot better after a day by the sea.

Russell's ideal beach, however, has stood the test of time rather better than his medicine. A beach, he wrote, should be 'clean and neat, at some distance from the opening of a river that the water may be as highly loaded with sea salt, and the other riches of the ocean, as possible, and not weakened by the mixing of fresh water with its waves. In the next place, one would choose the shore to be sandy and flat for the convenience of going into the sea in a bathing chariot. And lastly, that the sea shore should be bounded by lively cliffs and downs to add to the cheerfulness of the place.'

Bathing chariots (or machines) were an essential feature of the seaside for generations, fading away only with the last Victorians. The picaresque (i.e. unreadable) novels of Tobias Smollett help us imagine how they would have looked in an early beach resort. Here he is at Scarborough:

> You have never seen one of these machines. Imagine to yourself a small, snug, wooden chamber, fixed upon a wheel-carriage, having a door at each end, and on each side a little window above, a bench below.
>
> The bather, ascending into this apartment by wooden steps, shuts himself in, and begins to undress, while the attendant yokes a horse to the end next the sea, and draws the carriage forwards, till the surface of the water is on a level with the floor of the dressing-room, then he moves and fixes the horse to the other end.
>
> The person within being stripped, opens the door to the sea-ward, where he finds the guide ready, and plunges headlong into the water.

Women were not excluded – it has always been entirely proper for a lady to worry about her health. Female bathing attendants were on hand, as were voluminous flannel bathing suits, plus screens extending seawards from the bathing machines, the better to protect one's modesty.

Scarborough, Smollett observed, was a 'paltry' town but '*romantic*', a category that gained currency at a rate of knots as the eighteenth century drew to a close.

For a Tudor, staring down at the sea from a cliff's edge was terrifying. Here's Edgar in *King Lear*: 'How fearful / And dizzy 'tis, to cast one's eyes so low! ... I'll look no more; / Lest my brain turn, and the deficient sight / Topple down headlong.' Two hundred years later that dizziness was recast as awe, and untamed landscapes were no longer terrifying, but a desirable (and modish) route to the sublime. For Lord Byron, the romantic *par excellence*, there was *rapture* on a lonely shore, *music* in the deep sea's roar; he *wantoned* in breakers, revelling in a *pleasing fear*.

Thanks to such enthusiasm, our shores were destined to become a lot less lonely, especially after George IV-to-be, the playboy heir to the throne, started work in the 1780s on the Royal Pavilion, his opulent pied-à-terre in Brighton. Soon anyone who was anyone wanted to exclaim Byronically over Britain's coast. Witness good Fanny Price and bad Henry Crawford, mid-rapture, in Jane Austen's *Mansfield Park*:

> ... everything looked so beautiful under the influence of such a sky, the effects of the shadows pursuing each other on the ships at Spithead and the island beyond, with the ever-varying hues of the sea, now at high water, dancing in its glee and dashing against the ramparts with so fine a sound ...

Not everyone was there for the view, however. If you were very, *very* bad, like Austen's arch-flirt Lydia Bennett, the seaside thronged with a different sort of danger: officers.*

'They are going to be encamped near Brighton,' she squeals in *Pride and Prejudice*, 'and I do so want papa to take us all there for the summer! It would be such a delicious scheme; and I dare say would hardly cost anything at all. Mamma would like to go too of all things! Only think what a miserable summer else we shall have!'

She even tries the health angle – 'a little sea-bathing would set me up for ever' – but we all know her heart is set on that other great seaside tradition: the *dirty weekend*. She gets her wish and arrives in Brighton, only to lose her head and elope with the *wicked* George Wickham.

Austen's final, sadly unfinished, novel also unfolds in an (embryonic) resort. Mr Parker, who has drunk deep from the well of Richard Russell, plans to turn Sanditon, 'a quiet village of no pretensions', into a 'small, fashionable bathing place'. He reckons it's a sure thing: fine pure sea breeze, fine hard sand, deep water but ten yards from the shore, no mud, no weeds, no slimy rocks.

Parker's aim is to attract 'regular, steady, private families of thorough gentility and character', perhaps an Emma Knightley née Woodhouse, displaying the sort of *snobisme* with which resorts differentiate themselves to this day.

Austen's characters were, of course, the one per cent of the age. Two things needed to arrive before the seaside could be enjoyed by everybody else: *railways* and *paid holidays*.

Trains reached Great Yarmouth in 1844, Scarborough in 1845, Blackpool in 1846 and Torquay in 1848, with holidaymakers often heading to their nearest stretch of

....

* What was catnip to Lydia, was anathema to John Keats: 'On the road from Cowes to Newport I saw some extensive Barracks, which disgusted me extremely with Government for placing such a Nest of Debauchery in so beautiful a place.'

coast: the East Midlands went to Skegness; the West Midlands to North Wales; Lancashire to Blackpool; Yorkshire to Scarborough; Bristol to Weston-super-Mare; and London to Southend. In 1835, 117,000 visitors came to Brighton. Come Easter Monday 1862, 132,000 arrived in a single day.

Proper paid holidays didn't exist until the twentieth century, so people relied on Sundays and (from 1871) bank holidays to get to the seaside, cramming the big-city stations. Some resorts – Bournemouth for example – actually *banned* Sunday trains, fancying themselves too posh for that sort of thing, but more down-to-earth resorts welcomed families on mass outings (often organised by paternalistic factory owners or inner-city charities) with open arms.

Above all, the Victorian seaside was fun. As well as food and drink of every stripe, there were photographers and musicians, fortune-tellers and phrenologists, conjurers and ventriloquists. You could trick your little son out in a cute sailor suit, just like the Queen had done. You could watch a Punch and Judy show or ride a donkey. You could stroll down one of the piers that were popping up all round the country. Ballrooms and pleasure gardens, fairgrounds and aquariums. It was a non-stop carousel of gaudy fun ... unless you were George and Weedon Grossmith's comic masterpiece Mr Pooter.

Poor Mr Pooter. Respectable, self-conscious, suburban, lower middle class, for him the summer holiday was a social minefield, as he confides in *The Diary of a Nobody*:

> I said to Carrie: 'I don't think we can do better than "Good old Broadstairs."' Carrie not only, to my astonishment, raised an objection to Broadstairs, for the first time; but begged me not to use the expression, 'Good old'.

Perhaps his wife was dreaming of something grander than Mrs Beck's apartments at Harbour View Terrace? Nevertheless, she relents, and Pooter sets about dandifying his holiday wardrobe:

> Ordered a new pair of trousers at Edwards's, and told them not to cut them so loose over the boot; the last pair being so loose and also tight at the knee, they looked like a sailor's, and I heard Pitt, that objectionable youth at the office, call out 'Hornpipe' as I passed his desk … I bought a capital hat for hot weather at the seaside. I don't know what it is called, but it is the shape of the helmet worn in India, only made of straw.

Once at Broadstairs, his son Lupin is so mortified by his father's get-up that he 'positively refused to walk down the Parade' with him. The week unfolds like every strained family holiday. Rain. Lupin sneaks out to 'common' sorts of entertainment. An attempt at sailing; Lupin mocks. Rain. Billiards; Pooter disapproves. Cloud. Awkward parlour games with friends from London. Home sweet home again.

At the close of the Victorian era, the editor of a collection of seaside cartoons, originally published in *Punch* magazine (which first serialised Mr Pooter's diary) wrote:

> It is … curious to notice how little seaside customs, amusements, troubles and delights, have varied in the last half-century. Landladies are at the end what they were at the beginning; the same old type of bathing-machine is still in use; our forefathers and their womenfolk in the days when Mr Punch was young behaved themselves by 'the silver sea' just as their children's children do to-day. Nothing has changed, except that the most select of seaside places is no

longer so select as it was in the pre-railway days, and that the wealthier classes, preferring the attractions of Continental resorts, are less in evidence at our own watering-places.

The sort of people who populated Jane Austen's novels had indeed hightailed it for the French Riviera, but abroad remained inaccessible to everyone else until well after the Second World War. This allowed the British seaside to prosper, while also adopting freer, easier, French-er ways. Adieu bathing machines; hello bronzed glamour, backed up by the medical establishment, for whom the sun's rays were an ally in the fight against tuberculosis and rickets.

Lidos – the stylish outdoor pools named after Venice's prestigious bathing beach – were the apotheosis of this new cult of youth and health. According to John K. Walton, the *sine qua non* of the seaside's social historians, these classics of art deco architecture offered 'frolic, sport, scope for display of physical pride and prowess and (the other side of the coin) acceptable voyeurism'. The modern seaside had arrived.

Some might now, Pooter-like, turn up their noses at Butlin's holiday camps, but when they were launched at the end of the 1930s, they tapped into this new relaxed aesthetic, complete with palm trees, tubular steel furniture and lots and lots of chrome. Butlin's freed the holiday-maker, soon to be armed with a week's paid holiday a year, from the tyranny of the seaside landlady, offering instead reliable, egalitarian fun: wrestling, waterslides, and once Britain really started to let its hair down, knobbly-knee competitions and kids' discos.

But towards the end of the century, a new era of individualism made the Redcoats' communal fun feel excruciatingly passé, ripe for satire in the TV series *Hi-de-Hi!* After all, who'd go to Barry Island now the Med was within reach?

For back in 1950, Horizon Holidays had launched an all-inclusive trip to Corsica for £32 10s: a flight (no laborious journey by boat and train), plus tents on the beach, 'delicious meat-filled meals' and as much local wine as you could put away. The first eleven customers, who flew from Gatwick in a noisy, uncomfortable Dakota DC-3, were trailblazers for the package holiday boom. Like Cliff Richards in *Summer Holiday*, the British, with money in their pockets thanks to post-war economic growth, were ready to wave their rainy summers goodbye.

But what was good news for sales of retsina and ceramic donkeys was a terrible blow to the British seaside. In the decades that followed, its confidence and swagger drained away, all too often replaced by edginess and blight, perfect fodder for the ever-jovial Morrissey, who in the 1990s was singing about wet sand and greased tea in 'the coastal town / That they forgot to close down'.

Today, some resorts have more of a swing in their step, buoyed by big-city escapees, second-home owners and people seeking a riotous good time, but the roots of gentrification don't always run deep. Nevertheless, as we turn towards the future, let's hope that whatever the world throws at us, the seaside will be somewhere we can pack up our troubles – if only for a few hours. It's easier to feel optimistic with an ice cream in your hand and the sun on your back.

ROCK

It's like those sticks of rock: bite it all the way down, you'll still read Brighton. That's human nature. *

Rock – pink, sticky and helpfully lettered to remind you where you are – was dreamt up in the 1870s by a miner-turned-confectioner called Ben Bullock. Originally an inland delicacy, rock found its way to Blackpool and thence to national fame.

It's made from a toothsome blend of sugar and glucose syrup, heated above 130°C. When made on an industrial scale, a giant spherical boiler on four spindly legs would disgorge the finished product from its bowels. Today production tends to be more artisanal: a big pan on a big gas hob. Once cooked, it's poured onto a tray to cool slightly, after which most – but not all – is attached to a 'pulling machine', a Heath Robinson contraption which uses rotating arms to stretch, pull and aerate the sugar mix, creating a sort of white, malleable rock-dough.

....

* Graham Greene, famously, in his thriller *Brighton Rock*.

All well and good. *But how on earth do you get the tiny letters into it?*

You work fast, dying the mixture that's been set aside with food colouring and rolling it out into flat sheets. You fold these sheets into letter shapes, using the white rock-dough to fill the gaps. You place your letters, which aren't tiny at this stage, perhaps a couple of fingers across, in order to spell Blackpool or Brighton or Kiss Me Quick,* around an inner cylinder of white dough, before wrapping the whole lot in another coloured sheet. This resulting rock-sausage might be a metre long, 30 cm wide, and weigh more than 100 kg.

Finally, of course, you have to *stretch* it.

Once upon a time you might have hoisted one end to the ceiling and yanked it down by hand; nowadays spinning rollers do the hard work for you. When you've expanded your original sausage some 150-fold, it'll be thin enough for you to lop it up into dozens of little sticks. Time now to wrap it nostalgically and dispatch it to seaside shops, ready to extract children's wobbly teeth and grandparents' gold fillings.

....

* There are, naturally, tales of industrial saboteurs spelling less savoury phrases.

THE VICTORIAN SEASIDE

This sketch, published in the satirical *Punch* magazine during the reign of Queen Victoria, gives a flavour of what might have been preying on the minds of our forebears as they packed for their summer holidays: some of it familiar (rain, over-packing), some a little more recherché ...

Shall we like Pierpoint, to which favourite and healthy seaside resort we finally resolved to come, after a period of much indecision and uncertainty, and where we arrived, in heavy rain, in two cabs, with thirteen packages, on Saturday?

Shall we be comfortable at 62, Convolution Street, dining-room floor, two guineas-and-a-half a week, and all and perhaps rather more than the usual extras?

Shall we like Mrs Kittlespark?

Shall we find Kate all that a Kate ought to be?

Shall we lock everything up, or repose a noble confidence in Mrs Kittlespark and Kate?

Shall we get to know the people in the drawing-room?

Shall we subscribe to the Pier, or pay each time we go on it?

Shall we subscribe to that most accommodating Circulating Library, Pigram's, where we can exchange our books at pleasure, but not oftener than once a day?

Shall we relax our minds with the newest novels, or give our intellects a bracing course of the best standard works?

Shall we dine late or early?

Shall we call on the Denbigh Flints, who, according to the Pierpoint Pioneer, are staying at 10, Ocean Crescent?

Shall we carefully avoid the Wilkiesons, whom the same unerring guide reports at 33, Blue Lion Street?

Shall we be satisfied with our first weekly bill?

Shall we find in it any unexpected and novel extras, such as knife-cleaning, proportion of the water-rate, loan of latch-key, &c.?

Shall we get our meat at Round's, who displays the Prince of Wales's Feathers over his shop door, and plumes himself on being 'purveyor' to His Royal Highness; or at Cleaver's, who boasts of the patronage of the Hereditary Grand Duke of Seltersland?

Shall we find everything dearer here than it is at home?

Shall we be happy in our laundress?

Shall we be photographed?

Shall we, as Mrs Kittlespark has a spare bed-room, invite our Cousin Amelia Staythorp, from whom we have expectations, and who is Constance Edith Amelia's Godmother, to come down and stay a week with us?

Shall we be praiseworthily economical, and determine not to spend a single unnecessary sixpence; or shall we, as we have come to Pierpoint, enjoy ourselves to the utmost, go in for all the amusements of the place – pier, public gardens, theatre, concerts, Oceanarium, bathing, boating, fishing, driving, riding, and rinking – make excursions, be ostentatiously liberal to the Town Band, and buy everything that is offered to us on the Beach?

A month hence, shall we be glad or sorry to leave Pierpoint, and go back to Paddington?

THE ART AND SCIENCE OF SKIMMING STONES

THE STONE

A good skimmer blames his stones. Be ruthless. If the stones on offer aren't up to scratch, don't bother. But what is the right kind of stone?

1. Flat and smooth
2. As round as possible. Oval will do
3. Clean – no sand, seaweed or barnacles

4. About 1 cm thick, perhaps 2 cm if you're strong or it's windy
5. Heavier than you might think
6. Small enough to nestle between your index finger and the crook of your thumb, resting on your middle finger

THE STANCE

When you release the stone from your hand, it's important that it's close to the water. This ensures the shallow angle of first contact that is key to a good throw. You can achieve this simply by standing *in the water*, but then it's hard to take a good step forwards as you throw, which is what helps you achieve distance. Good skimmers, therefore, often stay *out of the water*, but manage a good release height by taking a long, *low* stride as they throw. Either way, stand side-on to the direction you want the stone to travel.

THE ACTION

Stand on your back foot, coil yourself up – a bit like a baseball pitcher – and then uncoil, taking a big step forward onto your front foot and throwing all in one go.

THE RELEASE

The most important part. Your forearm should be parallel to the water with the elbow leading the wrist, the wrist leading the hand, and the hand leading the index finger. You're aiming to *whip* or *flick* your wrist and hand on release, like a forehand frisbee throw.

Make sure your index finger stays in contact with the stone for as long as possible. This achieves two things. First, it gives the stone lots of spin, stabilising it as it flies through the air. Each time the stone skims, it loses some rotational energy, so the more spin, the truer it will fly, even after lots of bounces. Second, maximum stone-finger contact means more acceleration, similar to the effect achieved by a pelota player's *xistera* (a sort of long hooked glove) or by those plastic ball-throwers that make playing fetch extra fun for dogs.

This might sound counter-intuitive, but if you try too hard, if you put all your weight into it, the results are often strangely disappointing. Holding a bit back gets you a bit more.

FIRST CONTACT

If the stone makes contact with the water too close to you, the angle will be too steep. The stone will either disappear or rise sharply in an impressive first hop, followed by an unimpressive *plop* as it sinks.

If the stone makes contact too far away, the risk is that it starts to turn over in the air, makes poor contact with the water and doesn't skim very far, if at all. In this case, the first skip sometimes jags at a perfect right angle before plopping into the water. If this happens it's best to nod approvingly, giving the impression that's what you meant to do all along.

In general, you want the stone to hit the water three to four metres in front of you. This distance, combined with the height at which you release the stone, determines the angle at which it enters the water. There's been a surprising amount of scientific – and some less scientific – research into this, and the conclusion is that 20 degrees is best.

THE CONDITIONS

The ideal is no wind and flat water. If there's a breeze, skim downwind. If there's tide or current, throw with the flow. Of the two, wind (and the accompanying wavelets) has more impact.

CHILDREN

Just because skimming stones sounds simple, doesn't mean it's easy. Small children are rubbish at it. Don't bother trying to teach them before the age of seven.

Having children in tow, however, needn't diminish your skimming pleasure. Challenge them to find the perfect stone, allowing you to focus on the job in hand – skimming – while your minions scour the beach. Keep them interested by telling them how well their stones are doing. 'Oh, I can never find any that good! Oh, that really was the best stone ever!'

When that starts to pall, fall back on the great stalwart: who can make the biggest splash?

COMPETITIVE SKIMMING

Inevitably, there are stone-skimming championships. Some are won by distance. Some are won by number of bounces. Much as we endorse anyone's dedication to their craft, we fear they're missing the point of skimming entirely.

BRITISH WEATHER

*Caelum crebris imbribus ac nebulis foedum.**

To understand our British weather in all its wet, windy and occasionally bewitching glory, we must first take a diversion and travel south to the equator: ultimately, all weather

....

* 'Their sky is obscured by continual rain and cloud.' The Roman historian Tacitus's verdict on our weather.

derives from the sun, and the equator is where the sun shines the most.

The sun heats the air and the hot air rises, leaving behind a 'gap' or area of *low pressure*, which cooler air to the north and south rushes to fill, creating the reliable *trade winds*. In the northern hemisphere these are found between about 5° and 30°N (i.e. from close to the equator up to the same latitude as North Africa). Thanks to the rotation of the earth, they blow northeast and southeast, rather than due north and south.

Travelling north from the trades, we meet a mid-Atlantic area of *high pressure*, often called the *Azores high*. Air 'leaks' (or, to put it another way, *wind blows*) from this area of high pressure towards areas of lower pressure which, thanks again to the rotation of the earth, it does in a circular fashion, causing air to move clockwise around the North Atlantic, generating the *westerlies* that blow from the eastern seaboard of Canada across to us in Britain.*

It is these prevailing winds shepherding *depressions* (or low-pressure systems) and their associated *fronts*** to our doorstep that make the British weather so ... unique. But just when we're about to give up and hightail it to sunnier climes, a high-pressure 'shield' can form on top of the British Isles, forcing the depressions to detour north, gifting us glorious settled weather: cold, crisp winter days and warm, soft summer evenings.

....

* Britain isn't as cold as Canada thanks to the Gulf Stream, a current of tropical water which travels from the Gulf of Mexico, up the east coast of the US, before ricocheting off a cold current coming down from the Arctic, and setting off across the Atlantic. It keeps us warm, and as warm air can hold more water than cold air, it keeps us watered.
** The term *front* came into existence just after the First World War, capturing the idea of two air masses of air 'warring' with each other.

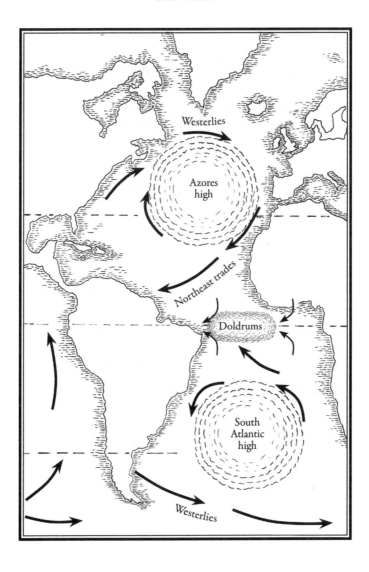

THE FORMATION OF A DEPRESSION

The north North Atlantic (i.e. the latitudes between the UK and Iceland) marks a boundary where two air masses meet:

1. warm, tropical air travelling north
2. cold, polar air travelling south

The line or *sheet* where they meet (they don't mix, but bump up against each other like drunks in a harbour bar) is called the *polar front*. If the sheet wrinkles, the front becomes unstable, with warm air trying to drive north, and cold air trying to drive south. The warm air and the cold air wrap around one another and start to *spin*, forming the depression, which will have both a *warm front* (a boundary with warm air behind it) and a *cold front* (the opposite). The cold front moves faster, meaning it can eventually catch up with the warm front, creating an *occluded front* (so called because the cold air pushes the warm air upwards, hiding or *occluding* it).

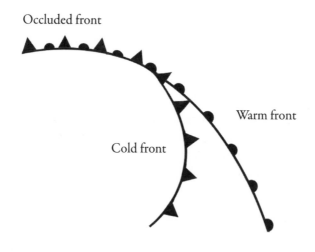

Occluded front

Warm front

Cold front

THE PASSAGE OF A DEPRESSION

As the warm front approaches, warm air rises up over denser colder air. As it rises, so it cools, and the moisture in the air condenses to form clouds. You'll see high wispy *cirrus*, followed by *cirrostratus, altostratus* and *nimbostratus*, making the sky look progressively lower and greyer, until drizzle or light rain arrives with the front.

If you also see *altocumulus* (known as a *mackerel sky* because it looks like fish scales*) after the cirrus clouds, more dramatic weather than usual is probably on its way.

Once the warm front passes, you're in the *warm sector* or *inter-frontal area*, which usually brings steady westerly or southwesterly winds, dense *stratocumulus* clouds and perhaps more light rain.

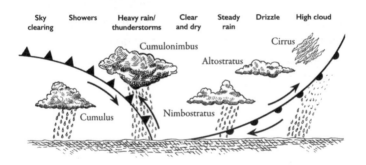

The cold front acts a little differently. It drives a wedge *underneath* the warm air in front of it, forcing it to rise much more steeply: clouds form faster and the rain is often heavier. If you can see nimbostratus (low, dense cloud covering the whole sky) then you're in for a long, steady

....

* Other European languages compare *altocumulus* perhaps more accurately to sheep or cobbles.

soaking, whereas *cumulonimbus* (fluffy towers with dark, angry bottoms) means torrential downpours, perhaps with thunderstorms.

The wind *backs* to the south or southeast just ahead of the cold front, *veering* sharply southwest and becoming very gusty as the front arrives, before veering further to the northwest once the front passes.

The change in weather as the depression rolls away to the east – the *clearance* – is thrilling: rain gives way to clear skies and sunshine, perhaps even a rainbow if you're lucky.

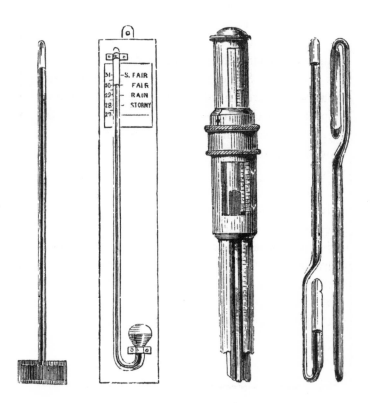

SEA BREEZE

In the summer, the maximum sea temperature in the UK is around 14–19°C. It warms gently over the day, but the land gets hotter, quicker. This temperature increase causes the air above the land to rise, creating an area of low pressure, which the cooler air above the sea rushes in to fill, causing an onshore wind: a *sea breeze*. At night the effect can go into reverse, resulting in a (usually much weaker) *land breeze* blowing offshore.

If you're out at sea, fluffy *cumulus* clouds building over the land are a good tip-off that a sea breeze is developing. Sometimes, though, it seems to arrive out of nowhere. The air is still. Your sails hang limp. Suddenly, dark patches ripple the surface, marching in a line towards the shore and – as at the flick of a switch – your sails fill and you're scudding through the water.

Sea breezes are more common in hotter parts of the world (because there's more likely to be a steep temperature gradient between land and sea), and they always help make coastal areas cooler and more inviting.

THE BEAUFORT SCALE: IN THEORY

Beaufort scale	Wind	Sea	Wind speed (knots)	Wind speed (mph)
0	Calm	Calm (glassy)	<1	<1
1	Light air	Calm (rippled)	1–3	1–3
2	Light breeze	Smooth (wavelets)	4–6	4–7
3	Gentle breeze	Slight	7–10	8–12
4	Moderate breeze	Slight–moderate	11–16	13–18
5	Fresh breeze	Moderate	17–21	19–24
6	Strong breeze	Rough	22–27	25–31
7	Near gale	Rough–very rough	28–33	32–38
8	Gale	Very rough–high	34–40	39–46
9	Strong gale	High	41–47	47–54
10	Storm	Very high	48–55	55–63
11	Violent storm	Very high	56–63	64–72
12	Hurricane	Phenomenal	64+	73+

Probable wave height (metres)	Sea description
0	Sea like a mirror
0.1	Ripples with appearance of scales are formed, without foam crests
0.2	Small wavelets still short but more pronounced; crests have a glassy appearance but do not break
0.6	Large wavelets; crests begin to break; foam of glassy appearance; perhaps scattered white horses
1.0	Small waves becoming longer; fairly frequent white horses
2.0	Moderate waves taking a more pronounced long form; many white horses are formed; chance of some spray
3.0	Large waves begin to form; the white foam crests are more extensive everywhere; probably some spray
4.0	Sea heaps up and white foam from breaking waves begins to be blown in streaks along the direction of the wind; spindrift begins to be seen
5.5	Moderately high waves of greater length; edges of crests break into spindrift; foam is blown in well-marked streaks along the direction of the wind
7.0	High waves; dense streaks of foam along the direction of the wind; sea begins to roll; spray affects visibility
9.0	Very high waves with long overhanging crests; resulting foam in great patches is blown in dense white streaks along the direction of the wind; on the whole the surface of the sea takes on a white appearance; rolling of the sea becomes heavy; visibility affected
11.5	Exceptionally high waves; small- and medium-sized ships might be for a long time lost to view behind the waves; sea is covered with long white patches of foam; everywhere the edges of the wave crests are blown into foam; visibility affected
14+	The air is filled with foam and spray; sea is completely white with driving spray; visibility very seriously affected

THE BEAUFORT SCALE: IN PRACTICE

Use the guide cautiously, taking into account air and sea temperature, the state of the tide and the sea, and your own competence.

Activity	Minimum force	Maximum force (sheltered waters)	Maximum force (open sea)
Swimming	0	4	3
Rowing dinghy	0	4	3
Dinghy with outboard engine	0	5	3
Motorboat (e.g. Plymouth pilot)	0	6	4
Motorboat (e.g. RIB)	0	7	5
Sailing dinghy	2	6	4
Sailing day boat	2	6	4
Yacht	3	7	8
Surfing	0	n/a	7
Kitesurfing	3	7	6
Windsurfing	3	7	6
Paddleboarding	0	4	3
Canoeing	0	4	3
Kayaking	0	6	4

Notes

Can be done at higher wind speeds with a support boat

Assuming a reasonable size dinghy

Assuming oars as backup

Remember lifejackets, a VHF and spare fuel if heading out to sea

Remember lifejackets, a VHF and spare fuel if heading out to sea

Very experienced sailors can cope in stronger winds, particularly with support boats

Make sure you have decent charts

Yachts can endure winds up to hurricane force, but they should never set out in anything stronger than a force 7

Novices and children should be much more cautious

Dependent on having a small enough kite to manage strong wind

Again, you need a small enough sail

Sea state is critical. You're generally fine in waves smaller than 3 feet

Beware offshore winds

Beware offshore winds

SEA FOG

Sea fog – known as *haar* in Scotland and *fret* in the north of England – is most common in Britain's northeast between the Humber Estuary and Aberdeen. It has sabotaged many a promising jaunt to the seaside in early summer.

Just as the sea warms more slowly than the land over the course of a day, so it takes longer to shake off winter's chill (as anyone who's leapt into the water on a balmy Easter Sunday will know). So, if land-warmed air moves out over the still chilly North Sea, it cools rapidly, meaning the moisture in the air condenses to become fog, which can roll back over the land, ruining your lovely walk.

SEA FEVER

~~~~~~~~

by John Masefield

I must go down to the seas again, to the lonely sea and the
   sky,
And all I ask is a tall ship and a star to steer her by;
And the wheel's kick and the wind's song and the white sail's
   shaking,
And a grey mist on the sea's face, and a grey dawn breaking.

I must go down to the seas again, for the call of the running
   tide
Is a wild call and a clear call that may not be denied;
And all I ask is a windy day with the white clouds flying,
And the flung spray and the blown spume, and the sea-gulls
   crying.

I must go down to the seas again, to the vagrant gypsy life,
To the gull's way and the whale's way where the wind's like a
   whetted knife;
And all I ask is a merry yarn from a laughing fellow-rover,
And quiet sleep and a sweet dream when the long trick's
   over.

WEATHER PROVERBS ...

Mackerel skies and mares' tails
make tall ships carry short sails

Mackerel skies = altocumulus = blotchy, tufty patches of high cloud, often at right angles to the wind. Mares' tails = cirrus = wispy streaks of very high cloud. Both are sure-fire warnings that the warm front of a depression is on its way, bringing with it the sort of windy weather that prompts the wise captain to reduce sail. If you spot them against a perfect blue sky on a perfect summer's afternoon, it's time to pour cold water on other people's optimistic plans for the next day.

Red sky at night, sailor's delight,
Red sky at morning, sailor's warning

This proverb has a long pedigree, with a version of it appearing in the New Testament.* Some say it's a late interpolation, but it's not *that* late, so we think it has historical – if not divine – authority.

....

* 'When it is evening, you say, "It will be fair weather, for the sky is red." And in the morning, "It will be stormy today, for the sky is red and threatening." You know how to interpret the appearance of the sky, but you cannot interpret the signs of the times.' Matthew 16:2–3.

Red skies are caused by a phenomenon called *Rayleigh scattering*. Shorter light waves, the ones at the blue end of the visible spectrum, are more likely to bump into dust and other particles. In the middle of the day, this light scatters in all directions, which is why the sky normally looks blue. Come the evening, when the sun is low in the sky, its light has to travel through more atmosphere before it reaches our eyes, scattering so much blue light that we only see the red end of the spectrum.

In areas of high pressure, even *more* blue light scatters (denser air = more particles to bump into), so a particularly red sunset implies high pressure to the west, and high pressure to the west often means good weather. Conversely, although less reliably, a particularly red *sunrise* implies high pressure to the *east*, where it can no longer act as a barrier to Atlantic depressions, meaning bad weather could be on the way.

First rise after very low only foretells a stronger blow

Very low here means *very low pressure*. A plummeting barometer tells you a depression is on its way, so you might think the worst must be over once it bottoms out and starts to rise. But this hope often proves premature because the wind is often particularly squally behind the cold front. Rising pressure will bring relief eventually, just not immediately, as Rudyard Kipling knew well:

> Stand by! The lull 'twixt blast and blast
> Signals the storm is near, not past;
> And worse than present jeopardy
> May our forlorn to-morrow be.*

....

* From his poem, 'The Storm Cone'.

When halo rings moon or sun, rain approaches on the run

Haloes occur when tiny ice crystals in the air reflect and refract sunlight or moonlight. These crystals occur in the cirrus clouds that precede the warm fronts of a depression.

When dew is on the grass, rain will never come to pass

Dew forms when clear skies mean a large temperature difference between night and day. When the air cools rapidly overnight, it can hold less moisture, which is why dew forms. Clear skies = high pressure = no rain.

When clouds appear like rocks and towers,
the earth's refreshed with frequent showers

Rocks and towers = cumulonimbus = the big, heaped-up clouds that mark the wet and windy passage of a cold front.

When the wind is in the east,
'tis neither good for man nor beast;
When the wind is in the north,
the skilful fisher goes not forth;
When the wind is in the south,
the bait jumps in the fish's mouth;

And when the wind is in the west,
then 'tis at its very best

This proverb works. But as to why ... nobody's quite sure. Here's an explanation which could apply to the Atlantic-facing side of Britain. Northerly and easterly winds are associated with high pressure, light winds and fine weather. Westerly and southerly winds mean low-pressure systems, wind and rain. Bad weather means good fishing because heavy onshore winds dislodge food (worms, mussels, sand eels and the like) from the seabed, encouraging fish to feed close to shore, making them easier to catch, whereas good weather and offshore winds send the fish out to sea in search of food, frustrating the amateur angler.

But why *particularly* the west ...? Good question.

... AND WEATHER MYTHS

If cows lie down it means rain is coming

Nonsense. They're probably tired.

Lightning never strikes the same place twice

Dangerous nonsense. An object that is much taller than everything around it (a lighthouse, a ship's mast, a clifftop tree) is perfectly likely to be hit more than once.

St Swithun's day if thou dost rain
For forty days it will remain
St Swithun's day if thou be fair
For forty days 'twill rain nae mare

Superstitious nonsense. It derives from the legend that St Swithun was so cross when his corpse was dug up from its preferred resting place outside Winchester Cathedral that he made it rain, a feat he can repeat for a biblical forty days if it rains on his saint's day, 15 July. Fortunately the Met Office has studied the historical record and found no basis in statistical fact.

WHAT'S THE DIFFERENCE BETWEEN A BOAT AND A SHIP?

It's tempting to ape the words of a long-dead US judge, pronouncing on what did or did not count as obscenity, and reply, 'We know it when we see it.' Tempting, but we'll try to do better.

One might try arguing that ships are for work, whereas boats are for pleasure. At first blush, that sounds pretty good. But then again: commercial fishing *boats*, tug *boats* ... and what about cruise *ships*?

Or how about this: 'A ship can carry a boat, but a boat cannot carry a ship.' A solution pleasing in its parabolic simplicity? Perhaps, but it's not without problems. What about the enormous ships whose sole purpose is to carry other ships? How do we know when the vessel being carried stops being a ship and becomes a boat? Or does being carried automatically demote it from ship to boat? What if the boat being carried is also carrying a boat? Does that turn it into a ship again? A minefield.

You might hope that in the Age of Data, the answer would lie with how the authorities categorise vessels. Unfortunately, that doesn't quite work either. While there is an obligation for *ships* over a certain size to register with the Maritime and Coastguard Agency, *boats* can also register, thereby becoming *ships*, in the eyes of the government at least.

Perhaps the finest distinction between a boat and a ship is that *a boat leans in* when it's cornering and *a ship leans out*. This is how it works. When any vessel turns there are two competing forces:

1. *Conservation of momentum*, which you might be more familiar with as *centrifugal force*. This is what you experience when you corner a car too fast and the passengers in the back seat are flung to the outside of the bend.
2. The second is a bit more subtle. Let's call it the *pivoting force*. Most vessels are moved by a propeller below the waterline, so if the bow is turning to port, the propeller is pushing the stern to starboard, and vice versa. But the propeller *also* makes the boat lean *into* the turn because it's pushing the boat sideways *below* its centre of gravity. (If you don't believe us, imagine standing next to somebody you don't like and kicking their feet out from under them: they'll fall inwards.)

When it comes to boats and ships, these two forces counteract one another.

On a large vessel with a big superstructure (i.e. lots of containers or deluxe cabins), the centre of gravity is higher, which means a more powerful centrifugal force, which means the vessel leans out: *ship*.

On a small vessel with only a mast or a fish-spotting tower above deck, the centre of gravity is lower, which means the pivotal force wins: *boat*.

(Lastly, submarines are always referred to as boats. Don't ask why, they just are.)

SEA LEVEL RISE

By now, we all know the basics. Industrialisation = more carbon dioxide and other greenhouse gases in the atmosphere = fewer of the sun's rays escaping back into space = a hotter planet. A hotter planet = rising sea levels because:

1. warmer water molecules in the oceans move further apart: *thermal expansion*
2. land glaciers are melting
3. polar ice sheets are melting

At the moment, scientists calculate that sea levels are rising at a rate of at least 3 mm/year, meaning an increase of more than 30 cm over the course of the century, although some predictions come in as high as 100 cm. What happens thereafter depends on how radically we change the way we live – and how the heating already taking place plays out.

Nobody can offer a definitive answer to either of those questions, but we do know that the south and east of Britain are more at risk than the north and west – with thousands of homes threatened. In some places, the government plans to hold the line, pouring money into sea defences. In others, the policy is managed retreat: an admission that the sea has already won. What makes some areas particularly vulnerable? Three main reasons:

1. GEOLOGY

The British coastline is made up of a bewildering variety of rocks, laid down at dramatically different periods of the earth's history. It is this variety which gives us golden sands, dank estuaries, beetling cliffs – and everything in between.

As a (very) general rule, the further north and west you go, the older the rocks, and the further south and east, the younger (although young is a relative term for geologists).

Old rocks are tough, don't erode easily and mean a complex wiggly coastline, with lots of stacks and shattered cliffs, the sorts of places that looks good under a louring sky with a westerly gale rising. Examples are St Kilda, the Western Isles, Duncansby Head and Tintagel.

Young rocks are soft, erode easily and mean crumbly cliffs, gentle bays and shallow inlets, the sorts of places that look good basking in spring sunshine. Examples are Aldeburgh, Whitstable and Rye.

This division is known as the *Tees-Exe* or *Severn-Wash line*, and the geological distinctions apply broadly inland as well. To the north and west, you meet igneous and metamorphic rocks that form the basis of our uplands. To the south and east, you find a gentler lowland landscape of mostly sedimentary rocks.

The granites and gabbros of the Highlands and Islands will exist for millennia to come; not so the southeast. It's calculated that a mere seven per cent of Scotland's coastline is eroding, compared with nearly a third of England's.

2. GLACIATION

Sea level rise is complicated by something called *isostatic uplift* or, perhaps more comprehensibly, *post-glacial rebound*. The earth's mantle (the section between crust and core) is so hot that although it's technically a solid, over the slow drip-drip of geological time it acts a bit like a liquid: it's ductile, viscous or even squashy. The weight of ice during periods of glaciation compressed the mantle, but as the ice melted, it started to expand again. This means, approximately, that (previously) ice-covered Scotland is rising, while (always) ice-free southern Britain is falling. Sea level rise, therefore, will have a greater impact in the south.

3. CLIMATE FEEDBACK

If summers get hotter and winters get wetter, as many climate models are predicting, it will exacerbate erosion. Droughts could mean fewer plants holding crumbling shores together. Wildfires could weaken soil and make land more prone to collapse. Heavy rains, seeping into cracks left by dry summers, could fragment cliffs. Wilder storms, with big waves and powerful surges, will only make matters worse.

LYING LOW

Open an online tool which shows how sea level rise will affect different parts of the country, and you'll immediately notice that the Fens and the Somerset Levels face an especially uncertain future. Both are places people have turned from sort-of-sea into sort-of-land.

They remain liminal, flat landscapes of marsh and birds and sky, with Ely Cathedral and Glastonbury Tor floating above them. In fact, they've never quite shucked off their watery nature. Ely is the Ship of the Fens. The Tor is the Isle

ROCK TYPES

IGNEOUS

The word comes from the Latin *ignis*, meaning fire. Igneous rocks are cooled lava or magma that once erupted from now-dead volcanoes, creating the gabbro hills of Skye, the basalt hexagons of Staffa, the basalt dykes of the Isle of Man, Cornwall's pillow lava and the granite of southwest England.

METAMORPHIC

As the name suggests, these are rocks that have changed after being subjected to extreme heat or pressure: gneiss, slate, schist or quartzite. Five hundred million years ago, for example, Welsh and Cornish slate was mudstone on the sea-floor. Tectonic movements gradually lifted these rocks up, folding and compressing them, and eventually turning them into slate.

SEDIMENTARY

Sedimentary rocks are made up of mineral or organic debris which has been compacted over time. Sandstone and mudstone, for example, were once tiny particles of silicate or clay dumped at the bottom of rivers or lagoons, whereas chalk and limestone contain the remains of microscopic marine life which died and sank to the beds of now vanished seas. These (relatively) young rocks are, of course, where you find fossils.

of Avalon. Roads in the Levels ripple like the imprints of waves on a beach.

Both were luxuriant landscapes for our Neolithic and Bronze Age ancestors. Later, they became places to hide and fight against invaders, perfect for a mythical King Arthur battling the Saxons, or for Hereward the Wake, a real Saxon, fighting a doomed guerrilla war against William the Conqueror. They attracted monks and hermits seeking a contemplative life among the alder thickets, reed beds and eel marshes. Later on, energetic men drained the land, and now cows graze the Levels, while the fields of eastern England fill our warehouses with wheat and vegetables.

But the newly dry Fen peat has been contracting and the wind blows away the exposed topsoil, meaning large areas now lie below sea level. The Levels are a little higher, but that won't remain the case as sea levels rise. How long until the waters return?

LOST LANDS, TALL TALES

This isn't the the first time these islands have contended with rising seas. Hundreds of thousands of years ago, a *glacial lake outburst flood*, the dramatic escape of dammed meltwater, reconfigured our coastline, gouging out the Straits of Dover and severing us from the continent in an irreversible geological Brexit.

Back then, the *Weald-Artois anticline** formed the southern ridge of a vast glacial lake. Part of that ridge is still with us today, most famously visible at the White Cliffs of Dover. To the north of the ridge, the level of the lake rose, a result of meltwater and the outflow of rivers which would

....

* Formed during the Alpine orogeny (*mountain-birth* in ancient Greek) at the same time as the rather better-known Alps, Pyrenees, Caucasus and Himalayas.

eventually become the Thames and the Rhine. Twice the lake breached the ridge, and unimaginable torrents of water cascaded south, scarring what is now the sea-bed between England and France so dramatically that millennia later scientists have been able to piece together what happened.

That ridge, however, wasn't the only piece of land that once connected Britain to Europe. At the peak of the last ice age, around 20,000 years ago, sea levels were some 120 m *lower* than they are now. Ice sheets covered northern Europe, including the UK, with only southern Britain poking out. As the climate warmed (nothing to do with humanity back then), the ice began to melt and sea levels rose, stabilising a few thousands years ago.

The retreating ice exposed a large tract of land which now lies beneath the North Sea between England and the Netherlands and Germany. This territory – picture lagoons, reedbeds, saltmarshes, mudflats – made a good home for some of our ancestors. It's known as Doggerland after Dogger Bank,* the shallow patch in the North Sea which is all that remains.

That bank had always been a happy hunting ground for fishermen, but they often hauled up a strange by-catch: bones. Bits of mammoth, lion, bear, wild horse, wisent bison, elk, reindeer, hyena, wolf, sabre-tooth cat, woolly rhino – all have come up in their nets. And where animals were plentiful, people followed: a scrap of skull and prehistoric tools have also been recovered.

....

* The fishing bank which, in turn, takes its name from *doggers*: Dutch sailing boats used for catching cod.

51

These hunters would have been badly hit by the *Storegga Slides*, when parts of Norway's continental shelf collapsed around 6,000 BCE, triggering a series of massive tsunamis, before the inexorable post-glacial sea level rise swallowed Doggerland altogether.*

Doggerland has joined other drowned lands that stalk our collective imagination. Indeed, there's a lovely proposition (far from universally accepted) that the world's dazzling array of flood myths represents a folk memory of long-ago rises in sea level. Perhaps stories were passed down, generation to generation, until they became Mesopotamia's Gilgamesh or the Noah of Genesis. It's a nice thought, anyway.

The most famous drowned island, *Atlantis*, is ancient Greek in origin, debuting as a fable in two of Plato's dialogues, before enjoying a long afterlife in Western culture and literature, especially in the more freebooting corners of sci-fi and fantasy. Atlantis, already a mighty empire, set about trying to subdue the Greeks, but was rebuffed.

> [T]here were violent earthquakes and floods, and in a single unlucky day and night all your warlike men in a body sank into the earth, and so too the island of Atlantis disappeared into the depths of the sea. That's why the sea in those parts is impassable and impenetrable, because there is a shoal of mud in the way, which was caused by the subsidence of the island.**

But we need not be in thrall to a Greek tale: we have our own home-grown lost lands. Once upon a time, so the

....

* If this idea tickles you, there's a trilogy by Stephen Baxter – *Stone Spring, Bronze Summer* and *Iron Winter* – which imagines the sea doesn't swallow up 'Northland', which instead becomes a great empire.
** From Plato's *Timaeus*.

stories say, Cornwall was a lot longer than it is now, stretching all the way to the Scillies, a remote and prosperous peninsula called *Lyonnesse*.

Lyonnesse flourished during the golden age of King Arthur, only to die with him. It was the birthplace of Tristan, whose adulterous love affair with Isolde,* an Irish princess married to King Mark of Cornwall, inspired the infamous Lancelot-Guinevere-Arthur love triangle. It was also where, according to Alfred Tennyson, the cuckolded Arthur fought a climactic battle against his treacherous son Mordred:

> Then rose the King and moved his host by night,
> And push'd Sir Mordred, league by league,
> Back to the sunset bound of Lyonnesse –
> A land of old upheaval from the abyss
> By fire, to sink into the abyss again;
> Where fragments of forgotten peoples dwelt,
> And the long mountains ended in a coast
> Of ever-shifting sand, and far away
> The phantom circle of a moaning sea.

Lyonnesse couldn't outlast the legendary king: Merlin drowned it to help save Arthur's soldiers after he and his son killed one another. It's powerful stuff, as the writer Beckles Willson mused a century ago:

> To sit at Land's End on a summer's day, watching a west-bound ship under full steam or crowded canvas, and not find some magic in the thought that beneath her swiftly gliding keel there stretch once-verdant hills and dales,

....

* ... or Iseult or Yseult, etc., etc. There are almost infinite retellings of most aspects of Arthurian myth, with different spelling to keep it interesting.

ruined towers and castles, towns and villages, is to be
wanting imagination indeed.

There are similar tales around the Welsh coast centred
on *Cantre'r Gwaelod* (the Lowland Hundred in English),
another legendary kingdom that thrived in Cardigan Bay.
Prosperous like Lyonnesse, Cantre'r Gwaelod was protected from the sea by a dyke, with sluice gates that were
closed at high tide. One night, though, a storm blew up
from the southwest, driving the spring tide hard against the
dyke. The watchman, a heavy drinker, was carousing at the
king's palace and failed to shut the gates in time. The land
drowned.

These stories, like all the best ones, shimmer with truth.
Around the coast of Wales, and again in Cornwall, especially in Mount's Bay, lie acres of submerged forests: pines,
alders and oaks. After storms or at low-water springs,
fossilised stumps emerge from the sand, whispering of vanished kingdoms. It is easy to persuade yourself that a line
of exposed rocks might be the ruins of ancient walls, or
perhaps that ridge isn't a glacial moraine, but an ancient
causeway. And if you shut your eyes and concentrate hard,
you might no longer hear a keening wind, but instead the
echo of church bells, tolling mournfully underwater.

Our seas will rise, and our memories of what we must
lose will leave a lingering afterburn. As the centuries unfold,
the list of drowned places is only going to grow. Already
Dunwich, Old Winchelsea, Eccles-on-Sea and Hallsands
are ghosts. Perhaps our descendants will wonder whether
they were there at all, or did we just imagine them?

KING CANUTE

A parable for our times ... as told by the twelfth-century historian, Henry of Huntingdon.

[A]t the summit of his power, he ordered a seat to be placed for him on the seashore when the tide was coming in. Then, before a large group of his flattering courtiers, he spoke to the rising sea, saying, 'Thou, too, art subject to my command, for the land on which I am seated is mine, and no one has ever resisted my commands with impunity. I command you, then, O waters, not to flow over my land, nor presume to wet the feet and the robe of your lord.'

The tide, however, continued to rise as usual, dashing over his feet and legs without respect to his royal person.

Then the king leaped backwards, saying, 'Let all men know how empty and worthless is the power of kings, for there is none worthy of the name, but He whom heaven, earth, and sea obey by eternal laws.'

THE GULF OF CORRYVRECKAN

The Corryvreckan whirlpool is Scotland's answer to mighty Charybdis, the mythical site of maritime peril described in Homer's *Odyssey*. If only the Loch Ness Monster could decamp to lour over the strait from the heights of Jura, a Gaelic Scylla plucking day trippers into her gaping maw, the Scottish tourist board would *really* be in business.

Glimpsed on a chart, the Gulf of Corryvreckan could be any other common-or-garden Scottish strait, meekly tucked between two islands, Jura and Scarba. But peer closer and you'll see that it bristles with wiggly lines – *overfalls* or *races* – and that the normally unflappable Admiralty has stamped *dangerous tidal streams* right across the middle.

The tides off the west coast of Scotland are as complex as they are strong, thanks to the Atlantic having to funnel up so many lochs, through so many straits, and in and out of so many islands. In some places this simply equates to extremely swift-flowing water – eight knots or more. What makes the north-setting flood tide through Corryvreckan so particularly dangerous is that the sea floor is very uneven, creating all manner of eddies, upthrusts and standing waves, as well as the famous whirlpool.

Even the fringes of a tidal race are scary. Waves break out of nowhere, for no good reason, and vanish just as fast. Your boat takes a beating from every angle. The normal rules of physics, motion and gravity seem to vanish as the sea lurches and groans and swills and sucks.

If you go through in slack water in fair weather, the gulf (disappointingly) in no way resembles the gates of Hell.

But if you can visit with professional Corry chasers – or if you muddle your tide times – it's a very different story.

One person who did misjudge the Corryvreckan was Eric Blair, better known as George Orwell. With *Animal Farm* under his belt, the writer had hunkered down on Jura, trying to finish *Nineteen Eighty-Four*. Rather extraordinarily, he took his son (Ricky), niece (Lucy) and nephew (Henry) out in a little boat into the gulf. This is how Henry later recounted the tale in a local paper:

> [W]hen we turned round the point there was already a fair swell, the boat was rising and falling a lot, but we were not worried because Eric seemed to know what he was doing and he did spend a lot of time mending and caulking the boat, and we had an outboard motor. But as we came round the point obviously the whirlpool had not receded. The Corryvreckan is not just the famous one big whirlpool, but a lot of smaller whirlpools around the edges. Before we had a chance to turn, we went straight into the minor whirlpools and lost control. Eric was at the tiller, the boat went all over the place, pitching and tossing, very frightening being thrown from one small whirlpool to another, pitching and tossing so much that the outboard motor jerked right off from its fixing. Eric said, 'The motor's gone, better get the oars out, Hen. Can't help much, I'm afraid.'*

Henry got the oars out and tried to steer them towards the shore.

> We got close to a little rock island and as the boat rose we saw that it was rising and falling about twelve feet. I had

....

* He was weakened by the tuberculosis which eventually lead to his death.

taken my boots off in case I had to swim for it, but as the boat rose level with the island, I jumped round with the painter in my hand all right, though sharp rocks painful on the feet, turned but saw the boat had fallen down. I still had my hand on the painter but the boat had turned upside down. First Lucy appeared, Eric appeared next and cried out, 'I've got Ricky all right.' Eric had grabbed him as the boat turned and pulled him out from under the boat. He had to swim from the end of the boat to the side of the island, still hanging on to Ricky. He seemed to keep his normal 'Uncle Eric' face the whole time, no panic from him or from anyone. And they were all able to clamber up on to the island ... 'I thought we were goners,' he concluded. He almost seemed to enjoy it.

Not something we'd recommend trying yourself.

THE NORTH SEA FLOOD

The North Sea flood of 1953 devastated communities up and down the east coast of England, killing hundreds of people and ruining the lives of many more. You'd need to travel back in time to the Great Storm of 1703 or to the Year Without a Summer in 1816 to find a British natural disaster on the same scale. Yet, somehow, the horror of that winter's night, when men, women and children drowned in their beds, has faded from our national memory.

The night of Saturday 31 January to 1 February was always going to see a big spring tide, but a deep Atlantic depression curved round Scotland and into the North Sea, sending a massive surge of water south. As the storm tracked down the coast, nobody knew what was coming.

The first casualties were aboard the *Princess Victoria*, a ferry that crossed the North Channel from Scotland to Northern Ireland twice a day. Two hours into the thirty-five-mile journey the ferry was overwhelmed by waves, its car deck flooded, and it began to list dangerously. The captain sent out an SOS, and a lifeboat was launched from Portpatrick, but the weather was so bad it couldn't find them. Back on board, the order was given to abandon ship.

In one of many acts of heroism that day, radio operator David Broadfoot stayed at his post while the ship started to sink, transmitting the vital Morse code signals that could help rescuers work out where they were. He was awarded the George Cross after his death.

At great risk to themselves, a cattle ship, a trawler, a tanker and a cargo ship also put out to sea from the protection of Belfast Lough to try to help, but they were too large to pluck passengers from the *Princess Victoria*'s lifeboats. All they could do was hope to shelter them a little in their lee.

The lifeboat, when it did arrive, was only able to save 43 out of the 176 people on board. No women or children survived.

Sadly, that was only the beginning.

The coast of Lincolnshire, Norfolk, Suffolk and Essex is low-lying and liable to flooding, plus the Thames Estuary wasn't as well defended as it is now. As Hilda Grieve explained in *The Great Tide*, her meticulous work of social history: 'Essex and the sea have been antagonists for centuries.' The county's creeks, estuaries and rivers are 'the arms of the sea restlessly probing the heart of the county'.

That Saturday afternoon, people whose business (or pleasure) it was to keep a weather eye on the sea were unsettled by 'the poor ebb of the afternoon, the persistence of the wind, and the weather forecast'. When you know a particular patch of sea intimately, it is deeply unnerving when it behaves beyond normal bounds.

The centre of the depression was as low as 964 mb, and for every 1 mb drop in pressure, sea levels can rise by 1 cm. The storm winds (gusts of up to 126 mph were recorded in Scotland) also had a long fetch over the North Sea, giving the waves time to build, especially as the water shallowed and the surge piled up against the bottleneck of the Dover Straits.

As high tide moved clockwise around the country, records were smashed. The Tees overflowed its banks at 3.30 p.m. although high tide wasn't due until an hour later. By the time it reached Skegness, high water was nearly eight feet higher than predicted; by Kings Lynn, more than eight feet. Every automatic tide gauge between the Wash and Southend-on-Sea was either broken or destroyed.

Today, we'd be better prepared for such a disaster, but in 1953 not only was forecasting less sophisticated, but there was no official warning system in place. Also, the Second World War had ended less than a decade previously, so flood defences hadn't been a spending priority.

Harwich lies at the northeastern tip of Essex, opposite Felixstowe at the mouth of River Stour. By 9.20 p.m., its harbourmaster knew that with half the flood tide still to come, the sea had already topped predicted high water. The town, which sits on a little peninsular, curving across the river mouth, had walls, but walls have weak points.

By 11 p.m., water was already spilling over the bank which protected the Bathside area from the Stour estuary, and police were going house to house warning people that their basements might flood. This prompted one man to go and check on his boat, which lay in Gas House Creek, where the local sailing club is based today. According to Grieve, he said:

> I got as far as Stour Road and looking to the west was a sight I am never likely to forget. Away to the west the sky was a dirty yellow and the whole length of the protecting sea wall was one wall of spray, which was flying several feet skywards. As I look back to that night it was a marvellous sight, although at the time I had the chills which were not all due to cold. After a few minutes I started back home, knowing that if I continued my journey to the creek I should never make it.

In the Old Town, an atmospheric tangle of little medieval streets, the constable who was trying to rouse people found himself cut off at every turn by water that was now spilling over the quay to the north and the esplanade to the east. By midnight the sea was in charge. Said one resident:

> Looking out of the upstairs window we could see the water rushing down the street and my husband thought of our cat and came downstairs to get him. He was just returning when what appeared to be a wave struck the house. With a noise like an explosion the downstairs windows were smashed in. Then the front door came in and the water poured in like a waterfall.

As water topped the railway embankment, others compared the waves rolling down the streets to the Severn Bore. By 1 a.m. the electricity sub-station had flooded. The lights went out.

Further south, near Colne Point, a stretch of low-lying saltmarsh, shingle, mudflats and shell banks, a holiday estate manager (crucially, an ex-seaman) was waiting out the storm in one of the bungalows with his wife, their small daughter and two fisherman sons. Luckily they were awake, saw how high the water was rising, and had a boat ready to row themselves to higher ground.

One of the sons was nearly washed away as he tried to cut the boat free from a barbed-wire fence. Eventually the water rose high enough to sweep them over the top, swirling them inland until they beached in a brussels sprout field at Lee Wick Farm, well over a mile from where the sea ought to have been.

That family had the know-how to save themselves; others were not so fortunate. Many people living on Canvey Island, built on reclaimed land in the Thames Estuary, were hit without warning when the water breached the sea defences. Wrote Grieve:

> They were awakened by the sudden roar as the wall burst, by the swish of the water as it rushed past, by the clatter and crash of debris striking the house, by the noise of splitting timber and splintering glass. Half-awake, dazed and bewildered, as they struggled to escape from this violent, engulfing nightmare, to reach the outdoor staircases to their lofts, or to fight their way through the tumult outside to go to the aid of elderly relatives or neighbours living nearby, successive waves charging through the walls swept them off their feet, breathless and numb from the icy impact.

With water attacking from all sides, the only escape was upwards.

> Many who clambered on chairs, tables, cookers, mangle-tables and step-ladders, to keep their heads above water or to make holes in the flimsy ceilings in order to escape into the roof space or out onto the roof, found their supports swept

away under their feet, leaving them fighting in the dark with floating furniture, clutching desperately at fanlights and the tops of doors and wardrobes, and trying to hold children up above the suffocating water.

In one bungalow, there lived a family with nine children under sixteen. The father, standing on the table, lifted one after another into the roof space, until seven were safe. After that, the table disintegrated. The mother was left standing in water trying to hold up her two youngest boys. Both died in her arms.

In total, fifty-eight people drowned on Canvey Island, with 307 dying along the coast.* The country, its wartime Blitz spirit still strong, rapidly mobilised to help, with looting and profiteering given very short shrift. Work began first on caring for the destitute: most people didn't have insurance, so relied on kindness, official and unofficial.

Hundreds of thousands of acres were inundated with seawater, the salt destroying the land's fertility for several years. Animals drowned in large numbers. Roads and railways, water supplies and sewage works, power stations and gasworks – masses of infrastructure was damaged or destroyed.

Closing *The Great Tide*, Grieve quotes a line from the Song of Solomon in the Old Testament: 'Many waters cannot quench love, neither can the floods drown it.' But, as she reminds us, courage and love alone cannot keep the sea out.

....

* We shouldn't forget that however bad it was in Britain, the even lower-lying Netherlands suffered worse: 1,836 people died.

THAMES BARRIER

One of the consequences of the North Sea flood was that planning started on the 520-metre-long Thames Barrier, designed to protect the capital from similar surges. Crossing the river near Woolwich, it has ten steel gates, five storeys high, which can be raised when high water coincides with a storm surge. Since it was finished in 1982, it has been closed some 200 times – fully a quarter during the exceptionally stormy season of 2013–14.

TIDES

Tides, you don't need us to tell you, are a very big deal in Britain. You get some rise and fall in the Mediterranean, but by and large a cove will ripple, azure and complacent, the same way, day after day after day. Here, though, the beach that was pounding surf while you picnicked can be trickling rivulets by the time you're packing up to go home. For your safety, if nothing else, you must *always* take tides into account, but that aside, there's something very consoling about watching the seascape remake itself before your eyes.

THE PHYSICS BEHIND TIDES

The basic premise is this: gravity creates tides. We are used to thinking of the earth's gravity as the force which keeps our feet firmly on the ground, but it is also one way of looking at the relationship between two celestial bodies, e.g. the earth and the sun, or the earth and the moon.

Sir Isaac Newton explained that this *gravitational attraction* is directly proportional to mass (the bigger the mass = the more gravitational force exerted), and *inversely* proportional to the square of the distance between them (the further apart = the less gravitational force exerted), which explains why the earth orbits the sun (333,000 times heavier than the earth), and the moon orbits the earth (eighty-one times heavier than the moon).* The mathematically minded among you might prefer to put it like this:

....

* Strictly speaking, they orbit each other; it's just that the larger object doesn't move anything like as much.

$$F = \frac{Gm_1m_2}{r^2} \text{ *}$$

Tides are a bolt-on effect of gravity, the crucial difference being that *distance is relatively more important than mass.* The power of one celestial body to affect another tidally (the *tidal force*) is inversely proportional to the *cube* of the distance between them. So, even though the sun is much bigger than the moon, its impact on our tides is only half that of the moon's because it's so much further away.

Imagine a patch of ocean directly under the moon. Imagine the moon's tidal force sucking the earth's water towards it,** creating a bulge. That's a high tide. (It's technically doing the same to the land, but you don't notice it because land doesn't stretch like water.) Now imagine the bits either side of the bulge, where the water has been sucked away. That's two low tides.

So far, so good? The moon creates a high tide on the *near side* of the earth. But *why* is there also a high tide at the same time on the *far side* of the earth?

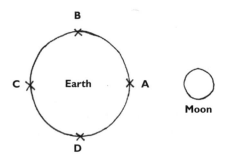

....

* F is the gravitational force; G is the gravitational constant; m_1 and m_2 are the masses of the two objects; r is their distance apart.
** Of course if there were oceans on the moon, the earth would be sucking them right back towards us – but more strongly, because we're bigger.

Take the sketch above. We have a high tide at point A, where the effect of the moon's gravity is strongest, a low tide at points B and D, where the effect is weaker, but what about point C, where the effect is weaker still? Why is there a high tide there?

Think of it this way. The water at point A experiences the *greatest* tidal force and *bulges towards* the moon. The water at point C experiences the *least* tidal force and is *left behind* as the earth itself is pulled moonwards. If you're standing at point C, it might appear that the water is bulging away from you, but in reality *you're bulging away from it*. Either way: a second high tide.

That's the basics; but it isn't the whole story. There are other forces at play which explain why the earth's tides are quite so *big*. Sketch 1 shows how point B is being pulled towards the moon.

I

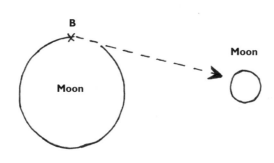

It is, however, possible to split any diagonal force into two parts. (In the language of vectors, any diagonal line is so many steps along a horizontal X axis and so many steps along a vertical Y axis.)

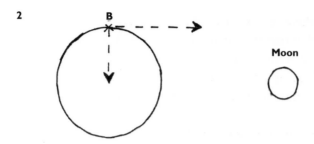

In (2) you can see that one part of the force sets off into space (along the horizontal X), while the other part sets off towards the equator (along the vertical Y).

But, of course, it's not just point B that's accelerating towards the moon, but the rest of the earth as well, which means that – see sketch (3) – the water sitting at the North Pole *doesn't notice* the horizontal force, only the downward force pulling it towards the equator.

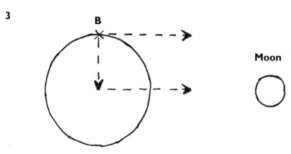

If we carry out the same exercise all over the earth's surface we come up with a series of forces that look like the sketch below.

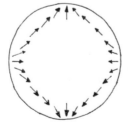

Tides, therefore, don't only exist because the force of the moon deforms the earth creating two high-water bulges. The force of the moon *also* squeezes the rest of the of water towards the middle (of the Earth), which makes the water bulge even more, which makes even bigger tides.

HOW DO TIDES WORK DAY TO DAY?

The moon takes 24 hours, 50 minutes and 24 seconds to 'orbit' the earth, meaning (mostly) that any given point on earth will have *two* high tides and *two* low tides each day, with the change from high to low (and low to high) taking about six hours. The difference between a solar day (24 hours) and the time it takes for the moon to return to the same point in the earth's sky (some 50 minutes longer), gives you the rough rule of thumb that a tide tomorrow will be a bit less than an hour later than the same tide today.

So if a high tide is due at 1100, a low tide will follow around tea-time, before a second high tide around 2330, a second low tide around dawn, with the next day's first high tide back again come 1150.

THE SUN

The sun's overall influence might be less than the moon's, but where it stands *relative to the moon* is very important because it determines whether you get *spring* or *neap tides*.

Spring tides occur when the sun and moon are in line* with the earth (either sun-moon-earth or sun-earth-moon), because the sun augments the moon's tidal force. When they're in cahoots like this, around either a full or

....

* *Syzygy* is the word for this phenomenon. It comes from the ancient Greek *suzugos* meaning *yoked together*, and should definitely be added to your Scrabble arsenal. You'll need a blank for the singular, but the plural *syzygies*, *doesn't* need a blank and could score you upwards of 300 points (two triple-word scores and your seven-tile bonus).

new moon, you get higher high tides and lower low tides, plus the tides run *much* faster, seeming to turn at the drop of a hat.

When the sun and moon are at right angles, not pulling in harness, you get neap tides, with lower highs, higher lows, and longer periods of slack water at the top and bottom of each tide, when the water mills about, trying to remember what it's meant to be doing next.

A spring high tide or a neap low tide always come around at the same time of day, so if there's a patch of seaside you know well, you'll be able to tell at a glance whether it's springs or neaps, simply by seeing what the tide's up to.

THE RULE OF TWELFTHS

You know it's high tide. You know low tide will follow about six hours later. But what if you want to know how high the water will be in between? What if you want to know how fast the water will be flowing? That's where the *rule of twelfths* comes in.

If you plot the rise and fall of a tide on a graph, it will (mostly) resemble a *sine curve*, with the rate of change from high water starting off slow, increasing until half-tide (the midpoint between high and low water) when the rate is at its fastest, before decreasing to its slowest rate just before low water.

The rule of twelfths takes the six hours between each tide and divides them into twelve, sharing the rate of change out between each hour.*

....

* Beware, local variation can be dramatic. Poole Harbour, for example, actually has a double high tide.

Hour after high or low tide	Flow volume	Flow speed	Rise or fall
1	1/12	slow	1/12
2	2/12	medium	3/12
3	3/12	fast	6/12
4	3/12	fast	9/12
5	2/12	medium	11/12
6	1/12	slow	12/12

WHY ARE BRITAIN'S TIDES SO BIG?

Geography, really. Britain is a) next to a big ocean, b) has relatively shallow coastal waters and c) has lots of long estuaries and narrow straits which water has to race up and down. (The Bristol Channel is the most extreme example: its tidal range is an extraordinary fourteen metres.)

Our weather also gives the tides a boost. Low-pressure systems cause higher tides, because the air *literally* presses down less hard on the water. Big storms can also pile the sea up against lee shores, creating dangerous storm surges, which can exacerbate an already big tide.

MAKING WAVES

A rising tide also can create a special kind of wave called a *tidal bore*. Globally, they're rare, but the UK has more than its fair share. Perfect conditions are a large tidal range and a long estuary, which is why the Severn Bore is our market leader.

Once upon a time, when boats plied the River Severn between Bristol and Gloucester, it was a serious hazard to navigation, but now it's just fun to watch – or to surf, if you're a real legend, like the local railway engineer who surfed the bore for more than seven miles, an awesome seventy-five-minute ride.

The bore forms in the Bristol Channel, with its height and appeal increasing as it surges upriver, becoming truly impressive as the Severn approaches Gloucester. You can expect a little bore when high water is more than 8 metres at Sharpness, a big bore when it's more than 9.5 metres, and a truly crashing bore if a spring tide follows heavy rain and powerful westerlies.

Other, less famous, bores can be found on the Dee, the Mersey, the Ribble, the Lune, the Kent, the Nith, the Eden, the Trent, the Great Ouse and the Parrett.

DEALING WITH TIDES IN PRACTICE

1 Check a tide table. On your phone. In one of the little booklets you can buy in seaside shops. On the blackboards outside lifeguard huts and sailing clubs.

2 If you're checking a booklet, make sure you adjust for British Summer Time if necessary. You might also need to adjust the times from a *reference port* to where you actually are.

3 Always leave stuff (cars, picnics, sleeping children) above the high-water mark (the line of seaweed, driftwood and flip-flops at the top of the beach).

4 If you're going for a walk along the bottom of some cliffs, beware walking round into a neighbouring bay when the tide is coming in. The water might seem far away in the middle of the bay, but it can easily cut you off at the edges.

5 If you have to swim or row across the tide, never try to fight it. You'll lose. Instead shape a course across it. You'll get swept a long way down-tide from where you started, but at least you'll make it across.

6 When you're swimming, surfing or dinghying near a beach, keep checking back at the shore to see if you're being swept up or down the coast or out to sea.

7   When anchoring or tying up a boat, make sure you put out enough line or chain to compensate for a rising or falling tide.

8   When wind and tide are strong and running in opposite directions, a vicious chop can develop that is dangerous for both swimmers and small boats.

9   If you're about to cast off into a strong tide in a boat, check your engine is working before you let go of the shore. Better to discover your outboard's out of petrol at the dockside, rather than halfway to Holland.

RIP CURRENTS

The bane of surfers, *rip currents* are found near beaches with breaking waves. After crashing onto the shore, the water needs to find a way back out to sea. If it finds a deeper channel somewhere along the beach – a path of less resistance – it will sluice out to sea by that route.

If you get caught in a rip current, it will try to suck you through its *neck* and out to its *head*, beyond the breaking waves, where its energy dissipates. Rips average 1–2 mph, but can reach 4–5 mph which, we promise you, is scarier than it sounds: even an Olympic swimmer at full tilt would struggle.

Don't try to swim against it back to shore: you'll exhaust yourself. Instead, swim at right angles to the current, parallel to the shore, until you find normal water again. From there you can, let's hope, get back to shore, using the waves to help you.

Some rip currents are predictable. Others come and go without warning. They can also can be tough to spot, but here are some clues: fewer breaking waves, darker water, a rippled surface, discoloured or sandy water beyond the breakers.

Grown-ups can make their own decisions about what risks to take, but when it comes to children playing in surf, be *hawklike* in your supervision and *boooring* on the subject of staying in between the lifeguard's flags.

UNDERTOW

A strong *undertow* is often found on steeper beaches as breaking waves rush back out to sea (the *backwash*). When this water (plus churned-up sand and pebbles) is travelling especially fast, it can pull you under the next wave. For a robust adult, it's not that serious, unless you're exhausted, e.g. after escaping from a rip current. You might get knocked off your feet and bashed around a bit, but you should be able to right yourself. It can, however, be very dangerous for smaller children.

SPANISH LADIES

This famous shanty enjoyed an early airing in *Poor Jack*, the 1840 novel by the naval-fiction pioneer, Captain Frederick Marryat, who wanted to 'rescue it from oblivion'. He could hardly have been more successful. It has since appeared in many different guises, from *Moby-Dick*, to a film based on Patrick O'Brian's novels, to *Swallows and Amazons*, with Titty encouraging her shipmates to sing it to Mother, Nurse and Vicky (waving her fat little hand) as they set sail for Wild Cat Island. In fact, 'Spanish Ladies' remains the perfect way to mark any embarkation.

Farewell and adieu to you Spanish ladies,
Farewell and adieu to you ladies of Spain,
    For we're under orders
    For to sail to old England,
And we may never see you fair ladies again.

We'll rant and we'll roar, like true British sailors,
We'll rant and we'll roar across the salt seas,
    Until we strike soundings
    In the channel of old England –
From Ushant to Scilly 'tis thirty-five leagues.

Then we hove our ship to, with the wind from sou'west, boys,
Then we hove our ship to, for to soundings to take;
    'Twas 45 fathoms
    With a white sandy bottom
So we squared our main yard and up channel did make.

Chorus

The first land we sighted was callèd the Dodman,
Next Rame Head off Plymouth, Start, Portland, and Wight;
    We sailed by Beachy,
    By Fairlight and Dover,
And then we bore up for the South Foreland Light.

Chorus

Then the signal was made for the Grand Fleet to anchor,
All in the Downs that night for to lie,
    Let go your shank painter,
    Let go your cat stopper,
Haul up your clew garnets, let tack and sheets fly.

Chorus

Now let ev'ry man drink off his full bumper,
And let ev'ry man drink off his full glass;
    We'll drink and be jolly
    And drown melancholy,
And here's to the health of each true-hearted lass.

WHO OWNS WHAT?

On a typical stretch of our coast, you will have walked through three different ownership 'zones' in the short time it takes you to, say, park your car, set up base on the beach, pull on your wetsuit and paddle out for a surf. Four, if you get caught in a rip current and sucked far out to sea.

ZONE 1: THE LAND

Once upon a time, a coastal landowner would have assumed that his title went right down the sea. But from Elizabeth I onwards, cash-strapped monarchs tried to argue that the beach or foreshore had never been included in royal land grants, and still belonged to the Crown, which would allow them to sell lucrative fishing rights.

Charles I ratcheted up the pressure so much that foreshore appropriation ('the taking away of men's right, under the colour of the King's title to land, between high and low water marks') was number 26 out of 204 grievances dished up to him by parliament – and we don't need to tell you what happened next.

Nevertheless, after the Restoration the law gradually shifted in favour of Crown ownership of the foreshore, unless the landowner could prove otherwise, which brings us to where we are today.

ZONE 2: THE FORESHORE

So the foreshore belongs to the Queen? Well, no, not exactly. Originally it *was* the monarch's private property, but when George III failed to stump up his share of the money his government needed to run the country, great swathes of his assets were parcelled up into something called the Crown Estate. The money generated by what is now a £14bn portfolio – which includes the lion's share of our foreshore, as well as other gems such as Regent Street and Ascot Racecourse – is turned over to the Treasury to be spent on the grateful nation.

The next most significant foreshore owners are two even more arcane entities: the Duchy of Cornwall (large parts of Devon and Cornwall, plus the Isles of Scilly) and the Duchy of Lancaster (from the midpoint of the River Mersey to Barrow-in-Furness). The former, as you probably know, belongs to Prince Charles, and the latter belongs ... to the Queen.

Neither mother nor son can touch the capital, but they can spend the income how they want, whether on themselves or their charities. The Duchy of Cornwall is fascinating, but hard to do justice to without a lengthy legal excursus. Suffice to say that it enjoys extraordinarily generous – some might say extraordinarily archaic – privileges, including the right to vet legislation affecting it.

The rest of the foreshore belongs to smaller owners, including local authorities, the RSPB, the National Trust, the Ministry of Defence, the Beaulieu Estate and the Duke of Beaufort.

All the major foreshore owners are by and large delighted for you to roam around their beaches and, subject to local bye-laws and common courtesy, for you to land your canoe, have a picnic, dig for bait and collect a few seashells to take home. Sadly, drones are also allowed.

However, the moment you want to exploit the shore commercially, you'll need a lease or a licence. So if you want to harvest seaweed for your breakfast, that's fine, but if you plan to make your fortune extracting iodine from bladderwrack, the Crown Estate will want a piece of the action.

What makes all this even more interesting is that the boundary between upland and foreshore is a moveable feast, based on an imaginary line called *mean high water*. (In Scotland it's *mean high-water springs*, which adds a few extra feet to the foreshore.) Dig out any large-scale Ordnance Survey map and you'll see the mean high-water line neatly marked, as well as mean low water, which defines the other end of the foreshore.

What does this mean in practice? Here's one small example.

Two boat sheds sit side by side on a little quay in Devon. One floods regularly at high tide and belongs to the Duchy of Cornwall. One sits *just* high and dry, and belongs to the local landowner, who can earn a few quid charging people a fee for boat storage. What if the sea level starts to rise and the mean high-water mark spills under the second padlocked door? Ownership would technically pass to the Duchy, along with any associated revenue.

The boundary only officially shifts if the rate of change is slow and steady; if it's sudden and violent, it stays the same. There could be some interesting legal battles over what counts as steady once global heating and sea level rise intensify.

Finally, when does foreshore stop being foreshore and turn into plain old riverbank? Answer: when the water stops being tidal, which fluctuates with the weather, the seasons, and with how much fresh water is flowing down-river. For simplicity's sake, each tidal river has an agreed *head of tide*, or Normal Tidal Limit, which again you'll find marked on a detailed map (e.g. at Teddington on the Thames).

ZONE 3: THE SEABED AND UK TERRITORIAL WATERS

Once you cross *mean low water* (or the lowest astronomical

tide – there's some variation), even if you've been on a Duchy beach, you're back in Crown Estate territory. In other words, if it's low water and you've got wet feet, the Prince of Wales can't touch you. This is because the Crown Estate owns virtually all the seabed around the UK up to 12 nautical miles offshore, which makes it a big player when it comes to wind farms, tidal energy, pipelines and (more relevantly to most people) moorings.

You'll be pleased to learn that you – and other nations' shipping – have the right of *innocent* passage through the waters above the Crown Estate's seabed.

ZONE 4: THE HIGH SEAS

After 12 nautical miles, it's free swim, the rolling main. (So long as you're not planning on fishing commercially, drilling for oil or building an offshore wind farm, in which case you need to head out to 200 miles, beyond the economic exclusion zone.)

ORKNEY AND SHETLAND: A LAW UNTO THEMSELVES

These islands haven't always been Scottish. They were settled more than a thousand years ago by Norsemen, eventually becoming part of a Scandinavian mega-state called the Kalmar Union. In 1468, a Scottish king was engaged to a Danish princess, and Orkney and Shetland were staked as collateral if her family didn't cough up her cash dowry. The money never materialised, the debt was never paid, and so both archipelagoes became part of Scotland, and later the United Kingdom. (Could they be redeemed by Denmark at some future date? A great plot for a geo-political thriller.)

Crucially, however, they retained some of the Norse legal system, known as Udal Law, under which a landowner's title does not stop at mean high water, but extends to the lowest low-water mark, or possibly even further: as far as a stone can be thrown, a horse can wade or a person can cast a salmon net.

The circumstances where you might fall foul of Udal Law are pretty niche – unless you're a major oil company. In the 1970s, Occidental Petroleum negotiated with the Crown Estate to bring a pipeline ashore on the Orkney island Flotta, near Scapa Flow. The landowner quite rightly kicked up a fuss, saying the foreshore belonged to him, not the Crown Estate, and the courts backed him up.

WRECK AND SALVAGE

If you stumble across something more lucrative than a flip-flop washed up on the beach, unfortunately it's not yours. You need to call the Receiver of Wreck, who'll return it to its rightful owner (or get in touch with the right museum), whether you've found:

flotsam: goods that have remained afloat after being lost from a ship that has sunk
jetsam: goods that have been cast overboard from a ship that was in danger of sinking
lagan: goods that have been buoyed (so they can be recovered) before being cast overboard from a ship that then sinks
derelict: property (whether a whole vessel or cargo) that has been abandoned at sea without hope of recovery

You have twenty-eight days to report your find, otherwise you risk a hefty fine. Wreck unclaimed within a year becomes the property of the Crown.

If you (the *salvor*) go to immense trouble – by, for instance, locating a sunken Spanish galleon filled with doubloons – you can claim salvage. How much you get will depend on how skilful you were and how dangerous it was.

In practice, people who lived by the coast long held a rather different view, seeing wrecked ships and their cargo as a natural resource, another instance of the sea's bounty.

Given Britain's meteorological and navigational idiosyncrasies, nobody needed to ape the murderous gang in Daphne du Maurier's *Jamaica Inn* and lure ships to their doom. Instead, a *wrecker* simply made the best of what fell into their lap, as Bella Bathurst explains in her engrossing book on the subject: 'They wrecked because they were poor, because they lived on the coasts, and because a ship on the rocks was irresistible during a Shetlandic winter or a Hebridean famine.'

Nor is wrecking a quaint historical quirk. We'll leave you with this late twentieth-century recollection of a fishing boat, stranded on rocks in Orkney, from Amy Liptrot's brilliant memoir, *The Outrun*:

> I watched Dad go first, long-legged, clambering aboard the boat, then helping others up. We held our breath, hoping their weight would not tip the vessel, before watching them disappear inside the cabin. They emerged a few minutes later and, although they were too far away to see properly, I could tell that they were beaming, arms full of computer equipment.

ROYAL FISHES

You're enjoying a bracing walk at the seaside, when you spot a whale carcass. Do *not* rush home for your blubber spade: beached whales, along with sturgeon and porpoises, are Royal Fishes and belong to the Queen herself. (It was Edward II who first arrogated the whales and sturgeons, with porpoises added in the seventeenth century.) Of course, these days the Queen doesn't want a decaying cetacean corpse so, as with flotsam and jetsam, call the Receiver of Wreck and leave it to them to sort out.

Scotland is different. A whale only belongs to the Queen if it's too large to be dragged by 'a wain pulled by six oxen' – by convention any whale over 25 feet long. Disposing of such a whale is now one of the Scottish government's more unenviable devolved responsibilities.

SANDCASTLES

We had sand in the eyes and the ears and the nose,
And sand in the hair, and sand-between-the-toes.*

Sandcastles are ineluctably appealing. Small children are electrified at finding themselves in a malleable habitat, free to riot in non-dirty dirt that has been laundered by the tide. Large adults, their spirits eroded by off-beach life, are relieved to lose themselves in the sort of meditative labour that leads to the profound state of tranquillity, known to the ancient Greeks as *ataraxia*.

Sandcastles are versatile, also functioning as land art, as territory marker, as invitation to play, and – if *ataraxia* isn't your thing – as stimulus for base competitive appetites. Moreover, if built correctly, they teach young and old important lessons about the implacability of nature and the fallibility of human endeavour. As Shelley observed after the incoming tide washed away his own creation:

> Nothing beside remains. Round the decay
> Of that colossal wreck, boundless and bare
> The lone and level sands stretch far away.

Yet even if no monument can stand the test of time, we should never stop building. Here's how:

....

* Christopher Robin having a good day out at the beach in A. A. Milne's *When We Were Very Young*.

1. Ideally, you want to locate your castle where the rising tide will engulf it at 4.48 p.m. (i.e. home time). You need to have laboured long enough over your construction to ensure the water's approach feels genuinely calamitous.
2. You *do* need a bucket. They provide both coherence and crenellation. Children may fill the bucket, but unless you are (overly) relaxed about build quality, upend it yourself, perhaps encouraging them to whack the base self-importantly before you wriggle it free.
3. You *do* need a spade, the smallness and pinkness of which should be in direct proportion to how large you are and how masculine a face you present to the world.
4. You do *not* need shop-bought flags or other fripperies. Castle decoration should be *objets trouvés*: shells, weed, attractive pebbles, plastic detritus, cuttlefish innards (excellent drawbridges), bleached crab exoskeleton (menacing gargoyles).
5. As you build, invest your sandcastle with the same love that Priam had for Troy – until your work is done, at which point, confusingly, you must briefly turn quisling and side with the sea. Bulldoze a trench from water's edge to castle's moat and wait.
6. As the first surge spills up the channel, leap to your castle's defence. Dig frantically, drawing the waves into side channels. Dredge an outer moat. Dispatch sappers to re-enforce the walls. Don't go down without a fight.
7. When doom comes, as doom must come, do *not* allow anyone to rebuild a few metres higher up the beach. It won't be the same. Promise everyone a whelk if they'll go home nicely.

You will, of course, have observed that this method only works on a rising tide. If you've mistimed your visit and arrived mid-ebb, don't panic. We can offer some alternatives which are (nearly) as fulfilling.

Sim city: Less military, more collaborative. The aim is to create a weird and wonderful array of urban amenities for sandhoppers. (Obviously, this only works if a) there are sandhoppers and b) sandhoppers don't freak you out.) *Talitrus saltator* has been known to enjoy racetracks, swimming pools, playgrounds and open-air art installations. Do not limit yourself – or them.

Dambusters: If there's no water coming *up* the beach, try to find some that's going *down* to the sea: a freshwater stream or a brimming rock pool. Dam this new water source, build a lavish settlement *below* it, open the floodgates, enjoy the destruction.

Cool runnings: You need small (preferably golf) balls and a steep beach. Start as high as you can with a helter-skelter tower, and from there build a series of tracks, tunnels and jumps. Racing the balls can consume *hours*.

ISLAND SAINTS

As well as straight roads, striking mosaics and a bewildering array of Mediterranean fruit and veg, the Romans introduced a new-fangled mystery religion to Britain: Christianity. After centuries of persecution, Emperor Constantine's conversion ushered in first tolerance and then imperial patronage, until by the end of the fourth century Christianity was *the* religion of the Roman Empire.

By then the western empire was, relatively speaking, on its last legs. Within a century, a barbarian king would be ruling in Rome, with obvious knock-on effects for Britain, a small frontier province. As Roman authority disintegrated, enterprising peoples – Angles, Saxons and Jutes – crossed the North Sea to take their chances in a new land, bringing their own rival pagan gods with them. Their success drove Christianity (and Britain's Celtic languages) to Ireland and the western fringe of Britain (Cornwall, Wales and the west coast of Scotland), where the faith endured far from its power centres in the east.

In 563, a young Irish priest, known to us as Columba, was exiled from his home in what is now County Donegal. He crossed the Irish Sea in a *currach*, a small wooden-framed boat, covered with hides. With the statutory twelve companions, he arrived on the Scottish island of Iona. It's tempting to think of Iona as a remote wilderness, and to picture Columba as a latter-day Luke Skywalker,* communing with a dying faith in a harsh new world, but we'd be wrong.

Iona soon became a sophisticated centre of healing and literacy, at a time when sophisticated wasn't a word you'd apply to much of mainland Britain. From Iona, Columba and his followers travelled to mainland Scotland, bringing the Picts the good news.

Columba died in 597 – the same year that Augustine landed in the south and set about converting the Anglo-Saxons – but Iona continued to thrive, with one of its sons, Aidan, travelling to Northumbria in 635 to found a

....

* See the final scene of *Star Wars VII: The Force Awakens*, filmed on Skellig Michael off the west coast of Ireland.

monastery on Lindisfarne, one of Britain's most impressive tidal islands.

Such islands are a fine metaphor for a missionary Christian: of this world and yet not; with people and with God. Aidan was a saint worthy of the name, as wrote the Venerable Bede in his *Ecclesiastical History of the English People*:

> He cultivated peace and love, purity and humility; he was above anger and greed, and despised pride and conceit; he set himself to keep and teach the law of God, and was diligent in study and prayer. He used his priestly authority to check the proud and the powerful; he tenderly comforted the sick; he received and protected the poor.

His example inspired a lowly shepherd named Cuthbert. While tending his flock, he had a vision of St Aidan ascending to heaven, and immediately abandoned his sheep and dedicated his life to God. He settled himself on the Farne Islands, scraps of rock south of Lindisfarne, several miles from the mainland, with only the storms and seabirds for company.

According to Bede, demons were a problem, but Cuthbert drove them off and built himself a little hermitage. A freshwater spring miraculously appeared; it's still there but prosaically contaminated by guano. He also persuaded the birds not to eat what little barley he grew.

Unfortunately, if you abandon the world for a life of prayer and contemplation, the world has a habit of seeking you out. Wrote one biographer: 'His conversation, seasoned with salt, consoled the sad, instructed the ignorant, and appeased the angry, for he persuaded them all to put nothing before the love of Christ.'

Both Lindisfarne and the cult of St Cuthbert continued to prosper in the 100 years after his death, but according to the Anglo-Saxon Chronicle of 793, a dark power was rising.

> In this year terrible portents appeared over Northumbria, which sorely affrighted the inhabitants; there were exceptional flashes of lightning, and fiery dragons were seen flying through the air. A great famine followed hard upon these signs; and a little later in that same year, on the 8th of June, the harrying of the heathen miserably destroyed God's church on Lindisfarne by rapine and slaughter.

The Vikings had arrived.

TIDAL ISLANDS

It isn't quite as easy as you'd think to come up with a working definition of a tidal island, but Peter Caton, in his definitive *No Boats Required: Exploring Tidal Islands*, offers this:

> A named area of land of significant size, which supports vegetation, shows signs of human activity, can be safely walked to with dry feet at least once a month from the UK mainland, is totally surrounded by water on a minimum of one tide each month, but never totally submerged.

Here is his list of forty tidal islands around the coast of the UK mainland:

An Caol, Loch Linnhe, Fort William
Ardwall Isle, Fleet Bay, Dumfries and Galloway
Barlocco Isle, Fleet Bay, Dumfries and Galloway
Burgh Island, Bigbury, south Devon
Burrow Island,* Portsmouth Harbour, Hampshire
Burry Holms, Rhossili Bay, southwest Wales
St Catherine's Island, Tenby, southwest Wales
Cei Ballast, Porthmadog, north Wales
Chapel Island, Ulverston, Morecambe Bay
Chiswick Eyot, River Thames, London
Cramond Island, Firth of Forth, Edinburgh
Davaar Island, Campbeltown, Kintyre
Foulney Island, Barrow-in-Furness, Cumbria
Eileanan** nan Gad, Kentra Bay, Ardnamurchan***
Ynys**** Gifftan, Talsarnau, north Wales
Hestan Island, Dumfries and Galloway
Hilbre Island, Dee Estuary, Wirral
Horsey Island, Hamford Water, Essex
Eilean Ighe, Arisaig, west Highlands
Innis Mhòr, Dornoch Firth, northeast Scotland
Holy Island of Lindisfarne, Beal, Northumberland
Little Eye, Dee Estuary, Wirral
Ynys Lochtyn, Cardigan Bay, west Wales
St Mary's Island, Whitley Bay, Northumberland
Mersea Island, Colne / Blackwater, Essex
Eilean Mòr / Eilean a' Bhealaidh, Loch Linnhe, Fort William
Eilean Mòr, Loch Sunart, Ardnamurchan
Northey Island, Blackwater Estuary, Essex

....

* Known locally as Rat Island.
** *Eilean* is Scots Gaelic for island (plural *eileanan*).
*** Ardnamurchan is a peninsula in western Scotland. Glancing at a map you'd be forgiven for thinking it an island in itself, so surrounded is it by fingers of lochs.
**** *Ynys* is the Welsh for island.

Osea Island, Blackwater Estuary, Essex
Piel Island, Barrow-in-Furness, Cumbria
Ray Island, Blackwater Estuary, Essex
Isle Ristol, Summer Isles, northwest Scotland
Rough Island, Kippford, Dumfries and Galloway
Sandaig Islands, Glenelg, northwest Scotland
Sheep Island, Ballintoy, Northern Ireland
Eilean Shona / Shona Beag, Loch Moidart, Ardnamurchan
Skippers Island, Hamford Water, Essex
Sully Island, Penarth, south Wales
Eilean Tioram, Loch Moidart, Ardnamurchan
Worm's Head, Rhossili Bay, southwest Wales

EXCERPT FROM A MAN YOUNG AND OLD

by W. B. Yeats

III.
The Mermaid

A mermaid found a swimming lad,
Picked him for her own,
Pressed her body to his body,
Laughed; and plunging down
Forgot in cruel happiness
That even lovers drown.

SELKIES

I stare at the dark curve of what I thought was a wetsuit, and the smooth place where flesh like mine joins on to – what? It reminds me of something. It's not like the scaly fish tail you see in a kid's book. It's like the tail of another creature altogether. Powerful, glistening, sleek, made for water and nor for land.

'A seal,' I whisper.

Sapphy (short for Sapphire, no less), the heroine of Helen Dunmore's *The Ingo Chronicles*, is face to face with the alluring Faro, whose mammalian tail evokes the appealing Orcadian shapeshifter, the *selkie*. The word still means *seal* in Scots (English's northern sibling), but it also refers to a singular being: a seal in the sea, human on the land. Female selkies offer the landsman the hope of romance (a seal's soft brown eyes are enough to make anyone go weak at the knees) although he must hide her seal skin if he doesn't want to lose her to the sea.*

Fishwives also enjoy liaisons with male selkies, even giving birth to hybrid children, but such relationships often end in tragedy, as we learn from the ballad, *The*

....

* Using animal form to escape unwanted male attention has, after all, been a necessary female tactic since storytelling began.

93

Great Selkie of Sule Skerry. A selkie father takes his child back to the sea, warning the mother that:

> An thu sall marry a proud gunner,
> An a proud gunner I'm sure he'll be,
> An the very first schot that ere he schoots,
> He'll schoot baith my young son and me.

HOW TO ROW

You can sail the fastest boats, catch the biggest fish, navigate blindfolded into the most crevice-like anchorages, but if you can't row with dignity and purpose, all of that will count for nothing. As punctuation is to writing, so rowing is to the seaside. It might be hard and boring when you're learning, but it makes everything else *work*, plus it's dead easy once you've got the hang of it, and after a while you may even find it acquires a spare beauty of its own.

OARS

Don't use metal or plastic oars if you can help it: they flex too much. Choose wood instead. Longer oars give you more drive, but they need to be in proportion to the boat. Reckon on having one-third of your oar inboard and two-thirds outboard. Measure the *beam* of your boat at the rowing *thwart*. Subtract an inch or two to leave a gap between your hands. Multiply that number by about 1.5 to give you a sensible length.

A decent oar also needs a decent *collar* (the fat ring between the handle and the blade) to protect it from friction. A collar also has a helpful ridge which makes it less likely you'll lose the oar in the water if you let go. Leather collars look lovely. Plastic is fine.

ROWLOCKS

Rhymes, very satisfyingly, with bollocks.

A *rowlock* worth its salt is U-shaped, with a pin at the bottom. The oar sits in the U, and the pin goes into a hole in the *gunwale* of the boat.

Rowlocks should be made from galvanised steel. Anything else is a waste of time: they'll crack, split or ping out when you least expect it. Also shun the O-shaped rowlock. You might think it'll stop your oar popping out from its rowlock (good), but it won't have a proper collar, so your stroke will be slithery and unsatisfying (bad). Eschew, too, any oar with an in-built pin. It is trying to make you do away with the rowlock altogether, which might, on the face of it, appear to be a very neat solution, but will only lead to pain and disappointment.

BOAT

So long as you've got decent oars and rowlocks, when it comes to the boat, anything goes. Rowing is about getting from A to B. It doesn't need to be stylish: a snub-nosed fibreglass *pram** will do fine. (Although we're all allowed to dream about a 12-foot clinker-built wooden dinghy.)

GETTING STARTED

Make sure the boat is well *trimmed* (equal weight at the bow and stern). Make sure the boat isn't *listing* (leaning to port or starboard).

....

* A little rowing boat with a flat (or *transom*) bow, instead of a pointed one.

Choose a spot with neither wind, tide, obstacles nor spectators. There's no shame in poling yourself away from the shore, punt-like, until you find clear water and a little privacy.

Sit on the central thwart, *facing the stern*. With the blades of the oars a hand's breadth above the water, lean forwards towards the stern, extending your arms in front of you until they're straight. Your oars will have moved behind you. Raise your arms, dipping the blades into the water, until they're just submerged. Lean back, keeping your arms straight, pulling the blades through the water. When you're nearly vertical, bend your elbows to pull your hands in to your chest. That's the end of your stroke. (And the correct moment for a quick glance over your shoulder to check where you're going.) Lift the blades out of the water, repeat.

To turn the boat, pull on only one oar.

To reverse dip and push, rather than dip and pull.

TOP TIPS

1. Don't worry about rhythm at first. Concentrate on getting each part of your stroke neat and tidy.
2. Don't try too hard. Keep your strokes short. Keep your strokes gentle. If you yank too hard, you'll pop an oar out of a rowlock.
3. It's bad manners to focus so hard on your own stroke that you forget to look where you're going.

ROPES AND KNOTS

You're probably familiar with the dusty displays of knots with increasingly improbable names (the *sheepshank*?) that hang behind the bars of seaside pubs, designed, as with so many things nautical, to intimidate the uninitiated. The reality is that there aren't very many knots you actually *need* to know. You can count the essentials on one hand and learn them in a few minutes.

GROUND RULES

On a boat there is a no such thing as *rope*. The word immediately brands you a landlubber. For example, the rope that attaches a boat to the shore is a *line* or a *warp*. Lines can be further subdivided into *springs*, *bow lines*, *stern lines* and *painters*. The rope that pulls a sail up and down a mast is a *halyard*. The rope that pulls a sail in or out is a *sheet*. You can probably guess that halyards and sheets are also ripe for subdivision: *main sheets*, *mizzen halyards*, *spinnaker sheets*, *jib halyards*. And that's before you've tackled *guys*, *braces*, *cunninghams*, *outhauls*, *topping lifts* and *kicking straps*, which control sails and spars in ever more complicated ways.

If you're in doubt about what to call a rope, refer to it as *string*; sailors go in for exaggerated casualness because nautical pride means being (or pretending to be) relaxed about whatever the wind or sea throw at you.

Once you know what your rope – sorry – *string* is called and what job it's meant to do, you can decide which knot might be appropriate. The main families of knots are:

hitches: attach a bit of string to an object
stoppers: stop a bit of string slipping through an object
loops: create a loop in a bit of string
bends: attach one bit of string to another bit of string

THE BUILDING BLOCKS: FOUR BASIC KNOTS

First, a hitch. The *half-hitch* or *overhand knot*, is the most basic kind of knot. By itself, it isn't much use, but it becomes very useful when combined with others.

Second, a stopper knot called a *figure-of-eight*, which does what it says on the tin.

Before learning knots three and four, you need a little more jargon. The bit of the rope that's not getting tied (often the bit that's attached to something) is called the *standing end*. The other end, the business end, is called the *free end*. And a *bight* is where you create a kink like the Greek letter Ω in the rope.

The easiest loop is the *overhand loop,* which you make by tying an overhand knot on a bight of rope. To tie, form a bight and fold it under the standing end creating a circle. Take the loop over the standing end and pass through the circle and tighten.

A simple variant of this, which is slightly better because it doesn't jam as much, is the *fisherman's loop* or *figure-of-eight loop*, for which you tie a figure-of-eight rather than an overhand knot on the bight.

You can now combine these basics to achieve whatever your heart desires. Here are some examples to get you going.

HALF-HITCH ON A HALF-HITCH

Good for small, fiddly jobs, eg. tying string onto a kite. Tie a half-hitch in the end of your string. Loop the free end through the ring at the bottom of your kite and tie it off with another half-hitch. Wriggle and tighten until one half-hitch jams into the other.

ROUND TURN AND TWO HALF-HITCHES

This is what you need when you want to secure one thing (a rowing boat, a yacht) to something else (a ring on a quay, a tree in the Magellan Strait). Simply pass the line around the object to create a complete full turn (if in doubt an extra turn will do no harm), then tie off the free end onto the standing end using two overhand knots.

99

FISHERMAN'S KNOT

This very ancient knot, the easiest type of bend, is what you need when the bit of string in your hand isn't long enough for the job. Perhaps you're executing a daring life-saving manoeuvre following a man overboard. Or perhaps you've just misread the tide table and your crabbing line won't reach the bottom of the harbour wall.

It consists of two overhand knots tied in parallel on the standing end of the other rope. First, lay the two bits of rope next to each other. Pick up one free end and tie an overhand knot around the second rope. Then pick up the other free end and tie an overhand knot over your first bit of rope. Finally, take the two standing ends and pull tight. The two knots will slide into each other and tighten.

TRUCKER'S HITCH

This knot is a great two-for-one deal. You can use it to lash things down tight (your kayak onto a roof rack, your dinghy onto a trailer) and to hoist things up (your dinghy into a boathouse, your smuggled cases of claret into a cave).

Start by tying an overhand loop in the line. Thread the free end through the securing point, then thread the free end back through the overhand loop. At this point you have created a system with a 3:1 mechanical advantage. The free end can by tied off in a number of ways; perhaps the easiest is a round turn and two half-hitches on the securing point.

Tightening the system, which is how you achieve the desired lashing or hoisting, is simple. First, pull on the line going from the securing point to the loop, while keeping the free end taut. Next, keep both parts of the line taut and take up the slack on the free end that you just created. This can be repeated many times in a process called *sweating the line*. The natural friction in the system has an almost magical effect: you don't lose the gains you make by sweating provided you keep the whole thing reasonably tight.

Now for something a little more advanced. You can increase the mechanical advantage by introducing additional overhand loops. The advantage multiplies with each additional overhand loop, so with two loops you have a 6:1 advantage, with three you have 12:1 and so on. Of course, the friction and profusion of knots makes the system much more unwieldy, so don't overdo it.

THE HAZARDS OF HEMP

Question: if these knots can achieve pretty much anything, why did our forebears dream up so many complicated variations? Answer: knot-tying is much simpler with today's relatively thin, synthetic ropes, compared with traditional hemp. Modern ropes are easy to untie after being under a lot of strain, whereas hemp knits tight. Sailors needed all those fancy knots because they were easier to undo.

Here are a few classics that might come in handy if you're working with retro rope, or if you just feel like showing off.

BOWLINE

A bowline (which rhymes with no-sin, not wow-wine) creates a permanent loop which is useful if you want to tie yourself

to something. Fold a loop in the standing end, pass the free end down through the loop, over the standing end, down again and back up through the loop, pulling tight.

SHEET BEND

This is good for tying a thicker bit of string (say, a hemp warp) to a thinner bit (say, a nylon line). Make a bight in the thick bit. Pass the thin bit up through the bight, round the back, over the top, back under itself and pull tight. Though simple, it's surprisingly strong.

(If you're observant, you'll have noticed that the sheet bend's shape is identical to a bowline: a bowline tied with two pieces of string, if you will.)

FISHERMAN'S BEND

This knot is slightly more complex, and not one you'll need regularly. It's included here because there's nothing quite like it for tying fishing line to a hook and swivel.

It's similar to the round turn and two half-hitches, but you go round the object you are attaching to twice, then bring the free end over the standing end and up through the gap between the line and the object you are attaching to, in a sort of half-hitch. This tightens against this first half-hitch and holds it better in place. You finish the knot with a second half-hitch.

AND FINALLY ... THE REEF KNOT

This one *doesn't* work brilliantly under strain, but it's perfect for tying something down quickly and smartly.

Pass one end over the other in a half bow, then tie another half bow. Crucially you must do the opposite of what you did for the first half bow. So, if you went left over right you must then go right over left. The finished knot should look nice and symmetrical – if it doesn't you have tied a *granny knot,* which is not so much a knot as the international symbol of incompetence. To be avoided at all costs.

ARTHUR RANSOME

I will make, if possible, a book that a child shall understand,
yet a man will feel some temptation to peruse should he chance
to take it up.[*]

As Roald Dahl is to chocolate and J. K. Rowling is to wizards, so Arthur Ransome is to small boats. Unlike some other children's classics, his books still hold up remarkably well. He is neither precious nor preachy, neither arch nor wordy, and his heroes and heroines all exude an enviable resourcefulness, while remaining recognisably human.

....

[*] Arthur Ransome approvingly quoted these words of Walter Scott's.

The plots are taut, the resolutions pleasing, and there's no dumbing down when it comes to nautical lingo.

Yes, the books inhabit what is now a remote past, where people *jolly well know how to row*, and if they don't, they're *awfully* keen to learn, but we needn't dismiss Ransome's work as nostalgic cliché. Above all else, he loved adventures on the water, and the children who live these adventures aren't cyphers, proxies for some hypothetical Englishness: they're real.

Ransome, his background comfortable rather than upper class, spent his early adulthood knocking about Edwardian London, mingling with artists and poets, making a bit of money out of writing (children's nature books, sketches about Bohemia, some literary criticism), all the while reading voraciously, and – most importantly – summering in the Lake District.

He quit England in 1913, leaving behind a stressful libel case and a bad marriage, bound for St Petersburg, which provided fodder for *Old Peter's Russian Tales*, a collection of stories. Come 1914, first war and then revolution turned him into a foreign correspondent, something for which his readers should be grateful, since according to one biographer, 'Journalism ... knocked the whimsy out of Ransome's writing.'*

As one of the Western reporters closest to the Bolshevik high command, Ransome knew both Lenin and Trotsky, and he was more sympathetic to their cause than officials back in England quite liked. He relished the exciting circles in which he moved, as can be seen from this letter home:

....

* An astute observation by Christina Hardyment in *The World of Arthur Ransome*.

'My principal friends here are Radek* and his wife, and two young women, Bolsheviks, as tall as Grenadiers, who prefer pistols to powder puffs, and swords to parasols.'

One of those women was Evgenia Petrovna Shelepina, then working as Trotsky's secretary, later to become Ransome's much-loved sailing mate, critic and wife. After Russia became too dangerous for a foreigner, they moved to Estonia, where he wrote for the *Manchester Guardian*, and they both enjoyed adventures around the Baltic on a little yacht called *Racundra*, whose logbooks Ransome later turned into a popular memoir.

They married in 1924, with Ransome telling his mother, 'I have got one of the staunchest and most capable wives that any man could wish for,' an attitude borne out by the staunch and capable girls who populate his books.

Installed back in England by the late 1920s, living in the Lake District, Ransome reacquainted himself with some old friends from his youth. He'd known Dora Collingwood since she was eighteen, learning to sail with her family on Coniston Water, once even proposing to her (although apparently she didn't take him seriously). She was now Dora Altounyan, married to Ernest, an Armenian-Irish doctor. Normally they were based in Aleppo, but in the summer of 1928 they were holidaying in the Lake District: four children, one baby, two dinghies: *Swallow* and ... *Mavis*.

From this kernel grew a book now known far and wide as *Swallows and Amazons*, in which John, Susan, Titty and

....

* Karl Radek, a Bolshevik insider who was aboard the famous sealed train that took Lenin to Russia in 1917 (although Radek himself was stopped at the border). When Ransome knew him, he was Vice-Commissar for Foreign Affairs.

Roger,* holidaying in the Lake District, set sail in a little dinghy called *Swallow* to camp on Wild Cat Island. The most famous line in the book, in all Ransome's books, arrives in a telegram from the children's naval officer father, whose permission has been sought for this great adventure (mothers couldn't yet sanction adventures on their own account). His reply:

BETTER DROWNED THAN DUFFERS IF NOT DUFFERS WONT DROWN.

is *the* mantra all twenty-first-century parents should mutter through gritted teeth when their child is climbing spiky rocks, rowing across a fast tide, jumping through pounding surf or doing anything else that is dangerously worth doing. (Children can yell it back at their parents when they're told for the umpteenth time to *be careful* ...)

Out on the lake, the Swallows meet the Blackett sisters, racing towards them in the *Amazon*, close-hauled against a southwesterly wind, displaying enviable levels of seamanship. Nancy and Peggy, *definitely* not duffers, are way ahead of their (and sometimes our) time when it comes to blasting gender stereotypes out of the water. The two camps become enemies, then allies, recovering precious papers burgled from the Blacketts' Uncle Jim's house-boat.

The book was a big hit, both critically and with young readers, with Ransome receiving an especially delightful piece of fan mail from one girl: 'Please write another book exactly like the last, with the same people, the same places and the same things happening.'

....

* The Altounyan children were Harriet (known as Taqui), Susie, Mavis (known as Titty) and Roger. Their surname in the book, Walker, was – perhaps unexpectedly – Ransome's first wife's maiden name.

He didn't quite deliver on that, but the eleven books which followed didn't deviate too far from the winning formula – while never once becoming formulaic. There were new characters, most notably the very relatable Dick and Dorothea (townies, a bit geeky), new baddies (boo to the boorish Hullabaloos) and new settings (the British ones more successful than the exoticism of *Peter Duck* and *Missee Lee*), culminating in *Great Northern?*, a *cri de coeur* against the once common practice of egg collecting.

THE NIGHT SKY

Astronomy apps are a wonderful way to learn about stars and constellations. Point your phone at the night sky, and your screen will map the constellations over the otherwise mystifying array of stars before your eyes. But there are two celestial objects that everyone should be able to detect phone-free.

THE NORTH STAR

The North Star is useful because, well, it points north. Plus, it's bright and easy to find. First, you need to locate the Plough (or the Big Dipper as it's called in the US). If you've no idea what a plough or a dipper actually look like, try finding a frying pan instead.

Next, draw an imaginary line through the right-hand edge of the pan and follow it upwards (i.e. in the direction of a tossed pancake). Slightly to the right of that line, you'll find the North Star or Polaris, which is the brightest star in the Ursa Minor or Little Bear constellation.

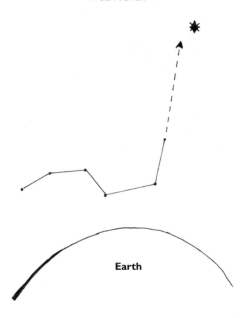

Earth

VENUS

Apart from the moon, Venus is the brightest object in the night sky. It orbits the sun on a similar track to our own, only closer, meaning we see it very close to the sun. By day, the sun is so bright that it's all but impossible to see Venus with a naked eye. At night, it has followed the sun round to the other side of the earth, so we can't see it either. Dawn and dusk are the sweet spots, which is why Venus is also known as the Morning or Evening Star – and why we see it so close to the horizon.

It's a rite of passage for a novice crew member, standing his first solo watch, to peer into the eastern sky, blink a couple of times, and call the skipper up on desk.

'Boat off the port bow. What d'you want me to do?'

The kind-hearted response to which is:

'Let's give her a moment and see what she does.'

Sure enough, a few minutes later, the mystery boat will soar into the sky, a graceful outrider for the sun itself.

TYPES OF RIG

A sailing boat can be a dinghy so small that a lone nine-year-old child could crew it, or a ship so large it needs dozens of experienced sailors to keep it in order. In between lies the classic 30–50 ft yacht, so versatile it can cross oceans (almost) as easily as hop to the next-door bay.

Over the years, designers have dreamt up different configurations of a sailing boat's three basic elements: masts, spars and sails, but these layouts (or *rigs*) can be broadly divided into three groups.

FORE AND AFT, TYPE 1: THE BERMUDA RIG

Developed on the island of Bermuda in the seventeenth century, the *Bermuda rig* is now the standard design for both modern dinghies (whether designed for pottering or racing) and modern yachts (ditto).

The mast is held in place by *stays*, which run from the masthead down to the deck (fore and aft, port and starboard). The triangular *mainsail* is attached to the mast from top (the *head*) to bottom (the *tack*), while the bottom edge (the *foot*) is held in place by the boom. A Bermuda-rigged boat usually carries one or two *headsails* in front of the mast: a *jib* or (larger) *genoa* if only one; a jib and (smaller) *staysail* if two.

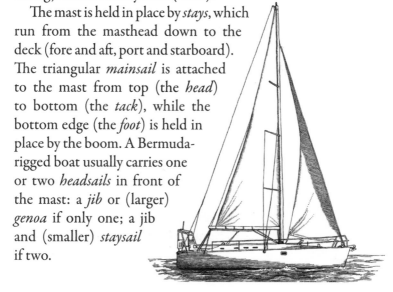

This rig is popular for three reasons: a) it can sail close to the wind, b) the sail is tall and thin, which makes it powerful and c) you don't need too many bits of string to handle the sails, which makes it easier to manage short-handed.

FORE AND AFT, TYPE 2: THE GAFF RIG

The gaff rig, and its friends and relations, is what you traditionally found on smaller working boats until their heyday came to a close early in the twentieth century. Nowadays you generally meet this rig on something wooden, beautiful and troublesome to maintain.

A *gaff* is a spar attached to the mast and the top edge of a four-sided mainsail, and is used to hold the sail aloft, getting round the challenge of providing extra sail area (and therefore power) without a taller mast.

You do need more bits of rope: two halyards, one for either end of the gaff, and possibly *running backstays* (meaning the wires or ropes that support the mast need to be set or stowed depending on which tack you're on).

Against this complexity, gaff-rigged boats are sturdier than Bermudans, don't *heel over** as much, are less prone to dismasting if they capsize, and – let's be frank – they look *beautiful*.

THE SQUARE RIG

A square rigger was *the* ocean-going merchant or naval ship in the Age of Sail, and carries lots of different square sails on lots of different masts. (Technically they're not square, but *trapezoidal*, i.e. longer at the bottom than the top). The sails hang from spars called *yards*, which are attached to the masts in the middle, so the sail falls symmetrically either side. A square rigger's headsails, on the other hand, are rigged fore and aft, no different from a modern boat.

They were most efficient running before the prevailing westerlies in high latitudes or the prevailing trade winds closer to the equator.

You can only sail a square rigger with a large and hoary crew. Shinning up *ratlines*, balancing (harness-free, naturally) on *footlines* below the yards, fighting to gather in handfuls of thrashing, storm-drenched sail ... working aloft was dangerous and demanding.

....

* Heeling over will be a familiar sight if you've ever watched racing yachts or dinghies pelting forwards while leaning over on what looks unnervingly like the point of capsize. Such a boat can be said to be *on its ear*.

TYPES OF BOAT

Once you've anchored those three basic rig types in your mind, you can now fit them onto an array of sailing boats:

Catboat. One mast, one large mainsail, no headsail. The mast is usually set well forward and the sail is frequently gaff rigged.

Sloop. One mast, one mainsail, one headsail. Bermuda or gaff rig. The headsail can either be a smaller jib or a larger genoa.

Cutter. One mast, more than one headsail, often a jib and a staysail. Bermuda or gaff rig. Can also carry a square topsail.

Yawl. Two masts, one headsail. Bermuda or gaff rig. The *mizzen* (mast nearest the stern) is shorter than the mainmast and stands *behind* the steering position.

Ketch. Two masts, one headsail. Bermuda or gaff rig. The mizzen is shorter than the mainmast and stands *in front of* the steering position.

Schooner. Two masts, the foremast slightly shorter than the mainmast. Once gaff rigged, now more likely to carry a Bermuda rig. Can also carry a square topsail.

Brig. Two-masted, square-rigged schooner.

Brigantine. Two-masted schooner. The foremast usually gaff rigged. The mainmast square rigged.

Ship. Three masts, square rigged. The mainmast (the one in the middle) is tallest.

Barque. Three masts. The foremast and mainmast are square rigged. The mizzen is rigged fore and aft.

Barquentine. Three masts. The mainmast and mizzen are rigged fore and aft. The foremast is square rigged.

GRACE DARLING

For twenty-two years, Grace Darling lived quietly on one of the Outer Farne Islands off the coast of Northumberland. Her father was the lighthouse keeper, trimming the lamps by night, catching fish and shooting a few birds by day. He was a dour sort, disapproving of novels and card play, and he saw no reason for his daughter to go to school. Occasionally, Grace would row ashore for supplies, but otherwise her life unfolded far from public view.

But in the small hours of 7 September 1838, this retiring girl's stouthearted seamanship transformed her into a national heroine, feted in poems, plays and books, idolised in paintings and sculpture. Bars of chocolate and of soap were emblazoned with her image and the mail bag overflowed with passionate letters begging for locks of her hair.

On Wednesday 5 September, a paddle steamer called the *Forfarshire* had left Hull at 6.30 p.m., bound for Dundee.

The captain was called John Humble, and he was joined on board by his wife, some forty passengers and twenty crew.

That night, as the ship passed Flamborough Head, he realised the starboard boiler was leaking, but instead of putting into shore, he decided to carry out repairs at sea. As he steamed north, leaving the Farne Islands behind him, the boiler failed again. The ship's pumps couldn't cope, so he gave the order to put out the engine fires and hoist the emergency sails.

Unfortunately, both a north-northeasterly wind and a south-setting tide united to drive the ship back towards the Farne Islands, until before dawn on the Friday morning the *Forfarshire* struck Big Harcar, an islet in sight of Grace's lighthouse. The ship broke up, drowning the majority of the passengers and crew, but twelve people managed to scramble onto the southern side of the islet. Three people, two of them children, died of exposure, but the remaining nine made it to the southern side of the rock where they found a scrap of shelter from the northerly wind.

It was then that Grace woke, saw the wreck and alerted her parents. It was still too dark to see whether there were any survivors, but by 7 a.m., with the tide falling, they spotted people still alive.

The more souped-up versions of the tale now have bold little Grace, passionately pleading with her stern father to allow her to row to their aid. The truth may be more prosaic. The lighthouse keeper earned bonuses for spotting wrecks, rescuing people and recovering dead bodies and his sons had certainly helped out before. The young men weren't there, but Grace could row perfectly well. Why *shouldn't* she help? A no-brainer to us, perhaps, but to Victorian sensibilities what followed was nothing short of miraculous.

Father and daughter took an oar each of their 21-foot boat, keeping in the lee (i.e. to the more sheltered south) of Blue Caps, Little Harcar and Big Harcar. Reaching the rocks, her father scrambled out to help the survivors, leaving Grace to manage the boat alone for what must have been a nerve-jangling few minutes. Together, they returned to the lighthouse with the one surviving woman and four of the men, where Grace remained while her father and two of the men returned for the rest.

The news spread. By Tuesday 18 September *The Times* was soaring: 'Is there in the whole field of history, or of fiction even, one instance of female heroism to compare for one moment with this?' Painters arrived, the paparazzi of the day, delighted to discover that the nation's new heroine was petite, feminine and god-fearing. Day trippers crowded ashore, eager for mementos. There were medals, generous donations (including from the young Queen Victoria), endless letters to reply to, endless autographs to sign, all overseen by the family's august new patron, the Duke of Northumberland.

If this were fiction, fame would turn Grace's head. Lured to London by a handsome impresario, she'd turn her back on her family, only to be abandoned once her fifteen minutes of fame were over. But no. It was God, she said, who deserved all the praise. No, she said, to invitations to star on the stage. No, she said, to marriage proposals. No, she said, to all temptations, remaining on her island, frustrated only that her admirers interfered with her housework.

Such virtue went cruelly unrewarded. Four years after she shot to fame, she fell ill with tuberculosis, and declined fast. Even the duke's physician couldn't save her.

Her death moved William Wordsworth to write a poem (not one of his best) about her birth 'on bleak Northumbria's coast' where she might have remained 'known unto few but prized as far as known' until her 'single act' made her famous. She was a maid, gentle, firm, unflinching, bound to duty, earnest, full of faith and fortitude, pious and pure, modest and yet so brave, young and wise, meek and resolute.

She was incomparably, impossibly, perfectly Victorian.

THE EDDYSTONE LIGHT

The Eddystone lighthouse sits on top of some inconveniently located rocks, roughly twelve miles south-southwest of Plymouth Sound. Right in the way of any ship hoping to pass up or down the north side of the English Channel between the Lizard and Start Point, the rocks disappear from view during high spring tides, making them especially hazardous.

Building on the rocks was never going to be easy, but nevertheless a lighthouse was completed in 1698, the first tower to go up in such a tricky spot in the open sea. It was known as Winstanley's Tower after its wonderfully eccentric designer, Henry Winstanley, who had been fired up by the loss of two ships in which he'd been heavily invested.

Building took place while England was at war with France, and the works were supposedly under the protection of the Admiralty. One day, however, in the absence of the supposed guard ship, a French privateer turned up and spirited Winstanley away to France. Rather wonderfully, Louis XIV ordered his immediate release, saying, so the story goes: 'France is at war with England, not with humanity.'

That tower was destroyed in the Great Storm of 1703, and its builder along with it: Winstanley had been repairing the lighthouse when the storm struck. The next, built of wood, stood from 1709 to 1755 when it burnt down, an obvious hazard for lighthouses pre-electricity. Four years later a new one was in place, which stood until 1882. The designer, John Smeaton, decided to copy the shape of an oak tree (a very naval image), and succeeded in building it out of stone.

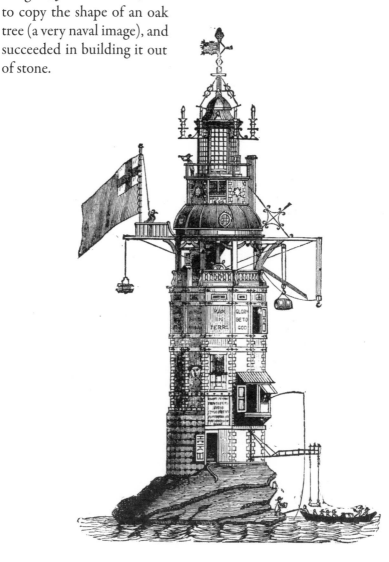

When it too started to fail, having stood for more than a century, it was shipped to stand as a monument on Plymouth Hoe.

The fourth incarnation of the Eddystone light was a much more sophisticated affair, becoming fully automatic on 18 May 1882. It remains there to this day, joyfully celebrated in this folk classic:

My father was the keeper of the Eddystone light
And he slept with a mermaid one fine night.
From this union came children three:
A porpoise and a kipper and the other was me.

Yo ho ho, the wind blows free, ho for a life on the rolling sea

One night when I was a-trimmin' of the glim,
Singin' a verse from the evening hymn,
A voice from the starboard shouted, 'Ahoy!'
And there was my mother a-sittin' on a buoy.

Yo ho ho, the wind blows free, ho for a life on the rolling sea

'Oh what has become of my children three?'
My mother then she asked of me.
'One was exhibited as a talking fish
The other was served in a chafing dish.'

Yo ho ho, the wind blows free, ho for a life on the rolling sea

The phosphorus flashed in her seaweed hair.
I looked again, and my mother wasn't there,
But her voice came echoing through the night,
'To hell with the keeper of the Eddystone light!'

HOW LONG IS THE
BRITISH COASTLINE?

Can geometry deliver what the Greek root of its name seemed
to promise – truthful measurement, not only of cultivated fields
along the Nile River but also of untamed Earth?*

Do we mean the coast of Britain *and* Northern Ireland?
Are we going to include islands and, if so, which ones?
When does an estuary stop being an estuary and become
a river? What's the state of the tide? Depending on how
you answer those questions, you'll get a different answer,
ranging from 10,000 to 20,000 miles.

Even if we lock down those parameters, the uncertainty
doesn't stop there. In fact, it's only the beginning. We're
about to fall, head first, into the mathematical thorn patch
that is the *coastline paradox*.

The first person, so far as we know, to really grapple
with this problem was Lewis Fry Richardson, a twentieth-
century mathematician, pacifist and weather forecasting
pioneer. While researching a theory proposing that the
longer the border between two countries, the more likely
they were to go to war, he noticed the measurements given
for border length varied wildly.

He realised, correctly, that this was down to a border's
roughness. When you're measuring a border – or a coastline
– how small is the smallest feature you should take into
account? That enormous bay? Obviously. That little cove

....

* *The Fractalist: Memoir of a Scientific Maverick*, Benoit Mandelbrot. The
Greek root he's talking about is *geo*: earth.

in the corner of the bay? Probably. That little crack in the cliff at the back of the cove in bay? Errr ...

Richardson chose a roundabout, and rather brilliant, way of tackling this problem. Rather than focusing on measuring his borders accurately, he focused on measuring them approximately, but with *increasing levels of precision*. Applying his method to our coastline, we start with a 100 km ruler. Round the coast we go, 100 km at a time, the ends of our ruler always touching two bits of coasts, until we arrive at our first answer. We repeat, this time with a 50 km ruler, which will give us a more accurate – and *larger* – figure. Why larger? Because with our smaller ruler, we've been able to take more of the variations into account. We then repeat with a 25 km ruler, a 10 km ruler, a 5 km ruler, and so on.

Richardson showed that there was an empirical relationship between the length of the ruler and the length of the coastline: the logarithm of the coastline was *directly proportional* and *negatively correlated* to the logarithm of the ruler. Smaller ruler; longer coastline.

This observation leads to two quite extraordinary conclusions. The first is that, in the words of the mathematician Benoit Mandelbrot (an expert in fractals and chaos theory), coastlines are *statistically self-similar*. In other words, if you zoom in on a patch of coast it doesn't look any less rough. Far out: wiggly bays. Middle distance: wiggly coves. Extreme close up: wiggly rocks. Whichever scale you choose, the roughness remains.

Intuitively, you might think that this relationship would tail off, that each extra increment of accurate measurement would yield less extra length each time, finally converging on a definitive length. But it doesn't work like that. The *smaller ruler; longer coastline* principle persists, leading to Mandelbrot's second rather stunning conclusion: *infinitely accurate* measurement of a coastline yields an *infinitely long* coastline.

Coastlines, therefore, are classic real-life examples of fractals, which are special kinds of curves whose lengths you can't measure using calculus because they get more complex the more you zoom in. For the full mathematical low-down, pop Mandelbrot's 1967 paper *How Long Is the Coast of Britain? Statistical Self-Similarity and Fractional Dimension* into your beach bag this summer, or to save time simply repeat with us: 'Geographical curves are so involved in their detail that their lengths are often infinite or more accurately, undefinable.'

WHISKY GALORE

In February 1941, deep in the Second World War, when there wasn't all that much to be cheerful about, a merchant ship ran aground in a rocky bay in the Outer Hebrides. When questions were asked about how an experienced captain could have made such a pig's ear of steaming through the Minch, a strait many miles wide, the ribald answer was often returned: well, he was drunk – wasn't he?

The *Politician*, you see, was carrying 20,000 cases of whisky.

When the lifeboat from Castlebay on Barra Island arrived to take the crew to safety, they couldn't help noticing the bottles poking out of their pockets, and naturally they asked a few probing questions.

Two days after the smash, the captain returned to the *Politician* to try to figure out whether he could refloat his ship. He wasn't successful, and a coaster turned up to offload as much cargo as possible, a tricky job as many of the holds were brimful of water. The whisky turned out to be particularly inaccessible, and the salvage team wrapped up their work without removing it. (Apparently, some of the workers swiped a few bottles, only to be busted when they got back to Glasgow. Next time round they were cannier, offloading their spoils in the Crinan Canal to pick up later.)

And so, little over a month after the accident, the local customs officer battened down the *Politician*'s hold and sealed it with his official customs seal. As if that was going to stop anyone.

Come low tide, little boats beetled out from North Uist and South Uist, from Barra and Eriskay,* perhaps even all the way from Lewis and Mull. On busy nights as many as fifty could be seen, bobbing around the stricken ship, islanders groping for a single rope ladder to get aboard.

Getting at the whisky wasn't easy. First, they had to haul bolts of cloth, household paraphernalia, and heaven knows what else out the way. Next, they had to figure out how to hoist the whisky out of the oily, murky water in the ship's hold and transfer it to their little boats. Once the booze was ashore, they had to stash it where neither officialdom nor greedy neighbours would unearth it.

And finally, you can be sure, they had to drink it.

'To say there was celebration on the islands would be something of an understatement,' writes Arthur Swinson in his fun account, *Scotch on the Rocks*. 'In the early days, life in some of the crofts was one long carousal. Parties blew up at the slightest excuse. Courting couples decided that this was the exact time to get married. Even chores like peat-cutting

....

* Today, Eriskay's only pub is called *Am Politician*.

were turned into a festival, the parties getting through a crate a day.'

A heartfelt toast, of course, was always due to the poor captain of the *Polly*, who'd done them all such a wonderful service.

But every good story needs conflict, and Charles McColl, the local customs officer, provided it in spades. He started inspecting crofts and found an extraordinary array of goodies swiped from the ship: soap, ink, disinfectant, rubber bands, notebooks, tin openers, shovels – but not much by way of whisky. The islanders, obviously, were keeping that better hidden.

Tales have been handed down of whisky stashed in the most outlandish places: in animal feeding troughs, in chamber pots, even in a coffin, and McColl, incandescent that the state's coffers were being done out of so much revenue, made it his mission to find every last bottle. (He didn't succeed. Today, a genuine bottle of *Politician* whisky can fetch thousands of pounds at auction.)

By then, the fun was over. The custom officer's garage was set on fire, and forty men wound up in court, with some serving a month or two in prison in Inverness. A shipbreaker arrived to dispose of the wreck, and the remaining whisky was dynamited.

The story was immortalised, first in Compton Mackenzie's book *Whisky Galore*, set on the fictionalised island of Todday, and then in the Ealing comedy *Whisky Galore!*, a classic tale of the underdog triumphant.

FINGAL'S CAVE

Fingal's Cave on the island of Staffa takes the UK's geological crown. Staffa, a couple of hours' sail west of Mull, was forged by volcanoes: lava erupted, cooled rapidly and created remarkable hexagonal basalt columns, best seen inside a sea cave on the south side.

Fingal is another name for the legendary Irish hero, Finn MacCumhaill (sometimes anglicised to Finn MacCool) who, amongst many other feats, was responsible for some of our quirkiest topography. He forged the Giant's Causeway so he could reach Scotland without wetting his feet; and when he hurled a piece of Ireland at an enemy, one chunk sheared off to become the Isle of Man, while another flew on to become Rockall.

There doesn't, alas, appear to be a proper legend linking him to the sea cave, but his name drew dozens of writers, artists, musicians and celebrities to admire it regardless. Most famous, perhaps, was the visit by the composer, Felix Mendelssohn, then aged twenty, who rode to the island aboard a paddle steamer in 1829. The friend he voyaged with wrote:

> We were put out into boats and lifted by the hissing sea
> up the pillar stumps to the celebrated Fingal's Cave. A
> greener roar of waves surely never rushed into a stranger
> cavern – its many pillars making it look like the inside of
> an immense organ, black and resounding, and absolutely
> without purpose, and quite alone, the wide grey sea within
> and without.

Apparently, they were all fearfully sick, but the cave impressed Mendelssohn so much that it inspired his great musical seascape, *The Hebrides* overture.

A SMUGGLER'S SONG

from *Puck of Pook's Hill*, by Rudyard Kipling

If you wake at midnight, and hear a horse's feet,
Don't go drawing back the blind, or looking in the street,
Them that asks no questions isn't told a lie –
Watch the wall, my darling, while the Gentlemen go by!

> *Five-and-twenty ponies,*
> *Trotting through the dark –*
> *Brandy for the Parson,*
> *'Baccy for the Clerk;*
> *Laces for a lady, letters for a spy;*
> *And watch the wall, my darling, while the Gentlemen go by!*

Running round the woodlump, if you chance to find
Little barrels, roped and tarred, all full of brandy-wine,
Don't you shout to come and look, nor take 'em for your
   play;
Put the brushwood back again – and they'll be gone next
   day!

If you see the stable-door setting open wide;
If you see a tired horse lying down inside;

If your mother mends a coat cut about and tore;
If the lining's wet and warm – don't you ask no more!

If you meet King George's men, dressed in blue and red,
You be careful what you say, and mindful what is said.
If they call you 'pretty maid', and chuck you 'neath the chin,
Don't you tell where no one is, nor yet where no one's been!

Knocks and footsteps round the house – whistles after
    dark –
You've no call for running out till the house-dogs bark.
Trusty's here, and Pincher's here, and see how dumb they
    lie –
They don't fret to follow when the Gentlemen go by!

If you do as you've been told, likely there's a chance
You'll be give a dainty doll, all the way from France,
With a cap of Valenciennes, and a velvet hood –
A present from the Gentlemen, along o' being good!

    Five-and-twenty ponies,
    Trotting through the dark –
    Brandy for the Parson,
    'Baccy for the Clerk,
Them that asks no questions isn't told a lie –
Watch the wall, my darling, while the Gentlemen go by!

SMUGGLING

Smuggling was once considered a forgivable sort of crime. For centuries, officials tried to make upright British citizens see it differently, but sneaking goods across the Channel without paying the government its due never really got people riled. After all, from whom does the smuggler steal? From faceless bureaucrats and spendthrift governments – and nobody feels sorry for them.

Once upon a time, being *anti-smuggling* could even make you appear priggish, prissy – a bit of a prude. No less an authority on human nature than the eighteenth-century economist Adam Smith once wrote: 'To pretend to have any scruple about buying smuggled goods ... would in most countries be regarded as one of those pedantic pieces of hypocrisy which, instead of gaining credit with anybody, seems only to expose the person who affects to practise it to the suspicion of being a greater knave than most of his neighbours.'

Duties, after all, are a *regressive* form of taxation, in that the earl pays no more for his tobacco than the labourer who works on his land. Jean-Baptiste Colbert, finance minister to France's Sun King, Louis XIV, declared that 'the art of taxation consists in so plucking the goose as to obtain the largest possible amount of feathers with the smallest possible amount of hissing'. Import duties were seen as excessively greedy; smuggling was a collective hiss.

British society didn't merely fail to condemn the smuggler; it even considered him charming. One prolific writer on all things maritime, Edward Keble Chatterton, called it a 'sneaking regard ... an instinct that is based partly on a curious human failing and partly on a keen admiration for men of dash and daring'.

Initially, though, smugglers focused on getting goods *out* not in. In the Middle Ages, sheep's wool was a top commodity, England's number-one raw material, but the best weavers weren't here: they were in Flanders. The Crown (needing money to fund its wars) slapped a hefty tax on wool exports, which smugglers around England's southeast coast did their best to dodge. And seeing as two-way trade is more profitable, wool-runners started to return with wine, silk, lace – all manner of fancy foreign goods.

From these beginnings, smuggling blossomed until its eighteenth-century peak when Britain was more or less constantly at war – against the Spanish, against the Thirteen Colonies (aka the United States), and of course against France.

Wars push up taxes. Wars push up prices. Wars mean governments and their navies have bigger fish to fry than chasing after men rowing brandy into moonlit coves in the dead of night. War, in other words, was good for smuggling.

Navigating the British coastline also required expertise that even the most upstanding seafarer could respect. Thus Captain Edward Brenton, in his *Naval History of Great Britain*:

> These men are as remarkable for their skill in seamanship
> as for their audacity in the hour of danger; their local
> knowledge has been highly advantageous to the Navy, into
> which, however, they never enter, unless sent on board
> ships of war as a punishment for some crime committed

against the revenue laws. They are hardy, sober, and faithful to each other, beyond the generality of seamen; and, when shipwreck occurs, have been known to perform deeds not exceeded in any country in the world; probably unequalled in the annals of other maritime powers.

The illicit trade also received such broad support because it majored in consumer luxuries, the sorts of thing everyone wanted: tea, alcohol, tobacco and covetable textiles. In his notebooks, the novelist Thomas Hardy recalled that even his respectable grandfather had spirits stashed in a dark closet, which had been delivered at night by men on horseback, who knocked at the windowpane and vanished, leaving tubs on the doorstep.

Booty flowed through dozens of little networks around the country: from ship to boat and boat to creek, along sunken lanes and narrow passages, ever onwards to expectant customers. A clifftop signal here or catcall there warned of revenue officers on the prowl, and if the warnings failed, magistrates could be threatened and jurors bribed.

Caves and secret tunnels are the stuff of legend, but the smugglers preferred to move their loot inland as quickly as possible. When short-term concealment was unavoidable ingenious solutions were found. Tobacco might be spliced into ropes or hidden in hollow loaves of bread. Barrels could be suspended under floats or rafts, to be retrieved once the coast was clear.

This sort of small-scale smuggling was immortalised in R. L. Stevenson's *Moonfleet*. Here our innocent young hero John is looking out to sea:

She was too small for a privateer, too large for a fishing-smack, and could not be a revenue boat by her low freeboard in the waist; and 'twas a strange thing for a boat

to cast anchor in the midst of Moonfleet Bay even on a
night so fine as this. Then while I watched I saw a blue
flare in the bows, only for a moment, as if a man had lit a
squib and flung it overboard, but I knew from it she was a
contrabandier, and signalling either to the shore or to a mate
in the offing.

That's the romantic side of the coin. Smuggling was, of
course, also carried out by well-organised criminals. The
uncompromising violence of the Kent-based Hawkhurst
Gang, for example, made them notorious in the early eighteenth century. Operating with impunity, they terrorised
anyone who stood in their way. In one particularly brazen
episode, they raided the Poole Customs House, which had
dared to impound their cargo. Later, a potential witness
and the customs official who was escorting him were kid-
napped by the gang, beaten up and brutally murdered: one
was buried alive, the other was thrown down a well. The
gang was eventually brought to justice, their bodies hung
in gibbets as a grisly warning to others.

In an attempt to regain control, the government banned
traders from using boats with shallow draughts (useful for
creeping into secluded creeks) or boats rowed by more than
four oars (useful for nipping to and from larger ships), and
forbade anyone from *hovering* within six miles of the shore.
Riding Officers (ashore) and *King's Cutters* (afloat) were
also established to play the smugglers at their own game,
with some success. Here's the epitaph on the Dorset grave
of one smuggler, killed near Poole in 1765:

A little Tea one leaf I did not steal
For Guiltless blood shed, I to God appeal
Put Tea in one scale human blood in tother
And think what tis to slay thy harmless Brother

The threat of a cross-Channel invasion during the Napoleonic Wars certainly made smuggling harder, as did the founding in 1809 of the Waterguard, which had watch houses and patrol crews around the coast. Ultimately, though, the government didn't quash smuggling by force, but by undercutting its profits with massively reduced tariffs. Once duty-paid goods are affordable, smugglers quickly go out of business.

Of course, these days, the word *smuggling* has far darker connotations: we're more likely to associate it with *people* and *drugs*. No celebrated national poet is exhorting you to *watch the wall* while those sorts of smugglers go by, nor would anyone think you puritanical for condemning them. No longer are smugglers the bold, mischievous figures of fiction and folk legend – if indeed they ever were.

TINTAGEL

The village of Tintagel on the north Cornish coast has a twelfth-century Welsh writer to thank for its fame, not to mention its King Arthur-themed gift shops.

Geoffrey of Monmouth's page-turner, *The History of the Kings of Britain*, is a trove of great stories, interweaving the almost factual with the altogether fictional: it covers, for example, Julius Caesar's invasion with the same seriousness as King Lear's troubles with his daughters. He also wrote one of the earliest – and one of the best – versions of the story of King Arthur, whose role as Britain's shining light during the Dark Ages no amount of bracing historical cold water has ever been able to douse.

Arthur may sleep in Avalon, but he was conceived and born at Tintagel. This is how the story goes ...

King Uther Pendragon is welcoming the British nobility to London to celebrate a triumph over the Saxons. Gorlois, Duke of Cornwall and the strategic mastermind behind the victory, has brought his wife Ygerna with him, the most beautiful woman in all the land. Her looks, as so often, turn out to be a double-edged sword. The king (conveniently forgetting the debt he owes to Gorlois) falls madly in love and/or lust, and tries to seduce her with food, wine and 'sprightly conversation'.*

Gorlois is no fool. Seeing which way the wind is blowing, he and his wife make an abrupt exit. Uther orders them to come back. They refuse. He musters his army, and sets off after them, burning towns and castles on his way. Gorlois digs in with his army, while Ygerna takes refuge in the safest place in Cornwall: Tintagel Castle.

An excellent choice – in theory. The castle is perched on an almost-island, high, high above the sea, accessible only by a narrow isthmus.** As Uther's sidekick Ulfius puts it (when the king says he will literally *die* without Ygerna), three soldiers could hold Tintagel against the entire might of Britain.

What is Uther to do?

Why, ask Merlin, of course.

The story now takes an even more sinister turn. Merlin can, he says, make Uther look exactly like Gorlois, allowing him to trick his way into the castle and Ygerna's bed. The king follows his advice, and so disguised, sets off to Tintagel where he sleeps with Ygerna, spinning tales all the

....

* *Banter* is the twenty-first-century equivalent of sprightly conversation.
** Today, there's a handy bridge.

while of how he ('Gorlois') loved her so much he'd snuck away from his camp (besieged by that *brute* Uther) to make sure she was all right.

Nine months pass, and Arthur arrives, a defining moment of British myth-making given a supernatural gloss by Tennyson, the Victorian poet superstar, in his *Idylls of the King*. Looking out to sea, Merlin waits ...

> Wave after wave, each mightier than the last,
> Till last, a ninth one, gathering half the deep
> And full of voices, slowly rose and plunged
> Roaring, and all the wave was in a flame:*
> And down the wave and in the flame was borne
> A naked babe, and rode to Merlin's feet,
> Who stoopt and caught the babe, and cried 'The King!
> Here is an heir for Uther!' And the fringe
> Of that great breaker, sweeping up the strand,
> Lashed at the wizard as he spake the word,
> And all at once all round him rose in fire,
> So that the child and he were clothed in fire.
> And presently thereafter followed calm,
> Free sky and stars.

Beneath Tintagel lies what we now call Merlin's Cave, which you can walk through at low tide, pondering the boundaries between fiction and reality.

....

* Singer-songwriter Kate Bush wrote a conceptual suite called *The Ninth Wave* about a person drifting lost at sea, quoting these first four lines on the cover.

DRACULA

Rip currents, storm winds, black rocks: you might think the sea delivered scares enough, without an overlay of gothic horror. But lit by the sickly glow of phosphorescence, there are maritime stories that rival anything a ruined castle and a windswept moor have to offer.

One unexceptional fishing town will be forever associated with a blood-sucking Romanian aristocrat, after Bram Stoker chose to wash Count Dracula ashore at Whitby, where a ruined abbey still lours eerily above the sea.

Stoker's heroine, Mina Murray, is innocently holidaying in Whitby, as the author did himself in 1890 (soaking up the atmosphere while his wife and son savoured high Victorian seaside society). She is charmed by everything.

'This is a lovely place,' she writes – mistakenly as it turns out – in her diary.

Meanwhile, Count Dracula has taken ship from a Black Sea port aboard the *Demeter*, which is loaded with boxes of his native soil (to keep up his demonic strength upon arrival). The ship is well named: Demeter is the Greek goddess of harvest and plenty, but her daughter Persephone was doomed to spend half the year with the vampiric Hades, god of the underworld.

The *Demeter* ignores various more conveniently located (but less atmospheric) ports in the southeast, and heads north to Whitby, with the crew dropping like flies.

Ashore, Mina is filled with foreboding: 'All is vastness; the clouds are piled up like giant rocks, and there is a "brool"* over the sea that sounds like some presage of doom.'

How right she was.

An easterly storm hits the schooner 'with all sails set',** driving it onto the lee shore. Says one old salt who is watching, 'she must fetch up somewhere, if it was only in hell.' A rush of sea fog obscures the view,*** until a wind shift blows the ship into the safety of the harbour. Here is the masterstroke:

> The searchlight followed her, and a shudder ran through all who saw her, for lashed to the helm was a corpse, with drooping head, which swung horribly to and fro at each motion of the ship.

A black dog, Dracula in canine disguise, leaps ashore, and from there unfurls a rich drama that ends with the count's death at the hands of a collection of fine, upstanding vampire hunters.

DANGEROUS BEASTS

One of the more appealing aspects of the Great British seaside (and indeed of Great Britain *in toto*) is the relative lack of creatures that are out to get you. The sea can be

....

* Perhaps one of the fruits of Stoker's research into local dialect.
** We'll forgive the captain for not keeping a weather eye out; an on-board vampire would have been distracting.
*** Sea fog in the middle of a tempest strikes us as unlikely, but again poetic licence, etc.

(as we hope we've said *ad nauseam*) incredibly dangerous, but as for our micro- and megafauna, they are by and large benevolent. With a few exceptions ...

JELLYFISH

Jellyfish predate dinosaurs by a considerable margin, surviving happily for millions of years with neither brains nor bones nor a central nervous system. Intriguingly, what we call a jellyfish is in fact the sexually active incarnation of a shape-shifting organism which also enjoys less intimidating larval, polyp and ephyral stages. Once transformed into an adult *medusa*,* it floats freely around the oceans until it reproduces and dies.

A charming sight when viewed from a boat or dockside, jellyfish induce panic when glimpsed through swimming goggles while neck-deep in water.

Their tentacles are covered with specialised cells, called *cnidocytes* or *nematocytes* which, if triggered, fire what is essentially a tiny harpoon on a thread loaded with venom.

The one thing that everybody knows about jellyfish stings is that you should pee on them. *Don't*. Instead:

1. Rinse the affected area with seawater.
2. Remove any stray bits of tentacles: they can still sting even if separated from the core jellyfish. Use tweezers if you are the sort of person who goes to the beach with a first aid kit, or a bank card if not.
3. Soak in water as hot as you can bear for at least half an hour.
4. Take painkillers.

....

* A reference to the mythical Greek gorgon who had tentacle-y snakes instead of hair; the word for jellyfish in the vast majority of European languages.

5. Present yourself to a lifeguard if it's bad or a doctor if it's worse.

Here are a few you might meet:

Moon jellyfish (*Aurelia aurita*): A translucent jellyfish with four easy-to-spot horseshoe shapes* on the top of its bell. Smallish with short, fine tentacles. They have stingers, but they're too small to hurt a human.

Blue jellyfish (*Cyanea lamarckii*): You can probably guess what it looks like. Small, unscary, most common around northern UK waters. Sting as mild as a nettle or as painful as a wasp, perhaps depending on where exactly it gets you.

Compass jellyfish (*Chrysaora hysoscella*): The distinctive brown markings around the fringe and on the top of its bell do indeed resemble – if you're feeling generous – a compass rose. They have frillier *oral arms* directly under the bell and thinner tentacles around the edge. Sting level similar to the blue jelly.

Lion's mane jellyfish (*Cyanea capillata*): Possesses an impressively bushy red/brown forest of tentacles underneath its bell. Can grow up to two metres in diameter, with tentacles forty metres long, but they're generally only about the size of a frisbee.

The lion's mane jelly did, however, enjoy a star turn in a Sherlock Holmes short story. A man is found *in extremis*, with dark red lines marking his back as if he'd been brutally whipped. His dying words are mysterious ... 'Lion's mane ... lion's mane ...' A few pages later, Holmes, unusually the

....

* Its gonads!

narrator in this story, unmasks the true culprit: 'It lay upon a rocky shelf some three feet under the water, a curious waving, vibrating hairy creature with streaks of silver among its yellow tresses ... "It has done mischief enough. Its day is over!" I cried. "... Let us end the murderer for ever."'

Holmes has it on good authority that the lion's mane sting is worse even than the bite of a cobra, but don't panic. There's some artistic licence at play, plus the plot depended on the dead man having a weak heart.

Portuguese man-o'-war (*Physalia physalis*). Not a jellyfish exactly, but a *siphonophore*: a floating colony of tiny organisms called zooids, which team up and function as a whole, in a sort of extreme *symbiosis*. What you see floating above the surface is the *pneumatophore*, a gas-filled sac or bladder, normally about 30 cm long. Below the surface, however, lurk trailing tentacles, which can reach up to 50 m, although 10 m is more typical. These are seriously venomous, but luckily the man-o'-war is only an occasional visitor to our shores from its traditional tropical waters. Stings are intensely painful.

MANY SHARKS, ONE FISH

There *are* sharks in UK waters, but thankfully none that are particularly interested in you. In fact, the most recent 'shark death' in British history occurred in 1956, off the

Lizard in Cornwall: two men were blown up by explosives they'd somehow attached to a shark's fin (apparently they wanted to kill it because they thought it was threatening a naval dive operation). The shark died as well. The coroner recorded a verdict of misadventure, which seems something of an understatement in the circumstances.

So, no great whites, tigers or bull sharks, but you could still come across: a smooth hammerhead, a blue shark, a smooth-hound, a starry smooth-hound, a shortfin mako, a tope, a porbeagle shark, a sharpnose sevengill shark, a Greenland shark, a kitefin shark, a bramble shark, a blunt-nose sixgill shark, a frilled shark, an angelshark, a thresher shark, a small-spotted catshark (aka sandy dogfish, lesser spotted dogfish, rough-hound or morgay), a nursehound (aka large-spotted dogfish, greater spotted dogfish or bull huss), a spiny dogfish (aka spurdog, mud shark, or piked dogfish) ... or a basking shark.

The basking shark (*Cetorhinus maximus*): Averaging around 7 m, or twenty-one mackerel laid nose to tail, is the second-largest fish in the world,* and quite the largest to frequent British waters. No threat to humans, these sweet, slow, small-brained sharks are filter feeders.

Their enormous mouths, with ridges inside that resemble a Halloween *Scream* mask, can gape more than a metre wide, allowing them to hoover up vast quantities of zooplankton (apparently basking sharks consider a tiny crustacean named *Calanus helgolandicus* to be a particular delicacy).

They visit from May until October, and you're most likely to spot them near the Outer Hebrides, around Mull and Skye, by the Isle of Man, off Malin Head, as well as

....

* Whale shark is number one; great white is number three.

up and down the Devon and Cornwall coasts. Special boat trips know where to look for them, but you might be lucky to run into one even while snorkelling or kayaking.

They're not aggressive, but – as you would with any large, wild animal – give them a wide berth (a *cable* should be plenty) because they can thrash their tails if they're upset. If there are lots of sharks following each other closely, give them an even wider berth. They could be mating.

Hunting basking sharks (for the oil in their liver) was only banned at the end of the last century. In the years after the Second World War, Gavin Maxwell (better known as the otter-loving author of *Ring of Bright Water*) tried to found a basking shark fishery on Soay, an island off the coast of Skye. Fortunately, his enterprise didn't prosper.

The three varieties of dogfish: You might come across these in two ways. Firstly, as food. You never read dogfish 'n' chips on a menu; instead you find one of these euphemistic alternatives: rock salmon, rock eel, huss or flake. The spiny dogfish (*Squalus acanthias*) is classed as vulnerable, so if you're feeling brave (and the queue behind you isn't too long) interrogate your fish batterer closely as to exactly which dogfish s/he is dishing up.

Secondly, as mermaids' purses. Most fish release thousands of eggs into the sea, many of which won't make it: remember the gory opening of *Finding Nemo*. A dogfish embryo, on the other hand, develops for months inside a special pouch, a sort of tough leathery capsule, which gives it a better chance of surviving once it 'hatches'. These egg cases have long tendrils, like rather stylish fringed handles, perfect for a discerning mermaid, and can often be found along the tide-line, especially after stormy weather.

Lesser weever or sting fish (*Echiichthys vipera*): These are a threat to anyone who is paddling barefoot at low water or playing in the waves on a sandy beach. They are small – only 8-12 cm – but *extremely* poisonous. They lie in ambush, hidden in sand, mud or light shingle, with only their eyes and spines sticking out. So if you see a rather pretty little fish with spines on its back in your shrimping net, *don't* pick it up. The pain is excruciating, and may be accompanied by swelling, redness, numbness, even paraly-sis. The advice is:

1. Get the spines out.
2. Rinse.
3. Put the bit that's been stung in water as hot as you can stand.
4. No vinegar, ice, petrol or pee.
5. Next time, invest in a pair of flip-flops.

MONSTERS

Tales of sea monsters are as ubiquitous around the world as flood myths. Perhaps, as some folklorists have speculated, they originate in our dim recollection of long-dead mega-fauna. It's a tempting hypothesis. Once upon a time, we did cohabit with sloths the size of elephants, with wombats as big as hippos, but it's doubtful that even our deepest memories go back to the *megalodon* or the *mosasaurus*, two reassuringly extinct aquatic carnivores.

The ancient Greeks gave us the monster *Cetus*, who attempted to devour Perseus's love interest, Andromeda, and whose name gives us the word *cetacean*, meaning sea mammal. They also gave us Scylla, the six-headed creature who lived in a cave opposite the whirlpool Charybdis, and who definitely *did* eat some of Odysseus's crew. In the Old Testament we meet the 'great fish' that swallowed Jonah, as well as the more mysterious *Leviathan*, glimpsed here in *Paradise Lost*, as Milton conjures up things that are as big as Satan:

> ... that sea beast
> Leviathan, which God of all his works
> Created hugest that swim the ocean stream:
> Him, haply, slumbering on the Norway foam
> The pilot of some small night foundered skiff,
> Deeming some island, oft, as seamen tell,
> With fixed anchor in his scaly rind
> Moors by his side under the lee, while night
> Invests the sea, and wished morn delays ...

In his novel *The Pirate*, Walter Scott made use of another creature that has long straddled the line between myth and reality: 'The *kraken*,' he writes, 'the hugest of living things, was still supposed to cumber the recesses of the Northern Ocean; and often, when some fog bank covered the sea at a distance, the eye of the experienced boatmen saw the horns of the monstrous leviathan welking and waving amidst the wreaths of mist, and bore away with all press of oar and sail, lest the sudden suction, occasioned by the sinking of the monstrous mass to the bottom, should drag within the grasp of its multifarious feelers his own frail skiff.'

The kraken is very large, has very long tentacles, and can swallow entire ships and lesser whales, not that anyone has ever seen a whole one. They were taken in deadly earnest as late as the 1750s when Erik Pontoppidan published his *Natural History of Norway*. Fishermen, he related, were wont to discover mysterious shoal patches far out to sea. Away they hastened, to watch the kraken rise from the depths, its body big as islands, its arms like masts.

We now think that sightings of the *giant squid* or the even bigger *colossal squid* are responsible for the kraken's place in folklore. We'll leave it to Herman Melville and *Moby-Dick* (its episodic structure makes it an unbeatable beach read) to conjure this most mysterious of real-life monsters:

> A vast pulpy mass, furlongs in length and breadth, of a glancing cream-colour, lay floating on the water, innumerable long arms radiating from its centre, and curling and twisting like a nest of anacondas, as if blindly to clutch at any hapless object within reach. No perceptible face or front did it have; no conceivable token of either sensation or instinct; but undulated there on the billows, an unearthly, formless, chance-like apparition of life.

THE DARK ART OF CRABBING

WEATHER

You don't crab on lovely sunny days, when you'll have better things to do. You crab in light drizzle, when the tide's too high to rock-pool, but too low to swim, when everyone's finished their ice creams, it's hours till lunch and you simply don't have the moral authority to force a bunch of under-nines on a clifftop walk.

KIT

You can of course fashion your own crabbing line by tying a piece of string round a rasher of bacon and weighting it with your house keys. Bacon is the classic option, but a sausage, a chicken drumstick, pretty much anything works. The European shore crab isn't fussy. It'll eat whatever it can get its claws (or *chelae*) on, right down to rotting fish. However, we're going to suggest saving your bacon for a barbecue when the weather clears up later: instead, buy a line and some bait from a small seaside shop. It'll probably seem overpriced, but that's the price you pay to keep small seaside shops in business, so they'll still be around to sell you ice creams next year. You should also buy a small treat to act as a prize for the *crab race* you'll have later.

LOCATION

Crabs like to lurk and skulk. Look for dank rocks covered in pungent bladderwrack or a rotting quay skirted with sea lettuce. If you're new in town, *ask.*

TECHNIQUE I: THE DROP

Swing the line far enough out that it hits the seabed, and then tug it close enough to your rocks/quay to mask the bait in weed. If a toddler is doing the swinging keep a tight grip on the scruff of its neck; they don't understand momentum. At this point, if you feel like some peace and quiet, tell the children that it's crucial the crabs *can't hear them*. Suggest they count *slowly* and *silently* to 100, which should be long enough for the crabs to find the bait, but not so long they'll devour it.

TECHNIQUE 2: THE LIFT

What you'll see when you haul the line up is a ball of crabs fighting over the bait (safe in a little string bag, if you bought it from the shop). When you lift the line clear of the water *all the crabs will fall off.* Don't worry. You're trying to spin things out till lunchtime. Repeat several times, berating yourself roundly and assuming poses of despair. Just when the children are starting to lose faith and/or get bored, slip your bucket underneath the crabs *before* they leave the water and crow in exultation as if you've just bagged a man-eating tiger.

ETHICS

The crabs are honourable prisoners of war and should be treated accordingly. Add seawater (not fresh; they will die) and a bit of weed to the bucket. Crabs breathe through gills, but unlike fish they can breathe on land so long as their gills are wet. People say keep the bucket out of the sun, but you're crabbing in the drizzle, so that won't be a problem. Don't put tiny ones in with monsters: that's certain death. Don't let children taunt the crabs.

TECHNIQUE 3: THE PICK-UP

This requires some sleight of hand, but the trick is accidentally-on-purpose to spill a crab forcing you *to pick it up*. Don't attempt this unless you are *sure* you won't scream and drop it. Come at it from behind, place your thumb behind one claw, your fingers behind the other. There are also eight legs, but don't mind them, they can't hurt you. If you've got hold of a big one, it will feel like it's about to twist round and *snap* your finger off, but hang in there. Nothing impresses a child (or future life partner) more than the sight of you insouciantly holding a crab.

READY, STEADY ...

The drizzle has stopped. The rocks are shimmering in weak sunshine. Not long till lunch now. Time for the *race*. Take your bucket anywhere a bit of shingle/mud leads into the sea. Plant yourself about ten paces from the water's edge. Get everyone to choose a crab. Upend the bucket in a way that's dramatic, but doesn't hurt the crabs. The children will either shriek in terror (especially toddlers with a poor grasp of scale) or explode with the effort of pretending they're not scared.

The crabs will camouflage themselves behind seaweed, squeeze into improbably small crevices, or freeze spookily still. Some crabs, if things get really tense, can eject a limb (*autotomy*), although we've never actually seen that happen. The remaining crabs will be scuttling fast for the water. (Why *do* crabs move sideways? Because that's how their legs bend. We wish there was a cooler answer.)

TECHNIQUE 4: THE GUARD
Crabs are plucky. Come too close to one and it will rear up on its hindmost legs and clack its pincers at you: 'Come and have a go if you think you're hard enough!' Immediately do the same thing back at it. Bow legs, tiptoes, hands pincing. Small children will think you are heroic. Larger children will think you are embarrassing. Both are good outcomes.

AND THE WINNER IS?
Somebody's crab will win. Congratulate them fulsomely. Present them with the prize you bought in the shop. Tell everyone else to *stop crying*. Promise to come back tomorrow.

BASKING SHARK

by Norman MacCaig

To stub an oar on a rock where none should be,
To have it rise with a slounge out of the sea
Is a thing that happened once (too often) to me.

But not too often – though enough. I count as gain
That once I met, on a sea tin-tacked with rain,
That roomsized monster with a matchbox brain.

He displaced more than water. He shoggled me
Centuries back – this decadent townee
Shook on a wrong branch of his family tree.

Swish up the dirt and, when it settles, a spring
Is all the clearer. I saw me, in one fling,
Emerging from the slime of everything.

So who's the monster? The thought made me grow pale
For twenty seconds while, sail after sail,
The tall fin slid away and then the tail.

POINTS OF THE COMPASS

COMPASS ROSES

The *8-point compass rose* is familiar to everyone. It shows the four *cardinal* directions, north (N), east (E), south (S) and west (W), plus the next four intersections, the *intercardinal* directions, northeast (NE), southeast (SE), southwest (SW) and northwest (NW).

The compass can be further divided into sixteen, adding eight new half-winds, which are north-northeast (NNE), east-northeast (ENE), east-southeast (ESE), south-southeast (SSE), south-southwest (SSW), west-southwest (WSW), west-northwest (WNW) and north-northwest (NNW).

This can be subdivided once again to give the 32-point compass, with north-by-east (NxE) now tucked between N and NNE, northeast-by-north (NExN) tucked between NNE and NE and so on. Any sailor worth her salt should be able to *box the compass*, i.e. reel off the 32 points in order.

One *point* – 11.25° (360° divided by 32 points) – also functioned as a unit of direction when giving instructions to the sailor on the helm. *Four points to starboard*, therefore, meant turn the boat 45° clockwise.

If that wasn't complicated enough, during the eighteenth century the system was subdivided further still. Each point was split in four, so between north and north-by-east, you'd now find N¼E, N½E, N¾E. Try boxing all 128 if you want to be *really* impressive.

MAGNETIC NORTH

We are sorry to have to tell you that *magnetic north* (whither your faithful compass points: the magnetic field caused by the earth's liquid and therefore *mobile* iron core) is *not* the same as *true north* (the actual North Pole; the axis about which we all spin).

True north is easy to locate: it's at the top of the map. Finding magnetic north is harder because *it moves*. To find it, you need to follow your compass north, north, north, until you arrive at the point where the needle wants to point *down* towards the earth's core. Of course, if you're holding your compass in the palm of your hand, it won't be able to do this. Turn it on its side, however, and it will spin *downwards*. This, very roughly, is what the explorer James Clark Ross did when he reached magnetic north on the Boothia Peninsula in the Canadian Arctic in 1831.

Since then it has been trundling towards Siberia, a neat geophysical metaphor for power struggles in a warming Arctic, accelerating (nobody knows *why*) from a few miles per year last century, to more than thirty miles per year currently, so that it is now assumed to lie under the Arctic Sea north of Canadian territory. (If this seems worrying, consider that at other periods of geological, if not human history, magnetic north was actually in Antarctica.)

MAGNETIC VARIATION (OR DECLINATION)
The difference between true north and magnetic north is called *magnetic variation* or *magnetic declination*, and it changes depending on a) where you are and b) where magnetic north is. Any chart you're using for navigation will include a compass rose showing both true north (pointing straight up) and magnetic north (as it applies for the area the chart covers). It will also include the date of publication, and how variation is changing each year: e.g. 7° 22 ' W, (2018) 8 ' E.

Right now, the position of magnetic north means that magnetic variation in the UK isn't that big (a degree or two depending on where you are), so it doesn't make much difference to anyone mooching around inshore UK waters. But in the past it was enough to land you in trouble if you didn't take it into account when setting a course.

Envisage this. You get out your chart and measure the course to steer from Sunny Beach to Charming Cove. It's due south, or 180°. You've forgotten about magnetic variation and tell the helm to steer 180°. If it was the 1980s, when magnetic variation might be 6°W, instead of heading due south, your boat would now be travelling south with a hint of east, or 174°. Of course, that doesn't make a massive difference over a mile, but over 100 miles you'd be off course by a serious margin, enough, perhaps, to land you on top of Spiky Rock or Shameful Shoal.

Therefore, you have to add 6° to your *true course* to arrive at a *magnetic course* of 186°, keeping in mind this handy chant: 'Variation west, compass best. Variation east, compass least.'

MAGNETIC DEVIATION

To complicate matters further, you also have to take *magnetic deviation* into account. Iron, or anything else that can be magnetised on a ship (marlinspikes, tins of bully beef, cannons and so on), can cause your compass to give inaccurate readings. On the upside, these inaccuracies are consistent. On the downside, they can vary depending on which way the boat is pointing, perhaps 5° E when steering north, 2° W when steering south, and so on.

The solution is to *swing your ship*. Moor it somewhere you can get a fixed bearing: e.g. lining up a particular buoy and a particular lighthouse gives you a magnetic bearing 270°. Point the boat's head north. What's the compass bearing? 270°? No deviation. Point the boat's head northeast. What's the bearing? 272°? You have deviation of 2°W. Repeat for the remaining cardinal and intercardinal points until you have a neat *deviation card*.

Thankfully, deviation is less of a problem on pleasure boats because they're largely made out of fibreglass, wood and aluminium, and the effect can be mitigated by the clever placement of little magnets around the compass.

MEASUREMENT AT SEA

LATITUDE AND LONGITUDE

Any point on the earth's surface can be described in terms of its *latitude* and *longitude*, which is especially useful when you're out of sight of land with nothing else on offer to tell you where you are.

Latitude is a set of imaginary concentric circles that wrap around the earth, travelling east and west. They are *always parallel*. Starting at zero at the equator, there are 90° of latitude going north until you get to the North Pole, and 90° of latitude going south until you get to the South Pole, making 180° in total.

Each degree of latitude is divided into 60 *minutes*, and each minute is divided into 60 *seconds*.* There is one *nautical mile* (or 6,076 feet, 2,025 yards, 1,852 m or 1.15 landlubber miles) between each imaginary minute of latitude, so the distance from anywhere on the equator to either pole is 90° × 60 minutes = 5,400 nautical miles.**

Longitude is another imaginary set of concentric circles, this time travelling north and south. They are *not parallel*, but pass through both of the poles. The line of zero

....

* Minutes of time, minutes of angle and minutes of latitude/longitude are different measurements with the same name. They are each *one-sixtieth* of a larger unit: the hour, the degree of angle and the degree of latitude or longitude.
** This isn't *precisely* true. The earth is an *oblate spheroid*, meaning that it bulges at the equator and is squashed at the poles. If you're standing on the North Pole, you're about 20 km closer to the centre of the earth than you would be on the equator. This means a minute of latitude near the poles is 1,862 m, but only 1,843 m on the equator.

longitude, called the *prime meridian*, runs due south from the North Pole, passing through the Royal Observatory at Greenwich,* continuing to the South Pole. There are 360° of longitude in total: 180° to the west of Greenwich and 180° to the east. They meet on the opposite side of the world to Greenwich at the *antimeridian*, which passes through Chukotka in Russia, close to the Nukulaelae atoll in Tuvalu and various Fijian islands, before finally arriving at Antarctica. *The International Date Line*, which separates today and tomorrow, roughly tracks the antimeridian, jigging east or west to allow island nations to stay in the same time zone.

The distance between degrees of longitude is widest at the equator, narrowing to zero at the poles. On the equator, a degree of longitude is the same as a degree of latitude, i.e. 60 nautical miles. But due to the curvature of the earth, by the time you get to Greenwich a degree of longitude is only 37.5 nautical miles.

Longitude and latitude, divided into degrees (°), minutes (') and seconds ("), using N and S to show whether you mean latitude north or south of the equator, and E and W to show whether you mean longitude east or west of the prime meridian, can be combined to give a precise location. For example, the Eddystone lighthouse is at 50°10'48"N, 04°15'54"W.

NAUTICAL MILES AND KNOTS
Since the maritime world has its own key unit of distance, the nautical mile, it follows that it has its own key unit of speed: the *knot*. One knot, simply, is *one nautical mile per*

....

* France bullishly carried on using Paris as its prime meridian until 1911, and even when it adopted Greenwich, it employed the wonderful circumlocution 'Paris Mean Time, retarded by 9 minutes and 21 seconds'.

hour. Just as a nautical mile is a bit longer than a land mile, so 1 kn is a bit faster than 1 mph.

The term dates back to the seventeenth century when people used a *log* to calculate their speed. Originally logs were ... logs. Sailors dropped a piece of wood into the water at the front of the boat and measured the time it took to pass a mark at the stern: distance divided by time giving them a rough calculation of their speed. Log design evolved until they mostly looked like a little parachute or sea anchor attached to a long line wound round a reel, plus an hourglass with enough sand to run for thirty seconds. A sailor would cast the log over the stern and see how much line paid out over the thirty seconds. The knots tied in the line gave rise to the term we use today.

CABLES AND FATHOMS

A nautical mile can be subdivided into ten *cables* and each cable into 100 *fathoms*, meaning:

1 cable = 185 m = 608 feet
1 fathom = 1.85 m = 6.08 feet

The word cable refers to the approximate length of a ship's anchor chain, 600 feet being a good bet if you want to be able to anchor reliably in 100 feet of water. Fathom is derived from the old English *fæðm*, meaning a person's outstretched arms. Like many traditional measurements, its exact distance for a long time was somewhat imprecise (*whose* arms?), but eventually the Admiralty defined it as 1,000th of a nautical mile, although it's also used to mean exactly six feet.

For a literary gloss, turn to the famous lines at the start of *The Tempest*, in which the spirit Ariel tells the shipwrecked prince Ferdinand:

Full fathom five thy father lies;
Of his bones are coral made;
Those are pearls that were his eyes:
Nothing of him that doth fade,
But doth suffer a sea-change
Into something rich and strange.
Sea-nymphs hourly ring his knell
Ding-dong.
Hark! Now I hear them – Ding-dong, bell.

NAVIGATION

There are two eras of navigation: before *Global Position-ing System* (GPS) and after. Before GPS, which became widespread from the early 1990s, to get a boat safely from A to B, you needed a solid grasp of navigational theory, hours of practice, a terrier-like attention to detail and a very strong stomach (so you could spend hours hunched over a bucking chart table below decks). Nowadays ... all those hard-won answers pop up on your waterproof tablet.*

Attempting satellite-free navigation in the early twenty-first century is like baking your own bread. Frankly, you don't need to do it. Nobody's going to look down on you for not doing it. In fact, people will probably think you're a bit of a show-off for doing it at all. Sometimes you won't be able to face it. But knowing you *can* do it ... that's some-thing to savour.

....

* Viz. the third law of science fiction writer and futurist Arthur C. Clarke: 'Any sufficiently advanced technology is indistinguishable from magic.'

Here are the bare bones of old-school navigation:

1. Work out where you are. Not as easy as you might think. If you get lost hiking, you can stand still and have a good think. If you get confused at sea, the wind, waves, tide and current will always be moving you on. Let's say you haven't left harbour yet, so at least one thing's certain.
2. Decide where you want to go, either by eye or by looking on your chart.
3. Check your chart to see whether any hidden obstacles (shoals, rocks) lie between you and your destination. If necessary work out a new interim destination to avoid them. Give yourself plenty of clearance.
4. Check your chart to see whether there are any helpful aids to navigation between you and your destination (buoys, cardinal markers). Use them to plan a safe route.
5. If you can see your destination, and you know there are no hidden obstacles, steer by eye.
6. If you can't see your destination, measure the course you need to steer on your chart (i.e. the compass bearing to your destination).
7. Take into account whether wind, tide or current are likely to affect your course. Adjust accordingly.
8. Steer your course.

Once you've set off, you need to find out whether the course you're steering *through the water* is the same as the course you're making *over the ground* (or in this case, over the seabed). They can be two very different things. Perhaps you're trying to steer across an estuary, but the tide is trying to sweep you out to sea. Perhaps you're beating into a heavy wind, and you're making a lot of *leeway*.* In both situations, your bow might be pointing at your destination, but your actual course is quite different – different enough to set you onto an unmarked rock you thought was half a mile off your starboard beam.

TAKING BEARINGS

To make sure that's not happening you *take bearings*. You need a *hand bearing compass* (or binoculars with an in-built compass), a *sharp pencil*, a *rubber*, a *chart* and a *navigation plotter*, which is a fat ruler with a free-turning protractor inside it. (Or you can use *dividers* and a *parallel ruler*, like Nelson would have done.)

Stand on deck, face the object on which you want to take a bearing (lighthouse, hill, steeple, buoy, etc.), hold the compass to your eye, wait for the dial to settle: that's your first bearing. Say it's 285°. Using your plotter, draw that line on your chart.**

Take a second bearing from a second landmark. Say it's 015°. Draw a second line on your chart. Where the two lines cross is where you are. Or rather, where the two lines cross is where you *might* be.

Take a third bearing to check. Say it's 230°. If you're a cyborg, your three lines will intersect perfectly, and you'll know your exact position. If you're human, they'll form a triangle, and you'll know you're somewhere inside that. Put a cross inside the triangle.*** Put the time next to it. That's a *fix*. Now, rub out all the lines so your chart doesn't get too messy.

....

* *Leeway* is a boat's tendency to slip sideways downwind, i.e. to leeward.
** (*whispers*) Of course you'll also need to take into account the difference between the *magnetic* north of your compass and the *true north* of your chart.
*** This triangle is often referred to as a *cocked hat*. Remember: the bigger the hat, the bigger the chance of a navigational cock-up.

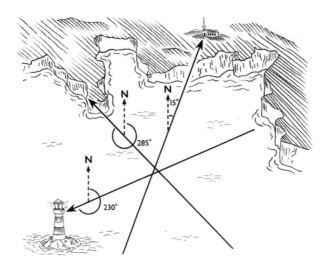

TAKING SOUNDINGS

Another way to check where you actually are is to *take soundings*. Once upon a time, this was done with a lead-line, but nowadays even the most *au naturel* navigator is likely to have an echosounder.

An echosounder works like a bat's echolocation, pinging a sound wave at the sea floor, and measuring the time it takes for it to ping back to give you a depth reading. Charts are marked with depths, and those depths are joined to form contours, just as for hills on an Ordnance Survey map.

You might, for example, have noted that the rock you're trying to avoid is inside the ten-metre line, therefore so long as you stay deeper than ten metres (always remembering to adjust for the tide), you can't hit the rock.

TRAVELLING BLIND

You'll have noticed that to take a bearing you need to be able to *see* whatever it is you're taking a bearing from. This is obviously harder:

1. **At night:** But luckily most aids to navigation are very well lit, often with individual sequences that will be marked on your chart. A buoy might be labelled *Fl R 3 (10s)*, meaning it flashes red, three times in ten seconds.

2. **In fog:** Radar, if you have it, can be a lifesaver here (likewise if you find yourself entering an unlit anchorage at night), although it's only good for a general picture, not fine-tuned pilotage, plus what appears on your display isn't always that easy to interpret. If in doubt, switch on your GPS or head away from shore until the fog lifts.

3. **When you're out of sight of land:** Which brings us to ...

DEAD RECKONING

Once you're out of sight of land, you have to start relying on the roughest of rough measures: *dead reckoning*, a notoriously inaccurate method.

Say your mid-morning 1000 fix put you five miles off the island of Harris. Say you've set a course of 240° that you hope will take you to St Kilda. Say your speed is 5 knots. At 1100 you can no longer see land, but you confidently put a cross five miles further down the line you've drawn from your last fix to St Kilda. Say the wind picks up and for the next hour you're travelling at 6 knots. At 1200 you put a cross six miles further down that line. Say the wind heads you and you can no longer quite steer 240°, but have to settle for 230°, and your speed drops to 4 knots. Draw a new line for the new course and mark yourself four miles down it.

Of course, you should also be taking into account tide, current and leeway. Perhaps your tidal stream atlas has informed you that for the first hour, the flood will be running at two knots up the west coast of Harris. You need to draw a *vector* to take into account the effect of that on your course. Perhaps you need to take the extra leeway into account in hour three.

That's dead reckoning, and you're right to be worried. It is – at best – educated guesswork. It can give you a rough idea of when you might make *landfall* (i.e. clap eyes on the coast you're making for), so you know when to start looking out for the flash of a lighthouse or clouds above a volcanic peak. But once you've made landfall, you have to approach very cautiously, waiting for clues as to whether you really are where you think you are.

SUN SIGHTS

More precise, if intellectually more taxing, is celestial navigation, which is an extension of the principle of taking bearings, only on a grander scale, using the height of the sun above the horizon to determine latitude and longitude. It relies on three things: a *chronometer* (in other words, an accurate clock), a *sextant* and a set of *sight reduction tables*.

Latitude has always been relatively easy to calculate (although easy is a relative term with anything involving a sextant, a wobbly deck and tables of numbers), because at noon on any given day, in any given place, the sun will be at the same height above the horizon. So long as you have the tables to hand, in which other people have already done all the maths for you, you measure the height of the sun in the sky (by fixing the angle between the sun and a horizon with your sextant), apply some adjustments to take the time of year into account (found in your nautical almanac) and – hey presto! – you have your latitude.

Longitude was much harder to calculate* until people invented accurate clocks which allowed navigators to compare noon where they were (i.e. the time when the sun was at its highest) with noon back at the Greenwich meridian. The earth takes twenty-four hours to turn 360°, or one hour to turn 15°, so if the sun is at its highest on your boat at 1200, but your Greenwich clock reads 1300, you know you're 15° to the west of Greenwich.

THANK YOU GPS

If this account of navigation sounds like doing increasingly hard maths exams while playing a high-stakes game of blind man's bluff ... you'd be right. For some people, that's *fun*. For everyone else, let's be grateful to the US Air Force for their Global Positioning System.

GPS is so brilliant that we sometimes forget to be amazed by it. As the French fabulist Jean de la Fontaine wrote in 'The Camel and the Floating Sticks':

L'accoutumance ainsi nous rend tout familier:
Ce qui nous paraissait terrible et singulier
S'apprivoise avec notre vue,
Quand ce vient à la continue.

... which translates as human beings can get used to anything, however weird and wonderful, even *camels*.

....

* This led to many deaths at sea. In 1707, for example, a British naval fleet led by Sir Cloudesley Shovell was wrecked on rocks to the west of the Scillies, drowning nearly 2,000 sailors. An accurate longitude reading might well have saved them. Seven years later, Parliament passed the Longitude Act, which offered large rewards for anyone who could solve this crucial problem.

HOW DOES GPS ACTUALLY WORK?

During the Cold War, two scientists in a US physics lab realised they could track the location of a Soviet satellite in orbit using the Doppler effect. Very roughly, this is how the frequency of any wave changes as the source of the wave moves past you: this could be a sound wave emitted by a car horn, or a radio wave emitted by a Sputnik. A change in frequency will tell you where the wave's source is in relation to a fixed point (you), but the inverse is also true. A change in frequency could also tell where *you* are in relation to a known wave source (a satellite).

From that beginning, GPS evolved through various (bewildering) iterations, until what we enjoy today became fully armed and operational in 1995. Twenty-four satellites are needed to provide full coverage of the earth, so that at any given time, at any given point on earth, you can 'see' four satellites. Each satellite, which knows precisely *where* it is and precisely *when* it is, broadcasts a radio signal which includes both pieces of information.

Pleasingly, GPS relies on Einstein's special theory of relativity, which says that the speed of light (and all electro-magnetic radiation, including, for our purposes here, a satellite's radio communications) is a constant and is independent of the speed of both the source of the light and the observer of the light. This allows you (or rather your phone/satnav) to calculate the distance between you and a satellite irrespective of how you and the satellite are moving.

Equipped with a number of distance calculations, you (or rather your phone/satnav) can now fix your location via *trilateration* (which is not quite the same as triangulation). Take a look at our simplified 2D sketch below.

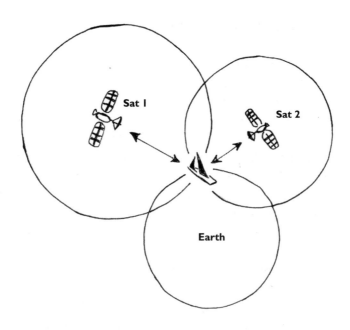

First, you know you are 22,000 km from satellite 1, which puts you somewhere inside circle one. Second, you know you are 20,000 km from satellite 2, which puts you at one of two points where these circles overlap. Finally, add a third circle to pinpoint your position.

As you can imagine, it's more complicated in three dimensions. The first satellite tells you that you're somewhere on a sphere. The second satellite creates interlocking spheres, which tell you that you're somewhere on a circle on the surface of both spheres. The third satellite narrows it down to two possible points. Often this will be enough, as one of the points is likely to be either in space or deep underground. (Knowing you are on the earth's surface counts as a fourth sphere.) Nevertheless, for absolute accuracy you do need that fourth satellite to determine your exact position.

SHIP FINDERS

The sea is best enjoyed analogue (unless you're up to your knees in quicksand, in which case you might find a mobile phone useful) – with one possible exception. Ship tracking websites. Head to ship-finder.co or marinetraffic.com or vesselfinder.com and see for yourself.

The details vary, but essentially you get a sky-god's-eye-view of the high seas, with jaunty little boat icons plying the waves. You can click and discover whether that smudge you can see from your clifftop vantage is cargo ship or ferry, tug or pilot, military might or pleasure seeker. You can find out where it's going, where it's been, what it looks like close up, whether it's underway, anchored, aground.

Neither do you have to be by the sea. You can snuggle up in front of a fire, listen to old shipping forecasts on loop, and 'watch' superyachts tacking up channel, fishing boats fishing, tankers tanking, icebreakers breaking ice.

All this tantalising information comes courtesy of their automatic identification systems (AIS), which the International Convention for the Safety of Life at Sea says all big ships and all passenger ships, big or small, must carry.

Highly recommended.

EXTRACTS FROM THE RIME OF THE ANCIENT MARINER

by Samuel Taylor Coleridge

An ancient mariner tells a wedding guest the tale of how once he shot an albatross. His ship is cursed.

Down dropt the breeze, the sails dropt down,
'Twas sad as sad could be;
And we did speak only to break
The silence of the sea!

All in a hot and copper sky,
The bloody Sun, at noon,
Right up above the mast did stand,
No bigger than the Moon.

Day after day, day after day,
We stuck, nor breath nor motion;
As idle as a painted ship
Upon a painted ocean.

Water, water, every where,
And all the boards did shrink;
Water, water, every where,
Nor any drop to drink.

*At the height of their desperation, the crew sees what they
think is their deliverance.*

There passed a weary time. Each throat
Was parched, and glazed each eye.
A weary time! a weary time!
How glazed each weary eye,

When looking westward, I beheld
A something in the sky.

At first it seemed a little speck,
And then it seemed a mist;
It moved and moved, and took at last
A certain shape, I wist.

A speck, a mist, a shape, I wist!
And still it neared and neared:
As if it dodged a water-sprite,
It plunged and tacked and veered.

With throats unslaked, with black lips baked,
We could nor laugh nor wail;
Through utter drought all dumb we stood!
I bit my arm, I sucked the blood,
And cried, A sail! a sail!

But their hopes are dashed.

And is that Woman all her crew?
Is that a DEATH? and are there two?
Is DEATH that woman's mate?

Her lips were red, her looks were free,
Her locks were yellow as gold:
Her skin was as white as leprosy,
The Night-mare LIFE-IN-DEATH was she,
Who thicks man's blood with cold.

Four times fifty living men,
(And I heard nor sigh nor groan)
With heavy thump, a lifeless lump,
They dropped down one by one.

The mariner looks on in horror.

The many men, so beautiful!
And they all dead did lie:
And a thousand thousand slimy things
Lived on; and so did I.

I looked upon the rotting sea,
And drew my eyes away;
I looked upon the rotting deck,
And there the dead men lay.

The dead crew come back to ghostly life.

The loud wind never reached the ship,
Yet now the ship moved on!
Beneath the lightning and the Moon
The dead men gave a groan.

They groaned, they stirred, they all uprose,
Nor spake, nor moved their eyes;
It had been strange, even in a dream,
To have seen those dead men rise.

The helmsman steered, the ship moved on;
Yet never a breeze up-blew;
The mariners all 'gan work the ropes,
Where they were wont to do;
They raised their limbs like lifeless tools –
We were a ghastly crew.

The mariner does penance and is forgiven. He sights land.

Oh! dream of joy! is this indeed
The light-house top I see?
Is this the hill? is this the kirk?
Is this mine own countree?

We drifted o'er the harbour-bar,
And I with sobs did pray –
O let me be awake, my God!
Or let me sleep alway.

A pilot approaches in a little boat.

The boat came closer to the ship,
But I nor spake nor stirred;
The boat came close beneath the ship,
And straight a sound was heard.

Under the water it rumbled on,
Still louder and more dread:
It reached the ship, it split the bay;
The ship went down like lead.

Stunned by that loud and dreadful sound,
Which sky and ocean smote,
Like one that hath been seven days drowned

My body lay afloat;
But swift as dreams, myself I found
Within the Pilot's boat.

Upon the whirl, where sank the ship,
The boat spun round and round;
And all was still, save that the hill
Was telling of the sound.

He is safe, but cannot forget.

Since then, at an uncertain hour,
That agony returns:
And till my ghastly tale is told,
This heart within me burns.

I pass, like night, from land to land;
I have strange power of speech;
That moment that his face I see,
I know the man that must hear me:
To him my tale I teach.

And so farewell ...

He prayeth well, who loveth well
Both man and bird and beast.

He prayeth best, who loveth best
All things both great and small;
For the dear God who loveth us,
He made and loveth all.

SAILING: THEORY AND PRACTICE

Picture a toy sail boat being blown across a duck pond. Picture shipwrecked sailors on a raft, a tattered shirt hoisted up a makeshift mast. Picture a Viking longship with one big square sail. In all these cases, wind pushes sail, and sail pushes boat.

That's more or less how sailing works *if* you're happy drifting where the wind blows. But how do you sail *across* or even *towards* the wind? In that case, you need *Newton's third law of motion*, which says 'To every action there is always opposed an equal reaction: or the mutual actions of two bodies upon each other are always equal, and directed to contrary parts.' Or, more simply: 'If you push something, *it pushes right back.*'

1. This is the wind, blowing down the page.
2. Wind hits sail.
3. Sail pushes wind away, and as we know from Newton, if the sail pushes the wind ...
4. ... the wind pushes back, which creates *lift.*

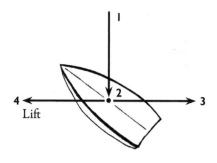

The direction in which number 4 is pointing is the direction in which the lift is trying to pull the boat: partly forwards (the *propulsion* force) and partly sideways (the *lateral* force).

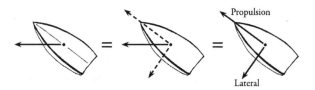

Not a bad start, but we only want the boat to go *forwards*, which is why you need a centreboard (if you're in a dinghy) or a keel (if you're on a yacht). When the lateral force tries to push the boat sideways, the centreboard/keel *resists* with all its might. The lateral force is curtailed, leaving the boat to enjoy the propulsion. Bingo: you go where you want to go.

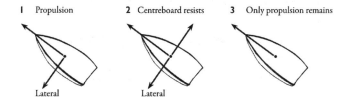

THE TIPPING POINT

Bear in mind though, that the lateral force (on the sails) is high up, while the counter-force (on the centreboard/keel) is low down, which is what causes the boat to tip sideways, or heel over.

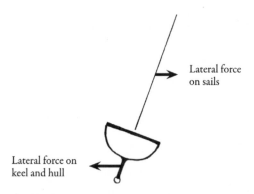

Lateral force
on sails

Lateral force on
keel and hull

A dinghy, whether a hi-spec racer or something slower and steadier, uses the weight of its crew to stop it heeling over so far that it capsizes. On a *Swallow* or an *Amazon*, it's enough to sit on the windward side. On something a little nimbler, the crew might stick their feet in *hiking straps* and lean out. On something sportier still, they might stand on the edge of the dinghy, wearing a *harness* attached to a *trapeze* attached to the mast, and *really* lean out.

If a dinghy does capsize, it's not the end of the world: simply swim round to where the centreboard is poking out of the bottom of the boat, haul yourself onto it, grab hold of a bit of rope or deck, lean backwards and your dinghy will right itself.

When a yacht heels over, perhaps so far that the leeward rail disappears into the sea, novice sailors (understandably) look extremely perturbed. Their more experienced crew-mates, on the other hand, remain nonchalant, knowing that in normal circumstances a yacht won't capsize because its keel is too heavy.* (You do see the crew of racing yachts arrayed along the windward rail, but this is primarily for speed rather than to stop the boat capsizing.)

....

* Most keels are made out of lead, although one designer took heavy to its logical conclusion and chose depleted uranium.

As the mast and sail tilt down to the right, say, the keel tilts up to the left, where it meets *gravity*, which stops it tilting any further. A breaking wave or violent squall *can* temporarily overcome gravity and knock a boat flat, but the weight of the keel almost always pops you back upright. (Admittedly, *pop* is not how it feels for those on board.)

ON THE WIND VS OFF THE WIND

That, in a nutshell, is how you get a boat to sail across the wind, but how *close* to the wind (i.e. how directly into it) can you actually go? Whatever wizardry you deploy, it's pretty much impossible to sail nearer than 45°. Past a certain point, the sail stops scooping and lifting, and instead *flogs* (i.e. flaps) loudly and menacingly to let you know it's had enough.

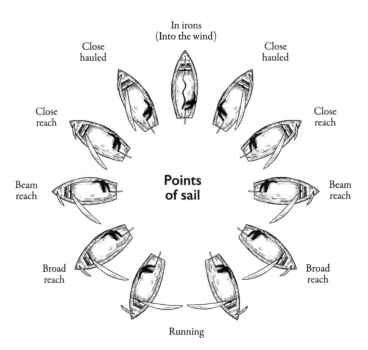

In irons
(Into the wind)

Close hauled

Close hauled

Close reach

Close reach

Beam reach

Points of sail

Beam reach

Broad reach

Broad reach

Running

The sweet spot where you're travelling as close to the wind as you feasibly can is called sailing *close-hauled*. Once you're no longer *hard on the wind*, you're on a *close reach*. If you *free* yourself further, you'll be on a *beam reach*, then a *broad reach*, and finally, when your boat is pointing pretty much dead downwind, on a *run*.

There are lots of ways to describe moving in either direction. If you want to tell the helmsman to turn closer to the wind, you might say *head up*, *point up* or *luff up*. If you want them to do the opposite, you might say *come off*, *ease off* or *bear away*.

When you're close-hauled, you pull (in a dinghy) or winch (on a yacht) your sails in hard – known as *sheeting in* – so they're at a very tight angle to the deck. When you're running, you let the sheets out, so the sails are almost at right angles to the mast.*

Sailing on and off the wind are two very different experiences. Close-hauled, the wind feels stronger than it is, because you have to combine the *true wind* that's actually blowing with the *headwind* generated by the boat moving to arrive at what's known as the *apparent wind*, which is what's experienced by the person on deck. This means that sailing *into* a force 6 is intense and exciting, because the wind feels like a force 7. The boat heels hard over, butting into waves. Spray lances down the deck. Sail *away* from a force 6, by contrast, and you'll find yourself swooshing serenely through the water.

....

* This means, incidentally, that once a boat is underway, the wind hits the sails at the same angle no matter which way you're going, almost as if the sails are fixed while the boat rotates beneath them.

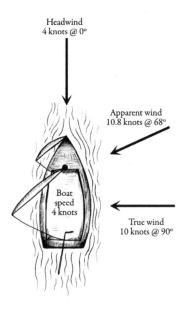

Headwind
4 knots @ 0°

Apparent wind
10.8 knots @ 68°

Boat
speed
4 knots

True wind
10 knots @ 90°

TACKING

With 90° of the compass (45° either side of the wind) effectively out of bounds to a sailing boat, you will often find that you can't *lay your course*, i.e. the wind's blowing from where you want to go. In that case you have to progress as Roger does at the start of *Swallows and Amazons*:

Roger, aged seven, and no longer the youngest of the family, ran in wide zigzags, to and fro, across the steep field that sloped up from the lake to Holly Howe, the farm where they were staying for part of the summer holidays. He ran until he nearly reached the hedge by the footpath, then turned and ran until he nearly reached the hedge on the other side of the field. Then he turned and crossed the field again. Each crossing of the field brought him nearer to the farm. The wind was against him, and he was tacking up against it to the farm, where at the gate his patient mother was awaiting him.

This dogged progress is called *beating*, and involves sailing as close to the wind as you can in one direction – on one *tack* – before turning the bow of your boat through the wind – *tacking* – and continuing as close to the wind as you can on the other tack.* Unless your destination is dead to windward, one tack will point you closer to where you want to go, which is called the *making tack*.

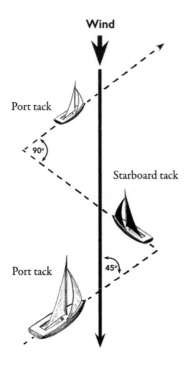

To tack, you spin your wheel (or put your tiller over),** driving the bow of the boat through the wind. The mainsail flips over to the new side automatically, but you need to
....

* When the wind is coming over your port side, you're on *port tack*. When it's coming over your starboard side, you're on *starboard tack*.
** By and large, dinghies and smaller yachts have tillers; larger yachts and ships have wheels.

let the headsails fly, wait until the wind blows them to the other side, and then sheet them back in. In a dinghy, you also have to scramble over to the new windward side of the boat to keep it balanced.

It's important to tack smartly, keeping as much *way* on the boat as possible, otherwise you end up *in irons* (i.e. stalled head to wind), which is both embarrassing and hard to extricate yourself from.

GYBING

What if you're travelling *away* from the wind, and you want to turn the *stern* through the wind? This manoeuvre, the opposite of tacking, is called *gybing* (or jibing if you're American), and is harder and more dangerous.

Since you're sailing downwind, you will have eased your mainsail out as far as it will go, meaning the boom is more or less at right angles to the deck. When the stern of the boat passes through the wind, the boom needs to travel in a wide arc all the way from one side of the boat to the other. (Compare this with a tack: the sail is sheeted in and the boom has a much shorter journey.)

The danger lies in an *accidental gybe** (i.e. the boom making this journey off its own bat). If there's a tiny wind shift or a wave slews you off course or you lose concentration, the wind can flick (in a dinghy) or slam (on a yacht) the boom from one side of the boat to the other, which can give you a nasty bump on the head, knock you overboard or even kill you outright.

....

* You're much less likely to tack accidentally: sailing close-hauled you're 45° off the point where the boat wants to tack, whereas on a run you might only be 5° off the point where the boat wants to gybe.

You can, of course, gybe perfectly safely by hauling the mainsail in as close to the centre of the boat as possible just before you put the stern through the wind, so the boom traces a small, controlled arc across the deck. Make sure everyone keeps their heads down, just in case. Many yachts are also rigged with *preventers*, which stop the boom in its tracks if it tries to gybe without permission.

SAILING ON A RUN

If you're running more or less dead downwind, you'll also find that the mainsail blocks the headsail, stealing all its wind, leaving it underemployed and liable to flap about annoyingly. This is your chance to *goose-wing*: haul the jib to the opposite side of the boat and use a *spinnaker pole* or *whisker pole* to hold it in place. If goose-winging isn't fast enough, you can also set a *spinnaker*, one of those big, billowy, colourful, photogenic sails.

A spinnaker is very large, very light, and (to put it mildly) quite a handful to hoist and lower, especially if it's windy. Once up, it's also a good deal less forgiving than your classic sails, needing constant, attentive *trimming* (i.e. adjustments to suit each tiny wind shift). To trim a jib, you need one rope. To trim a spinnaker, you need *four*: two to control the pole, two to control the sail. Spinnakers do allow you to sail a *lot* faster, especially in lighter airs, but they're more popular on racing boats because they're not very relaxing beasts.

REEFING

As well as adjusting your sails for wind direction, you also need to adjust for wind speed. If the wind gets up, a boat starts to feel *pressed*: over-powered and hard to steer. On a dinghy, you can slacken your sheets so your sails don't catch the full strength of the wind. Either that or head to shore. On a yacht, it's time to *shorten sail* or *reef*.

First, you lower the mainsail a few feet (using the halyard). Second, you secure the edge nearer the mast with some sort of hook-and-eye system. (You might have two, three, or even four hooks to allow you to shorten sail incrementally as the wind increases.) Third, you secure the end nearer the stern with a *reefing line*. Fourth, you tidy up the middle with *reefing ties*. Fifth, you re-tighten the halyard.

What sounds simple on paper is of course different in practice. To reef safely, you often need to turn head to wind, which requires one person who's a steady hand on the helm and another who's still got enough feeling in their cold, wet hands to jam the eye in the sail over the hook on the mast, while not losing their balance as the foredeck rears up and down.

On some modern boats, to make reefing more straightforward you only need to wind the mainsail onto a drum inside the boom or mast, which is also how the sail is stowed when you're not at sea.

Most modern jibs use the same system, which is a lot easier than having to drag a smaller headsail onto the foredeck, drop the old one, bundle it into a bag which will always be too small, *hank on* the new one, hoist it, check its sheets aren't tangled (they will be), all while waves break over your head and the skipper stands in the cockpit bellowing instructions you can't hear.

If the wind gets *really* serious, force 9-plus, you can rig a tiny *storm jib* at the front and a tiny *trysail* instead of the mainsail. They're often lifeboat orange, just in case you needed reminding that you might be in trouble.

FLAGS AND ENSIGNS

If you stick to messing about in rowing boats and little sailing dinghies, you can happily skip this section. Lucky you: flag etiquette, and especially *ensign* etiquette, is blighted by insider-outsider snobbishness that you could do without. But for the sake of completeness, we'll share both essential law and inessential tradition, and let you steer your own course.

WHAT IS AN ENSIGN?

An ensign tells you where a vessel comes from: its national identity. It's usually the largest flag on board and usually flown above or at least near the stern. Standard for a British vessel is the *red ensign*, which is a rectangular red flag with a Union Jack in the top left-hand quarter. If only we could leave it there.

Depending on who you are, you might be permitted to fly a special ensign. Perhaps you save lives (the Coastguard), or live in perpetual darkness (the British Antarctic Survey), or serve Queen and Country (the Royal Navy). If nothing like that applies, but you still want a special ensign, you can become a member of a yacht club: the more exclusive your club, the *smarter* your ensign.

Red ensign: The classic.

Defaced red ensign: This will have a little picture, probably a yacht club's badge or emblem, in the bottom right-hand corner. Posh.

Defaced blue ensign: Blue background instead of red. Little picture. Posher.

Blue ensign: Blue background. No picture. Poshest.

White ensign: White flag. Big red cross of St George, plus the Union Jack in the top-left corner. Only flown by the Royal Navy, Royal Yachts, and a single yacht club, the Royal Yacht Squadron.* Turbo posh.

DO YOU HAVE TO FLY AN ENSIGN?
According to the Merchant Shipping Act 1995, a vessel must fly an ensign if signalled to by 'one of Her Majesty's ships' or a ship under the command of a naval officer (the act is silent on what constitutes a signal); on entering or leaving a foreign port; or if you're a big ship entering or leaving a British port.

....

* The RYS only allowed women to become full members in 2013. Just saying.

In practice, if you're on board a boat big enough to have its own loo, you'll probably fly an ensign from dawn until dusk, whenever you're in sight of land and other boats.

HOW BIG SHOULD IT BE?
Just right: a huge flag on a bathtub looks just as ridiculous as a handkerchief on an oil tanker.

DIPPING THE ENSIGN
If you pass a Royal Yacht or a Royal Navy vessel it's meant to be good manners to *dip* your ensign: lower it by a third, wait until the frigate or whatever it is acknowledges you by dipping in return, and hoist it back up again.

Dipping should be low on your priority list if you're wrestling with some finicky pilotage, but it's quite fun if you're motoring along with nothing better to do. Don't worry about wasting the frigate's time: the navy likes tradition. Give them a friendly wave if you want to make the whole thing a bit less weird.

NIGHT-TIME
Again, it's good manners to lower your ensign at night-time. This is where affectation really kicks in. In theory, the *senior* boat in a harbour or anchorage lowers first (i.e. that frigate), followed by everyone else in descending order of ensign special-ness. Do ignore. Simply lower around sunset to salute the end of the day and hoist with your first cup of tea in the morning.

THERE ARE ALSO BURGEES ...
Burgees are small triangular flags, often with a club emblem on them, flown at the top of the mast, which is the second most important place to fly a flag after the stern. It used to be a very practical flag, because it showed your apparent

wind. They're becoming less common, given that mastheads now bristle with wind meters, communications equipment and lightning dissipators.* If people still want to fly a club burgee, they tend to move it to below the starboard *spreader* of the mainmast.

... AND COURTESY FLAGS ...

A courtesy flag is the ensign of the country you're visiting, if you're boating abroad. On a yacht, it should be flown below the starboard spreader, above the burgee.

... AND DRESSING OVERALL

On really special occasions – your birthday, the anniversary of the Battle of Trafalgar, etc. – it's the done thing to string all your signal flags (A to Z) in a line from the tip of your bow, up to your masthead(s), and down to your stern.

NAUTICAL PHRASES

The sailing lexicon is large and complicated. To the uninitiated it can seem wilfully obfuscatory. If you're reading an accomplished writer such as Patrick O'Brian, the intricate vocabulary braces the flourishes of the plot. If it's your first day out on a boat, it is a mind-numbing nightmare.

But being able to say *slack the port-hand backstay* or *luff her two points* and be certain of instant comprehension is essential not only for efficiency, but also for safety. You

....

* Looks a lot like a wire loo-brush. Helps reduce the build-up of static at the top of a mast, making it less prone to lightning strikes.

don't want to find yourself yelling *pull that rope, no not that one, that one* in a sudden squall.

Over time, this rich language has come ashore, finding its way into the broad compass of everyday English. Here are a few choice examples:

aback *adv.* of square sails: laid back against the mast by a headwind OR *fig.* disconcerted by a sudden check; discomfited

batten down *v.i.* strengthen or secure with battens (*n.* a strip of wood or metal for securing tarpaulin over a hatchway); fasten down hatches against bad weather OR *fig.* to prepare for a challenging situation

by and large *adv.* sailing with the wind ahead of the beam (by) and abaft the beam (large) OR *fig.* on the whole, generally speaking, all things considered

cut and run *v.i.* cut the cable and make sail without waiting to weigh anchor OR *fig. colloq.* run away, hurry off, scarper

fathom *n.* measure the depth of water with a sounding line OR *fig.* get to the bottom of, penetrate, comprehend fully

high and dry *adv.* out of the water OR *fig.* in a helpless or abandoned position

in the offing *n.* the part of the open sea visible from a shore or beyond an anchoring ground OR *fig.* nearby, at hand, in prospect, likely to appear or happen in the near future

keep a weather eye (open) *v.* look to windward OR *fig.* be watchful and alert, keep one's wits about one

(At sea, especially on a sailing boat, it's essential to keep looking to windward to see what the weather has in store. Is the weather, you want to know, about to get (any) worse? So ingrained is this practice, the words *windward* and *weather* are interchangeable: the *weather sheet* is a rope on windward side of the boat; *weather helm* is a tendency for the boat to round up into the wind.)

leeway *n.* the lateral drift of a ship to leeward (*n.* the direction towards which the wind is blowing) of the desired course; the amount of deviation produced by such drift OR *fig.* freedom of action within set limits; room allowed for this; a safety margin

mainstay *n.* the stay (*n.* large rope used to brace mast) which extends from the maintop to the foot of the foremast OR *fig.* a chief support, a thing or person that provides support; an object of reliance

on an even keel *phr.* with the keel (*n.* the lengthwise timber or metal structure along the base of a ship or boat, providing lateral stability) horizontal or level OR *fig.* balanced, harmonious, stable

sail too close to the wind *q.v.* taken aback; if you sail too close to the wind, you will be taken aback OR *fig.* to behave in a manner that is on the verge of being dangerous, improper or illegal

skylarking *v.i.* esp. of ship's boys and midshipmen: to return to deck after working aloft by sliding down the backstays (*n.* ropes extending downwards and aft from the top of the mast to the stern of the ship) rather than using the ratlines (*n.* small ropes fastened across the shrouds of a sailing ship like ladder rungs and used to climb rigging) OR *fig.* indulge in horseplay, frolic

take the wind out of somebody's sails *phr.* to pass to windward of another sailing vessel thereby stealing their wind, slowing them down, making them really cross OR *fig.* frustrate or deflate a person, esp. by making an unexpected remark or anticipating an action

turn a blind eye *hist.* 'I have only one eye, I have a right to be blind sometimes ... I really do not see the signal.' Spoken by Nelson to his flag captain during the Battle of Copenhagen. Nelson ignored his admiral's orders to disengage, and went on to win the battle OR *fig.* pretend not to notice

One final suggestion, not yet in common usage:

lose steerageway *phr.* to lack sufficient headway (*n.* ship's movement ahead or forward; *gen.* advance, progress) for a vessel to be controlled by the helm OR *fig.* of children, a serious crime; to dawdle, loiter; to misplace shoes; esp. to need a pee after putting on a wetsuit

THE LITTLE SHIPS OF DUNKIRK

Romans, Angles, Saxons, Jutes, Vikings, Norwegians, Normans, the Spanish, the Dutch, the French, the French, the French: we have not wanted for invaders, some stunningly successful, others less so. The last time the Channel acted as a bulwark against Britain's enemies was, of course, during the Second World War, when a fleet of Little Ships ploughed across a calm sea to pluck thousands of troops from the beaches of Dunkirk.

By May 1940 German troops had advanced through France, Belgium, Luxembourg and the Netherlands, driving the Allies back towards the coast. With the Germans already holding the major ports, Calais and Boulogne, the soldiers massed at Dunkirk were surrounded, cut off from all help. There they would have been either captured or killed, were it not for the daring evacuation.

As the Luftwaffe strafed the soldiers waiting on the beaches, some men were able to climb aboard the waiting destroyers from a large concrete breakwater, but that was never going to be fast enough. To speed things up, the Admiralty requisitioned all 'self-propelled pleasure craft between 30 feet and 100 feet in length'. These Little Ships, which could ferry men from the beaches out to bigger ships waiting offshore, have passed into legend.

Only a year later, they were starring in stirring adventure stories, such as *Dave Dawson at Dunkirk*:

Dave couldn't speak as he stared at the sight. The words were all too choked up inside of him to come out. The whole beach was practically covered with row after row of British and French soldiers ... And out there looking weird and grotesque in the glow of the burning Channel port were boats of every conceivable description. There were row boats, and yachts. Fishing smacks and pleasure yawls. Coastal vessels and ferry boats. Motor boats and canoes. Barges and British destroyers. Anything and everything that could float had been brought over to help in the evacuation. No, it wasn't the British Navy taking the British Army home. It was all England come to rescue her fighting men.

Of course, in reality it was a naval operation, with most of the boats manned by officers and ratings, not Blighty's have-a-go heroes. Nevertheless, nothing should dim the glory of their achievement. The number of men saved was staggering. Between 27 May and the 4 June, while the French held the perimeter, 338,226 soldiers were evacuated, allowing the Allies to fight on to victory.*

Only a very few Dunkirk veterans are still alive, but some of the Little Ships are still afloat, or preserved out of the water in appropriate dignity. The *Medway Queen* paddle steamer is moored at Gillingham; the *Sundowner*, a motor yacht, lies at Ramsgate; and the *Tamzine*, a 15-foot, clinker-built, open fishing boat, sits in the Imperial War Museum, looking almost unbearably small.

The success of the Dunkirk evacuation allowed Winston Churchill to deliver one of the most famous speeches of all time, a rallying cry when Britain's back really was against the wall:

....

* That the Allies, at this point, included Indian, Senegalese and Moroccan troops has often been overlooked.

We shall go on to the end, we shall fight in France, we shall fight on the seas and oceans, we shall fight with growing confidence and growing strength in the air, we shall defend our Island, whatever the cost may be, we shall fight on the beaches, we shall fight on the landing grounds, we shall fight in the fields and in the streets, we shall fight in the hills; we shall never surrender.

THE SCUTTLING OF THE GERMAN FLEET AT SCAPA FLOW

In a curious diminuendo after the guns had fallen silent at the end of the First World War, while politicians were haggling over the terms of peace in Paris, fifty-two German ships sank to the bottom of the sea in Scapa Flow.

Great Britain doesn't want for safe anchorages, but Scapa Flow, 120 square miles of sheltered water tucked inside the Orkney archipelago, has to be one of the best. Bounded on the north side by Mainland (the confusingly named largest Orkney island) and (moving clockwise) by Burray, South Ronaldsay, Flotta and Hoy, as a bolthole it is safe as houses – so long as you've read your sailing directions thoroughly.* The only possible downside is that it's rather grim to the untutored eye, as this piece of contemporary doggerel reveals:

....

* The Admiralty publishes sailing directions, also known as pilots, which are detailed guides to making safe passage around the British coast and in international waters. Yacht clubs sometimes publish their own versions, which are founts of invaluable local knowledge.

Have you ever heard the story of how Scapa got its name?
If you haven't then you're slow, because it's earned a
    world-wide fame.
It has caused a lot of howling amongst our tars at sea,
So I'll tell to you the story as a sailor told it me:
Sure a little bit of wastage fell from out the sky one day,
And it fell into the ocean in a spot up Scotland way.
And when the Sea Lords saw it, sure! it looked so bleak
    and bare
They said, 'Suppose we start to build a Naval Base up there.'

From 1914, the Admiralty beavered away, turning Scapa
Flow into a fitting base for its Grand Fleet. Ships were
sunk to block key pinch points. Booms were slung across
other channels. Gun batteries were built along the shore.
Underwater listening technology – hydrophones! –
was even deployed in anticipation of a new enemy: the
submarine.

From this watertight refuge, the navy could sally forth
to control access to the North Sea and enforce its blockade
of German ports. Indeed it was from Scapa Flow that
Admiral Sir John Jellicoe sailed in 1916 for the Battle of
Jutland, an indecisive and much-debated confrontation
that saw terrible loss of life, but did leave the British navy
with the upper hand for the rest of the war.

One of the conditions of the 1918 armistice was that
Germany surrender most of its fleet. Seventy-four German
ships therefore steamed to Scapa Flow, along with many
of their crew, who were forced into quasi-imprisonment
while the Paris Peace Conference (which led to the Treaty
of Versailles) got underway.

But when it came to determining the fate of the fleet,
the Allied powers were not of one mind. France and Italy
wanted to get their hands on some German ships, whereas

Britain, keen to cling on to its naval superiority, wanted them destroyed.

The German crews, as you can guess, were not happy. They'd lost the war. They couldn't go ashore. The food was dreadful. They were desperately bored, with nothing to do but sing (contemporaries reported hearing *Die Wacht am Rhein* and *Die Lorelei* drifting over the waters), gamble and drink whatever contraband they could barter with the British. Even worse, the smaller ships hadn't been designed for long-term on-board living, so conditions were extremely uncomfortable.

Rear-Admiral Ludwig von Reuter, the German commander at Scapa Flow, learnt in May 1919 that the draft treaty ordered all the interned ships be handed over to the Allies, with Germany henceforth to be allowed only the most nugatory of navies. Such a humiliation was too much for him and his officers to bear and so he told his captains in a (top-secret) letter to make (top-secret) preparations to scuttle the fleet.

They set about sabotaging their ships with great enthusiasm, deploying every stratagem to ensure that when the time came the chill Orkney waters would come cascading in to displace the air below decks. Portholes were loosened. Holes were bored through mighty bulkheads. Hammers and axes were readied to smash engine-room pipework. And, leaving nothing to chance, white flags were stashed aboard life-rafts ready to be hoisted when they abandoned ship.

Come 21 June, Reuter – clad in full dress uniform, complete with his Iron Cross medal – took up position on the deck of his ship, *Emden*. Luckily for him, many of the British guard ships were on exercise outside Scapa Flow. Using flags, he gave his order. Some ships hoisted the Red Flag: *advance on the enemy*. All opened their seacocks. By

1216 the first ship, *Friedrich der Grosse*, had flipped upside down and sunk.

'It was a clear afternoon,' wrote one British official, 'and probably no more wonderful sight has ever been witnessed than that of these huge vessels on all sides heeling over and plunging headlong – some with their sterns almost vertical above the water, others listing over to port or starboard, with steam and oil and air pouring out of the vents and rising to the surface long after the ships had completely disappeared beneath the water.'

The moment is more poetically rendered by Tim Pears, in his fictionalised account of the Great Scuttle in his novel, *The Redeemed*: 'The great ships were leviathans. They seemed to have altered their constitution, steel made flesh, to have come alive, like whales, vast grey creatures saying farewell to the upper air and leaving the world of men to sink into the deeps of the ocean.'

By the time the British fleet returned from their man-oeuvres, all but the largest ships had sunk.* Nine Germans were shot trying to make it to land (making them the unlucky last casualties of the war), and any pretence of civil treatment of the internees was abandoned, as sailors were roughed up, robbed of their meagre possessions and left in sodden clothes without blankets on iron decks.

The next day, Admiral Sydney Fremantle, the British commander, addressed a furious lecture to Reuter, saying that the war had begun with 'a breach of military honour in the invasion of Belgium' and had now ended with 'a breach

....

* The few German ships that weren't eventually salvaged can enjoy a surprising afterlife as a raw material for Geiger counters, which need to be made from *low-background steel*, i.e. steel uncontaminated by the radiation that spread around the globe in the wake of the bombing of Hiroshima, Nagasaki and later nuclear tests. The ships' sequestered location at the bottom of Scapa Flow makes them ideal candidates.

of naval honour' – a bit rich, seeing as: a) the British wanted the fleet sunk and b) if the situation had been reversed they'd have done exactly the same thing.

ETERNAL FATHER

a hymn by William Whiting

You don't have to be remotely Christian to appreciate this Victorian hymn. The melody of the penultimate line in each verse sounds like the insistent keening of wind in the run-up to a gale. It is often sung very movingly at seafarers' funerals.

Eternal Father, strong to save,
Whose arm hath bound the restless wave,
Who bidd'st the mighty ocean deep
Its own appointed limits keep;
Oh, hear us when we cry to Thee,
For those in peril on the sea!

O Christ! Whose voice the waters heard
And hushed their raging at Thy word,
Who walkedst on the foaming deep,
And calm amidst its rage didst sleep;
Oh, hear us when we cry to Thee,
For those in peril on the sea!

Most Holy Spirit! Who didst brood
Upon the chaos dark and rude,
And bid its angry tumult cease,
And give, for wild confusion, peace;
Oh, hear us when we cry to Thee,
For those in peril on the sea!

O Trinity of love and power!
Our brethren's shield in danger's hour;
From rock and tempest, fire and foe,
Protect them wheresoe'er they go;
Thus evermore shall rise to Thee
Glad hymns of praise from land and sea.

NAVAL TOASTS

A classic scene in *Master and Commander: The Far Side of the World*. Darkness outside. The captain's cabin lit by candles. The ship reeling drunkenly on a big sea. Captain Jack Aubrey, mock-serious, lifts his glass to propose the Royal Navy's Saturday toast: 'Gentlemen, to wives and to sweethearts ...' (cue snorts around the table) '... may they never meet.'

Thirteen years into the twenty-first century, *wives and sweethearts* were ditched in favour of *families* (cue galumphing about political correctness gone mad). Here are the toasts, new and old, traditionally drunk by officers on formal occasions after the loyal toast to the sovereign.

Sunday: Absent friends
Monday: Our ships at sea
Tuesday: Our sailors (previously, Our men)
Wednesday: Ourselves as no one else is likely to concern themselves with our welfare
Thursday: A bloody war or a sickly season*
Friday: A willing foe and sea room
Saturday: Our families (previously, Our wives and sweethearts)

AIDS TO NAVIGATION

From grand lighthouses on famous headlands to sticks in the mud of a little creek, we all need help negotiating Britain's complicated coastline. Luckily, we can rely on *aids to navigation*, which, large or small, all serve the same purpose. They show us how to find safe, deep water and how to avoid rocks, shoals and other menaces. They also help pinpoint your position: matching a neat symbol on a chart to a big, clanking, red buoy is very reassuring when you're approaching an unfamiliar anchorage.

Until 1977 there were around thirty different buoyage and navigation systems operating around the world, which had very obvious drawbacks. Thankfully, the comprehensively named International Association of Marine Aids to Navigation and Lighthouse Authorities got nearly everyone to agree to a single standard of buoyage:

....

* War and disease meant deaths; deaths meant vacancies; vacancies meant promotion.

today a submerged reef is marked the same way in the Tuamotus as it is in the Firth of Clyde.

The 500-year-old charity Trinity House is in charge of buoyage around the coasts of England, Wales, the Channel Islands and Gibraltar, plus sixty-six lighthouses and nine lightvessels, as well as inspecting local buoyage provided by smaller harbour authorities. Its counterpart for Scotland and the Isle of Man is the Northern Lighthouse Board, with the Commissioners of Irish Lights having responsibility for the island of Ireland.*

There are six main components to the system:

1. LATERAL MARKS

These line the sides of a safe channel or passage, often into a port or harbour, but also through a narrow strait or between shoals. A red buoy (or can, mark or stick) denotes the left-hand or *port* side of the channel. A green buoy (or can, mark or stick) denotes the right-hand or *starboard* side.**

But *whose left* are we talking about? The ferry heading into port? Or the one heading out to sea? Britain and much of the world marks a channel from the perspective of the boat coming *into* port, so the red buoys will be on your left as you arrive, and on your right as you leave.

But in North and South America, the Philippines, Japan, Korea and various Pacific islands, red buoys are on the *left* when you're heading out to sea and on your right when you're coming back to shore again. Chant 'red right

....

* This massive undertaking is funded by *light dues* which are levied on all commercial ships and bigger pleasure craft docking in UK ports. Historically, entrepreneurs could finance private lighthouses in a similar way, until Trinity House was given the right to buy them out in 1836.
** All the shorter words – left, port, red – belong together. As do all the longer ones – right, starboard, green. You're welcome.

returning, red right returning' if you ever find yourself negotiating these waters.

Also, if you're following a channel, but not actually putting into an estuary or harbour, remember that buoyage tends to follow the direction of the flooding tide. You'll find a large magenta arrow on your chart if there's any room for doubt.

2. CARDINAL MARKS

As with lateral marks, cardinals can either be floating buoys or fixed posts. They show where safe water lies relative to something dangerous, probably rocks or an area of shallow water. They're painted yellow and black, with two triangular cones on top, and come in four flavours – *north, south, east* and *west* – with different stripes and different triangles, depending on their position relative to the danger. Remember, a north cardinal lies north of the danger, so you need to go north of it to be safe.

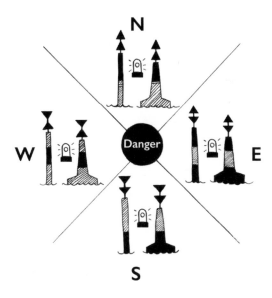

North and south cardinals are pretty easy to remember as the triangles helpfully point up and down. East and west are a bit trickier. Navigation instructors like to say you can draw a W over the west cardinal triangles, but frankly this is a bit tenuous. Better to think of it as an hourglass: as the day's time runs out, the sun sets in the *west*.

3. ISOLATED DANGER MARKS

These mark a rogue hazard in an otherwise safe patch of water. Unlike cardinal marks, they perch bang on top of the danger, and are painted black and red with two balls on top.

4. SAFE WATER MARKS

These jaunty, red-and-white striped marks tell you that you're in the clear, often when you've got to the end of a complicated buoyed channel threading you out of a busy estuary.

5. SPECIAL MARKS

Show an area reserved for a niche activity such as water-skiing or naval gunnery. Various shapes of yellow.

6. NEW DANGER MARKS

These warn mariners of a new hazard that hasn't yet made it onto charts. Blue-and-yellow vertical stripes.

LEADING MARKS

Often found in smaller anchorages, *leading marks* rely on two points which, when aligned, bring you inshore on a *safe bearing*, clear of any obstacles. The marks might be painted posts on the foreshore, a church spire and a flagpole, or the pair of lanterns which allowed the Swallows to land on Wild Cat Island after dark. Here's how to use them safely:

1. Line up your two marks and steer towards them.
2. If the lower one, the one closer to you, moves to *starboard* of the higher one, you're to *port* of your safe bearing. Alter course 10° to starboard until they line up again. Return to your original course.
3. If it moves to *port* of the higher one, you're to *starboard* of your bearing. Alter course 10° to port, line them up and return to your original course.
4. In other words, when they're out of whack, *steer at the lower one.*

RULES OF THE ROAD

Motoring out of a ferry port, crossing a shipping lane, weaving through a fishing fleet: all are scenarios every bit as intimidating as a first car journey through a big city. Cities have white lines, traffic lights and roundabouts to stop cars colliding. Boats have the *rules of the road*, officially known as the International Regulations for Preventing Collisions at Sea (1972), which apply wherever you are in the world. Mess with them at your peril.

PASS PORT TO PORT (OR, DRIVE ON THE RIGHT)

Unlike traffic, boats rarely stream along in two neat lines, one lot going one way, one the other.* So, if as often happens, you and another boat are 'meeting on a reciprocal or nearly reciprocal course', i.e. you're in danger of having a head-on

....

* Busy stretches of water, such as the Straits of Dover, do have designated shipping lanes for larger vessels.

crash, then you *both* alter course to starboard, meaning you pass each other port to port, *as if* you were driving on the right. Make sure your course alteration is unambiguous – as definite as your sea room allows.

OVERTAKING BOAT KEEPS CLEAR

Overtaking means any vessel which approaches another 'more than 22.5° abaft her beam', and it's up to the fastest boat to be sensible. We'd advise you not to insist on this if you're in a narrow buoyed channel with a ferry steaming up behind you.*

WINDWARD BOAT KEEPS CLEAR

This rule only applies to two sailing boats. If both boats have the wind coming over the same side, i.e. they're on the same tack, the boat that is closer to the wind (the windward boat) has to keep out of the way of the downwind (or leeward) boat, because it has more room to manoeuvre. In Age of Sail parlance, the windward boat has the *weather gage*, much favoured by Nelson et al. because it allowed a captain to swoop down on his enemy, all guns blazing.

PORT GIVES WAY TO STARBOARD

This is very simple if you're sailing. If you're on port tack, i.e. the wind is coming over the port side of your boat, you must avoid a boat on starboard tack.

Under engine, it's a bit more subtle. If you're approaching another boat *neither* head on (cf. pass to port) *nor* from astern (cf. overtaking boat), then whichever of you is to port of the other keeps clear. To port, you're the *stand-off*

....

* There's a brilliant Mike Peyton cartoon (one of many; he captures the absurdity of the sea better than anyone) showing a little yacht flapping about in front of the bow of a massive cruise ship. The caption? 'Don't alter course now, you'll only confuse him.'

or *give-way vessel*; to starboard, you're the *stand-on vessel*.

If this is hard to grasp (and it is a bit), picture the lights you would be able to see if it was dark. If you're to port, you can see the port lights of the other ship. Port lights are red, red says DANGER, time for you to take evasive action. If you're to starboard, on the other hand, you can see their starboard lights. Starboard lights are green, green says GO, maintain your course.

To give way in this situation, it's normally safest to alter course to steer immediately behind the stand-on vessel: you want to *duck under its stern*. As with passing port to port, make it really obvious what you're doing: one big course alteration is easier to see than lots of little ones. And don't just slow down either. It's hard to judge speed at a distance, whereas the change in a boat's profile as it alters course is very distinctive.

Both in this instance, and when passing port to port, you're turning to starboard, thereby opening up more of the red-lit, port side of your boat, which is why a skipper, peering anxiously through her binoculars, might grunt at the helm, 'Show that bugger a bit more red.'

POWER GIVES WAY TO SAIL

Obvious in theory, but it comes with a caveat. Many power boats are commercial, whether ferries, fishermen or freighters. Practically all sailing boats are at sea for fun. Technically, a yacht *could* enforce its rights of way over a working boat, but that would be spectacularly rude.

More formally, the rules say a sailing boat must give way to any vessel *restricted in its ability to manoeuvre*, which could mean a big ship in a tight channel or a trawler working its nets.

On the other hand, if you're belting down an estuary in a RIB, don't make it any harder for a yacht trying to beat out to sea.

AND FINALLY ...

The one overarching rule is to do whatever you can to avoid a collision. In practice, this means you shouldn't insist religiously on your right of way, and it's also worth considering who's likely to come off worse in a crash, as these delightful lines remind us:

> Here lies the body of William Jay
> Who died defending his right of way.
> He was right, dead right, as he sailed along
> But he's just as dead as if he'd been wrong.

BUT HOW DO I KNOW IF I AM ON A COLLISION COURSE?

For once, there is a beautifully simple answer. Take a bearing on the boat you're worried about. Wait thirty seconds. Take another. Wait thirty seconds. Take another. Has the bearing changed? *Yes!* You're fine. *No* ... Take evasive action.

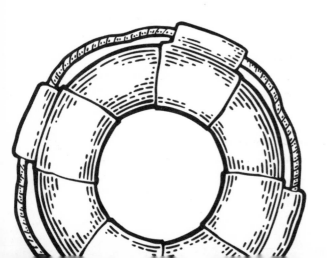

SOUNDING THE HORN

Despite all the above, sometimes it's really hard to work out what's going on. In theory, there are a very useful set of sound signals, which boats can use to help them manoeuvre round each other safely.

IN OPEN WATER

One short blast: I am altering my course to starboard
Two short blasts: I am altering my course to port
Three short blasts: I am operating astern propulsion
Five short blasts: What the bloody *hell* are you doing?*

IN A NARROW CHANNEL

Two long, one short: I intend to overtake you on your starboard side
Two long, two short: I intend to overtake you on your port side
One long, one short × 2: I agree (in response to the above two)

AND WHEN ROUNDING A BEND

One long blast: You can't see me but here I come!

In reality the only one you often hear is the long, nerve-jangling blast of a ferry careering towards you. If you *really* need to find out what another boat is up to, call them up on VHF channel 16 and hope somebody's listening.

....
* Please make your intentions clear.

THE *TORREY CANYON* DISASTER

During the last century, vast supertankers started to snake across the oceans, shunting the crude oil that still powers the earth's economies from where it is drilled to the refineries that prepare it for our factories, cars and homes. For most Britons, then as now, this happened out of sight, out of mind, until a tanker hit a rock off the Isles of Scilly, disgorging thousands of tonnes of oil onto some of the nation's most cherished coastline.

The *Torrey Canyon*, three football pitches long,* was owned by a Liberian company registered in Bermuda, which in turn was a subsidiary of the US oil company Unocal; a standard legal ruse that allows ships to fly *flags of convenience* which can reduce the number of rules (or red tape, depending on your point of view) to be complied with.

That said, the *Torrey Canyon*'s captain and crew were eminently experienced mariners, Italian seamen who knew their trade front to back – which makes what happened all the more excruciating.

Until the early hours of Saturday 18 March 1967, their journey from the Persian Gulf to the Welsh port of Milford Haven had been business as usual. At 0400 First Officer Silvano Bonfiglio came on watch. The weather was fine. The visibility good. The ship – guided by its automatic pilot – was steering a course of 018°, about north-north-east. Its speed was 16 knots.

....

* At the time, the thirteenth-largest merchant vessel afloat.

He was, quite correctly, keeping an eye out for the Isles of Scilly. This was long before GPS, but he did have radar. Sure enough, around 0630 the Scillies showed up – but not exactly where Bonfiglio expected.

Normally, a ship the size of the *Torrey Canyon* would pass outside the islands, leaving them comfortably to starboard, before turning east to Milford Haven. The radar, however, was showing them on the ship's port bow, meaning the current must have set the tanker further east than expected. The first officer changed course to the west, assuming his boss would want to stick to precedent, but when he telephoned down to Pastrengo Rugiati, he was told in no uncertain terms to stick to 018°.

Technically, there's no reason why even a big tanker shouldn't pass between the Scillies and Land's End. There are some legendary rocks, true, that lie in the middle of the seaway, but they're marked by the Sevenstones Lightship. True, the recommended passage is between Land's End and the lightship, not between the Scillies and the rocks, but there's space, so long as nothing goes wrong ...

Around 0700 hours, Captain Rugiati – his maritime record hitherto exemplary – joined the first officer on the bridge, who stood down at 0800 to be replaced by the rather less experienced third officer, Alfonso Coccio. Aged twenty-seven, Coccio wasn't cocky. He'd known he'd be on watch for this part of the journey and had dutifully prepared the route. Unfortunately, the route he'd prepared had been the one to the west of the Scillies, not through this relatively narrow gap.

Nevertheless, he started taking bearings to fix exactly where the tanker was. A bearing from the Peninnis Lighthouse on St Mary's Island, combined with a distance reading provided by radar, showed him they were shaping a perfectly respectable course. At 0818 he plotted their position on the chart, putting the lighthouse dead abeam.

Around about then, some fishing boats appeared off their starboard bow. Rocks are often fertile fishing ground, and these French boats were busy with their lobster pots. The fishermen on the boats later reported that they were a bit surprised to see such a big ship attempting the passage, but they weren't immediately worried. In theory, it had plenty of sea room.

The captain altered course to port, to 015°, a nudge he could do without turning the steering gear from automatic to manual. But although the ship's head was turning to the left, away from the rocks, the current and the wind were still sweeping the *Torrey Canyon* to the right – towards the rocks.

By 0830 the *Torrey Canyon* was steering 010°, which would have taken it clear of the rocks, but then the captain made a brief course alteration back to 013°, back towards the rocks, trying to avoid some fishing floats, and possibly another boat.

At this crucial moment, the third officer marked a fix on the chart in the wrong place. The Captain told him to do it again, and fast, and so it was that at 0840 they realised they were only 2.8 miles from the nearest rock: not worrying if you're a little motorboat, *very* worrying if you're a supertanker.

The captain – obviously – altered course to port, but the next fix still put them less than a mile from the rocks. He shouted to the helmsman to take the *Torrey Canyon* hard to port – to 350° ... 340° ... 320° – but the ship didn't answer.

Why? *Why wasn't it turning?*

The reason, both awful and prosaic, was that the steering gear had found itself in an unusual back-up mode, neither automatic nor manual, when you could only steer using a special handle, not the wheel. In the vital, panicked moments it took the captain to realise this, put it back into manual, and fling the wheel to port, it was too late. The *Torrey Canyon* hit Pollard Rock at 15.75 knots.

Oil gushed into the sea.

The spill was unparalleled in British history; indeed more than half a century later, it remains the worst disaster of its kind in UK waters. The Cornish coast, as well as parts of Brittany and the Channel Islands, were doused in oil, washing up so thickly that 'chocolate mousse' was the favoured journalistic simile at the time.

At first the task of salvaging the tanker went to a Dutch tug called *Utrecht*, which was poised in Mount's Bay on the south coast of Cornwall ready to respond to just such a call. Its terms were no-win no-fee: it wouldn't charge for its services unless it managed to float the ship off the rocks and return it to shore. It conspicuously failed.

Captain Rugiati and three of the crew remained on board, while the rest, fearing that it wouldn't take much for the oil to catch fire, were taken off the ship by helicopter, the seas being too rough for them to board a lifeboat.

While the *Torrey Canyon* crunched and scraped atop its rock, the oil came ashore with the highest tide of the year. Black waves swamped beaches, inundated pretty coves and busy harbours, and the reek of oil stained the air far inland. Seabirds began to die in their thousands.

One poignant tale among many is of schoolchildren turning out on Easter Sunday with watering cans, buckets and bottles to help marines scoop the oil off the beaches, in a clean-up operation called – bizarrely – Operation

Canute. To those on the ground, it felt futile.

By Tuesday it was obvious that the salvagers were losing the battle. The oil was still leaking, and the *Torrey Canyon* was starting to break up. Action was needed. Ships were ordered out of the area, people were warned not to come too close to the coast (advice everyone ignored), and in the afternoon planes swooped over the tanker, dropping bombs which ignited the oil, sending dramatic clouds of smoke and fire billowing into the sky. But even an oil fire is hard to keep going at sea.

The planes had to return the next day, this time with napalm, the petrochemical used to such devastating effect in the Vietnam War, and only on Thursday was it agreed that all the oil had burnt.

Detergent, two and a half million gallons of it, allowed clean-up workers to rinse the beaches clean, but it had horrific consequences for marine life: cockles and mussels, limpets and whelks, crabs and eels and baby flatfish – it killed everything. Soon the stench of decay mingled with the stench of oil.

The start of the tourist season was subdued. The spill had received a great deal of publicity and people didn't want to risk their precious holiday on oil-soaked beaches. However, by high summer, the hard work of the clean-up operation had paid off. If you were observant, if you went looking, there was a sheen of oil in secluded pools, underneath rocks or deep in the sand, but holidaymakers could still have their fun, and – more importantly – the local economy still had its vital annual income.

Even the blackest spills have silver linings. Thousands of people volunteered to help. Environmental consciousness increased. Pollution regulations were tightened. Unfortunately, it is often a disaster that ushers in change.

QUICKSAND

When encountered at an impressionable age, quicksand – a writer's last resort – can give you a childhood's worth of nightmares. The signs dotted around the British coast of a stickman stuck up to his waist, stick arms waving frantically, don't help. But while quicksand *is* incredibly dangerous, it's not because you sink over your head and vanish.

This is what actually happens.

Quicksand is sand and water, but with bigger gaps between the grains of sand than normal. When you place your weight on it, the sand comes alive,* sundering the illusion of solidity and turning the sand and water into an unstable gloopy mess.

Normal sand supports you because the friction between each tiny grain allows your weight to be distributed over a wide area. Add more water, and you have sandcastle sand, wetter, but still able to support you. Add more water (seeping upwards from an incoming tide, say), and the sand and water liquify and can no longer bear your weight.

The reason you get stuck is that the sand-and-water suspension disturbed by your weight resolidifies, trapping you. You can't sink over your head because a human body is less dense overall than quicksand. But if quicksand itself can't kill you, a returning tide can.

....

* The *quick* in quicksand means *alive*, not *fast*. As in Jesus sitting at the right hand of his Father to judge the quick and the dead.

WHAT TO DO IF YOU'RE STUCK?

1. Stay calm.
2. Discard anything heavy.
3. If possible, try to spread your weight.
4. Keep your hands above the level of the sand.
5. If you're in deep, lie backwards and hope your legs will float up.
6. Don't struggle: you'll work your way deeper. Struggling = applying more force = creating more of the quicksand that caught you in the first place.
7. Deep breaths will help to keep you buoyant (and calm).
8. Don't let other people try to rescue you. Tying a rope around your middle and heaving hard won't get you out because the pressure is too great. Instead, get them to call 999 and ask for the coastguard.

When help arrives (let's think positive), perhaps aboard one of the RNLI's mudflat hovercrafts, your rescuers will have special overshoes called *mudders* to help spread their weight. They will also bring stretchers or inflatable sleds which they can lay across the sand, allowing them to reach you without sinking. Finally they will have a *mud rescue lance* which injects water or air into the quicksand: water will loosen the consistency of the quicksand to a slurry, making it easier to get you out, while air will reduce the vacuum created by the quicksand.

You're free!

SEASIDE FOOD

Seaside food tends to set up camp at one of two extremes: sweet, fatty, easy to come by – or chewy, wholesome and hard-won.

In a battle between pillowy doughnuts, salty chips and the sweet kiss of a 99 Flake on the one hand, and squelchy limpets on the other, there's only one winner. It's hard to bribe children off the beach with a whelk. But for those brave of palate and curious of nature, a cornucopia awaits.

Helpfully, when it comes to flora, the law is very much on your side. Says the Theft Act of 1968: 'A person who picks mushrooms growing wild on any land, or who picks flowers, fruit or foliage from a plant growing wild on any land, does not (although not in possession of the land) steal what he picks, unless he does it for reward or for sale or other commercial purpose.'

With fauna, however, the rules and regulations are *legion*. In theory, you're allowed to catch fish, molluscs and crustacea. In practice, there are local and national laws restricting what you can do when, where and how. It's all in a good cause – preserving stocks and habitats – but it means you must do your homework thoroughly before sallying forth.* Armed with that proviso, let's begin with a few basic rules.

....

* John Wright, whose *Edible Seashore* is full of wise advice, suggests: 'If you ever find yourself in trouble, pretend you are Norwegian.'

Be prepared: When is high water? When is low water? What is the weather forecast? If you can't answer those questions, you're not ready.

Be healthy: Gather only where sea and shore are clean.

Be moderate (or, don't be greedy). Pick what you can eat that day, no more, and only from thriving populations.

Be thoughtful: Tread carefully and tidy up piles of sand.

Be careful: Watch your step. The going may well be slippery and spiky.

BLACKBERRIES

(probably *Rubus fruticosus*) Entry-level foraging. Easy to spot. Not poisonous. Great in apple crumble. Ensure you pick above the dog-pee line.

SLOES

(*Prunus spinosa*)

Sloes, the fruit of the blackthorn, are found all over the country, but the ones that grow in the sandy, salty soils of cliffs, dunes and hams are particularly flavoursome. You're not foraging for pudding, but for something even better: sweet sticky *sloe gin*.

You harvest sloes from early September (if it's been warm and you're relatively far south) until early November. The tradition used to be to wait for the first frost, but these days that might be leaving it too long.

A ripe sloe resembles a blueberry: plump, firm but not hard, with an attractive white-ish bloom dusting its skin. You should be able to squish it, but not too easily. And now to make the gin.

You need:
400 g sloes (washed, thorns and rotten sloes discarded)
150 g sugar
500 ml gin (supermarket not artisan)
1 litre Kilner jar, or similar (no need to sterilise: the gin does that for you)

1. Prick the sloes to allow the alcohol to leech the juices from the fruit while the gin matures. Use a needle or, for maximum authenticity, a blackthorn. If that sounds laborious (it is), freeze them, which splits their skins and does the same job in a fraction of the time. It can lead to sediment or cloudiness, but you can deal with that later.
2. Put the sloes, gin and sugar in your jar and mix well.
3. Leave the container in a cool, dark place to mature, stirring or simply upending every week or two. Although sloes bottled in October will *just* be ready for Christmas, it's better to wait around six months before decanting and bottling. Assuming you've frozen your sloes, you'll also need to strain your gin through a muslin to filter out the sediment.
4. Your sloe gin should be coloured a bright, clear ruby and taste sweet, tart and bitter all at once. Delicious on its own, it's even better with any kind of fizzy wine.

WILD CABBAGE
(*Brassica oleracea*)
This is the ur-green, the great-great-great-grandmother of the modern cultivars we know as cabbage, broccoli, cauliflower, kale, sprouts and savoy. It's happy in limey soil and salt, hence it grows well on cliffs. Treat it as you would any trendy green: stir-fry with lots of salt and oil, or crisp it up in a low oven.

SEA BEET
(*Beta vulgaris maritima*)
Another food ancestor, this time of spinach beet, Swiss chard, mangelwurzel, beetroot and sugar beet. Easy to identify. Grows like a cheerful weed. Late spring is a good time: the leaves will be fresh and young.

Treat it as you would spinach, but if you don't want to intimidate people with Popeye-sized mounds, try shredding it finely and incorporating it into savoury pancakes or cheese scones.

ALEXANDERS
(*Smyrnium olusatrum*)
An umbellifer, in other words a relative of carrots, parsley and celery, so
called because their flowers poke out
like little umbrellas. It arrived on the
south coast with the Romans, but
as the climate warms it's marching
northwards. Once a more common
ingredient, it's been sidelined in
favour of celery. Cliffs are a good
hunting ground.

In April and May enjoy the stalks as you would aspara-
gus. Later in the season, when they're tougher, dice them
with onions and carrots to make an interesting *sofrito*.
Or roast the flower heads as you would purple sprouting
broccoli.

SEA HOLLY
(*Eryngium maritimum*)
Its leaves are a beguiling blue-purple, particularly stunning
in the light of a westering sun. It grows in sand on beaches
and dunes, in places where the tide doesn't *quite* reach.

Colour aside, the leaves do indeed look like holly, while the pain if you step on one is reminiscent of a thistle.

You're after the root, so technically you need the landowner's permission. Once secured, cook as you would a carrot or parsnip. If you're feeling flash you can candy it, creating a once popular, now obsolete treat know as an *eryngo*. An aphrodisiac, apparently.

FENNEL
(*Foeniculum vulgare*)
A garnish rather than a square meal. Not the big bulbs of supermarket fennel, but wispy, fringy leaves which look a bit like dill. Delicious with fish or scattered over an Iranian-inspired rice pilaf.

MARSH SAMPHIRE
(*Salicornia europaea*)
You might have seen samphire, looking like rooted seaweed or a mini cactus, in a fishmongers during its summer season, or you can find it yourself on saltmarshes or mudflats. Bring scissors to snip leaves off the plants. You will get muddy.

You can eat it raw, but it tends, at the risk of stating the blindingly obvious, to be a bit salty. Better, then, to blanch in lots of fresh water and then fry in a little oil or butter. Or use it to garnish your seaside G&T now that lemon, lime and even cucumber are passé.

The cookery writer Meera Sodha says: 'It can be bitter, yes, but in a way that reminds you that you're not eating something grown in a polytunnel. It is stubborn, special and wild.'

SEAWEED
Seaweed is a loose, unscientific term for three types of macro algae: green, brown and red. Green variants are usually found higher up the beach as they need more sunlight, red are well submerged, and brown are in the middle. Superficially, seaweeds appear pretty similar, but they don't in fact share a common ancestor.

Several UK companies hand-harvest seaweed, and sell it on at a pretty stiff price, which you can avoid paying by heading to a (clean) beach with a string bag. Most seaweed sits below mean high-water springs, meaning it belongs to the Queen via the Crown Estate. We suspect she isn't going to miss a few fronds.

KELP
(*many different species*)
Kelp is a key ingredient in the Japanese stock *dashi*, which in turn is the base of miso soup. It was the original ingredient that led to the designation of *umami* as the fifth taste, alongside sweet, sour, bitter and salty.

Try baking kelp on a low heat in the oven to create a fashionable seaside rival to the kale crisp. Or take a leaf out of another seaside tradition and batter and deep fry.

DULSE
(Palmaria palmata)
These long red/brown flat fingers (a bit like pappardelle) have been used in cooking for generations, especially in Ireland and Scotland, where dulse was certainly harvested by St Columba's monks. Gather it off rocks at low water in the spring and summer, and leave to dry. Crumbled over pretty much anything – scrambled eggs, grilled courgettes, stir-fried rice – it gives a friendly umami boost. You can also fry it in bigger pieces and incorporate into, say, a salmon quiche.

LAVER
(Porphyra umbilicalis)
Thin, semi-translucent, brown/green, reminiscent of hair and wet paper. In situ, draped forlornly over rocks, laver isn't very appetising, but laverbread (or *bara lafwr*) is a classic dish if you're from Wales or the north coast of the Bristol Channel.

After harvesting, wash and simmer for around six hours until you've got a dark, lurid green, translucent mush. Squeeze off any excess water, as you would with spinach. Finely chop or whiz up in a food processor. Eat on hot buttered toast with lots of salt and pepper.

Or make laverbread cakes: take equal amounts of laverbread and rolled oats, mix and season, roll into little balls, flatten into patties, fry in butter or oil, two to three minutes each side. Best with leeks, cockles and bacon for breakfast.

MOLLUSCS

Human beings have been eating molluscs forever: their shells feature heavily in the prehistoric rubbish dumps or *middens* unearthed by archaeologists. Our forebears could enjoy these exemplary sources of protein and iron with a light heart, but today we have to be wary of their side effects: radically upset stomachs caused by pollution from agricultural run-off and human sewage.

1. Do your research on water quality: only collect from areas with attested clean water. No marinas or pig farms.
2. Stick to the old saw: only collect when there's an R in the month, i.e. September to April.
3. Make sure they're alive before you cook them: discard them if they don't *clam up* when you tap them.
4. Do cook them.
5. If you must eat them raw, buy from the professionals. Their molluscs will have been purified in tanks of artificial seawater.
6. Be extra careful with the bivalve filter feeders (cockles and mussels, oysters and clams).

LIMPETS
(*Patella vulgata*)
Inevitably, the easiest mollusc to catch is by far the least desirable. You won't struggle to find limpets, which are essentially snails despite their un-snail-like shape. Sneak up and knock them off their rocks with a swift, clean stroke. If you're too tentative, they get nervous and cling on tighter.

You *could* cook them in their shells over a fire, but unless you've been shipwrecked or the apocalypse is finally upon us, you might prefer to give them a miss.

WINKLES
(*Littorina littorea*)
A more recognisably snail-like marine snail. Small. Clings to rocks. Pluck, wash in lots of clean seawater, leave to soak for an hour or two, boil for three to four minutes. Use something spiky* to dig them out of their shells. As with all snails, they don't actually taste very nice, so it's advisable to pair them with a stronger flavour. Like vinegar. Or perhaps some early wild garlic.

DOG WHELKS
(*Nucella lapillus*)
A dog whelk is a carnivorous brute that terrorises the fore-shore. It latches onto its bivalve prey, bores a hole through its victim's shell using its *radula*, part tongue, part tooth. Thus primed, it injects the unlucky mussel (or similar) with an enzyme, which liquifies flesh to a soup, ready to be sucked out and devoured.

Fancy eating one now? No, us neither.

RAZOR CLAMS
(*Ensis siliqua* and *Ensis arcuatus*)
These, on the other hand, are a must. Hunting razor clams is both straightforward and comic, with a delicious outcome. Allow us to share this fine description of *Solen*-hunting from George Henry Lewes's** exquisite *Sea-side Studies at Ilfracombe, Tenby, the Scilly Isles and Jersey* (1858):

....

* A winkle-picker will be too big.
** Better known as the other half of Mary Ann Evans, aka George Eliot.

It is a hot, quiet afternoon. The tide is out, and a wide sweep of sand lies before us. We are armed with thin iron rods, each barbed at the end like a harpoon; we add thereto a paper of salt, basket, and jar. Over the yielding sand we pass, until we approach low-water mark, and then we begin peering about to find the trace of the *Solen*. This trace consists of nothing more than two small holes close together, sometimes broken into one, and presenting very much the appearance of the key-hole of a writing-desk ...

Having found a hole, we know that the *Solen* is at some distance underneath; it may only be a few inches, it may be many feet. The least disturbance will drive him irretrievably away. We must, therefore, allure him. Placing a pinch of salt over the hole, we await the result. In a minute or two the water begins to well up; this is succeeded by a commotion – the sand is upheaving – we hold our breath, and keep the hand ready to make a swift clutch – a final upheaval has taken place, and the *Solen* slowly shows the tip of his siphon; but he is still buried in the sand, and we must wait till he has thrust himself at least an inch above ground or we shall lose him. It may be that, having come thus far, he will suddenly change his mind, and, instead of advancing, make a precipitate retreat. But if he raised himself an inch out of his hole, and you are swift, he is your prize ...

As a technique, salting has stood the test of time, but on some beaches or in some conditions, it doesn't seem to work, in which case you'll need to deploy a *clam gun*: essentially a section of drainpipe, 3 feet long, with a lid and handle, and a hole in the lid to create a vacuum. (There are lots of DIY videos online.)

Find your keyhole. Place your gun over the hole and drive it down through the sand, twisting it back and forth as you go. Once the gun is as deep as it'll go, place a finger over the air valve and pull up the gun. Since it's now airtight, it should extract a core of sand, hopefully with the clam in the middle.

As for cooking: clam chowder, clam curry, clam linguine ... the world is your oyster.

COCKLES

(*Cerastoderma edule*)

Head to a legitimate cockling beach, often large, flat and sandy, remembering that is precisely the sort of beach over which tides rise exceptionally fast.*

Cockling takes place at low water, especially low-water springs. Armed with a robust rake, set off across the sand, keeping a weather eye out for empty shells that will mark a cockle bed. Your cockles will be lurking a finger's breadth below the sand. Rake out enough for a meal, and put them in a bucket filled with seawater to take home.

Leave them overnight in the bucket so they expel the sand from inside their shells, give them a scrub, put in a bowl of fresh salty water, tap and chuck any that don't close up smartly.

....

* Morecambe Bay, a classic cockling site, is now tragically associated with the deaths of twenty-one Chinese workers, hired out by gangmasters, who drowned harvesting cockles in 2004. So treacherous are the bay's shifting dykes and channels that since 1548 an experienced local has been appointed as the Queen's Guide to the Sands.

The British tradition is to cook cockles in boiling water and pickle with vinegar, but we'd encourage you to look more widely, to southeast Asia in particular. Or simply soften some onion and garlic in a frying pan, turn up the heat, add the cockles, a glass or two of white wine, parsley and lemon, and cook for two to three minutes covered. When the shells open, you know they're done, this time discarding any which *don't* open.

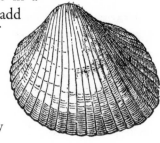

OYSTERS
(*Ostrea edulis* is the UK native)
Definitely leave to the professionals. Most oyster beds belong to licensed oyster farmers who won't appreciate you foraging.

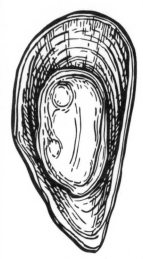

MUSSELS
(*Mytilus edulis*)
Mussels are able to survive in far fouler water than many of their relations, which should encourage extra caution. The mussels on a fishmonger's slab will have passed a hardcore set of purifying protocols which are

hard to replicate. At the risk of sounding a bit lame, we'd probably file mussels under *more trouble than they're worth* – unless you find yourself in the Outer Hebrides in January.

CRUSTACEANS

More challenging than molluscs: they can run away *and* bite back. To bag a lobster or a crab, you'll probably need some sort of permit *and* you'll have to wrestle with your conscience as to how you're planning to kill it.

Boiling alive, old-school, feels cruel. Some say there's a special place to poke its brain out, but the RSPCA helpfully points out that your lobster has thirteen brain centres, so unless you're absolutely sure you know what you're doing, brain-poking is not humane either.

If you have the appropriate kit and know how to use it, you can stun them, otherwise stick to shrimp (lots of peeling for not much flesh; it's hard to overcome the brutal mathematics of the shrimp's surface-area-to-volume ratio) and (the marginally more productive) prawn.*

BROWN SHRIMP

(*Crangon crangon*)
Unglamorous little creatures that dart away from you when you paddle in the shallows left by a retreating tide.

To catch, you need a likely location, a tide table, low water and a net. One from a beach shop will do, but if you're serious you need a *push net*, which has a bar at the bottom. Walk uptide, driving the bar through the sand, disturbing the shrimp so that they leap out of their hiding places slap bang into your net.

....

* Names are confusing. In the US they call prawns shrimp. In the UK shrimps are shrimpier and prawns are brawnier.

Simmer for a minute,* until they turn the familiar pink. Peel, at least the head. Fiddly but *just about* worth it. Let them make friends with hot melted butter, while you make friends with a fine manzanilla. Or you can roll up your sleeves and make potted shrimp, which calls for even more butter and mace.

COMMON PRAWN
(*Palaemon serratus*)
Hunt prawns from late summer into the autumn, seeking out long, sandy gullies between rocks which are covered at high tide, but are easily paddle-able at low water. There are two tactics: *beneath the fronds* and *march of the prawns*.

1. **Fronds:** Start two hours before low water and keep going for an hour afterwards. A neon child's net will do fine, although you can seek out something larger and more earnest. The prawns will be lurking in the cool shade under the fronds of seaweed dangling from the rocks. Work against any current, dragging your net under the weed, scraping along the bottom. Check your net frequently, removing captured prawns and inevitable debris. Keep your catch safe in a bucket of seawater lined with seaweed.

2. **March:** As the tide returns after low water, the prawns will stroll back up the middle of the gully, often several at once, in single file. Stand *very still*, net touching the bottom, and wait until the prawns have all but walked into your trap. Sweep your net forwards and gather them up. Be stealthy. Any clumsy movement and they'll dart out of sight.

....

* Why is it OK to boil a shrimp, but not a lobster? Good question.

We'll level with you: neither method is likely to produce a calorie surplus. If you want to improve your yield, you can make a *prawn trap* out of a water bottle, perhaps virtuously upcycling one you've found on the beach.

Cut the top off and shove the neck down inside the bottle. Punch plenty of holes in the sides so that it sinks. If you're feeling diligent you can use some of the holes to tie the inverted neck in place, but if you've shoved it in hard enough it should stay put.

Bait it with the stinkiest food imaginable. Fish food. Shrimp paste and hot water mashed into a ball. Fish guts and shucked limpets. If they aren't fresh, so much the better.

Sequester your trap under the fronds, weighted and lashed to a stone. Leave for a few hours over low water. Return and bask in success.

Eat your prawns as quickly as possible. Wash, blanch briefly in boiling water and serve with mayonnaise, a squeeze of lemon, salt and lots of pepper.

MACKERELING

The rules laid out by the UK's ten Inshore Fishing Conservation Authorities (IFCAs) are so byzantine and location-specific that we're going to ignore all fish, save one: the trusty mackerel.

1. They're a fair-weather fish, visiting the UK in the summer when it's a pleasure to be out in a boat.
2. They're no more endangered than we are.

3. They're *really* easy to catch.
4. They taste quite nice.

Mackerel are related to tuna, and there is something tunic about their appearance (beautiful green-and-black zebra stripes; iridescent blue shimmer) and behaviour (fast swimmers; fight hard when caught).

THE BAIT

The mackerel is not a clever fish, neither cunning nor subtle, meaning a number of different baits will work just fine. Catching sand eels for bait is fun, but you can get away with spinners (shiny bits of metal resembling a fish flicking away) or lures made out of plastic or feathers.*

FROM A BOAT

You only need 15 m of hand-line, a half-pound weight and your lure, plus a stretch of rocky coast that shelves steeply. Proceed at 2–3 knots (no faster than a brisk walk), with your line streaming out behind you. Late afternoon and early evening work well, but possibly because that's when mackerel fishing is most appealing.

It's hard to tell when a mackerel bites, so wind your line in every five to ten minutes to take a look. Odds are you'll have caught

....

* A punter is admiring the colourful, feathery lures in a fishing shop. 'Do fish really go for these?' he asks.
'I don't know,' comes the shopkeeper's reply. 'I sell lures to people, not fish.'

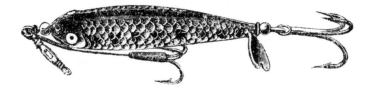

one. You can probably manage without a landing net, but you might want to slow the boat down. Once you've got it on board, you need to kill it, by hitting it over the head with a blunt object (pump handle, beer bottle).* Off it goes, into the bucket with saltwater and seaweed.

If you hit a mackerel shoal, it's easy to get over-excited and haul them in by the dozen. *Don't.* Mackerel are best eaten immediately, with their appeal decreasing exponentially every hour they spend polluting your fridge. Limit yourself to one mackerel per person, and don't kid yourself the children will eat any.

FROM LAND

From land, you need slightly more serious kit: a long, whippy rod that'll let you cast a reasonable distance. You can use the same sorts of lure, but choose a lighter weight (because you're *trolling* the bait more slowly with a rod than from a boat). You want a promontory or breakwater near the open sea, rocky and steep-to.

Cast your line as far as possible without overdoing it. Reel back in at a steady pace so that the lure sinks without catching on the bottom. If you hook something, reel it as close to shore as possible, and then either use a landing net or put a foot on your rod before pulling the last bit of line in hand over hand.

....

* The correct term is a *priest*: it delivers the last rites.

GUTTING

Gut in situ: no gore in your kitchen and it's a lot easier to dispose of the entrails. Mackerel don't really have scales so that's one thing you don't need to worry about.

1. Insert your knife into the mackerel's anus.
2. Cut along the belly until you arrive under the head.
3. Reach inside and scoop out its guts.
4. Cut out any bits still clinging on.
5. Chuck the innards into the sea.
6. Rinse your mackerel.

COOKING

Always barbecue them. Mackerel are oily: frying only makes them oilier, and not in a good way. Mackerel are also smelly: you want to keep them outside if you can.

1. Build a barbecue.
2. Salt and pepper inside and out. Slices of lemon inside.
3. Don't score them with pretty diagonal or diamond patterns: they'll disintegrate, utterly and stickily.
4. Give them about five minutes a side, depending on heat of fire and fatness of fish. To find out if they're done, cut into the chunkiest bit (probably above the pectoral fin) and check the flesh is dull white/grey not translucent pink/brown. Hopefully a few drops of fat

and oil will drip onto the embers, flaming up to add a tantalising smoky-oily flavour.

SERVING

Try this. It's not British, but it's great. Mash avocados (one per person), finely chopped fresh red chillis (half per person) or chilli flakes (good pinch per person), lemon juice, salt and pepper. Toast everyone a piece of bread (rye, sourdough, that sort of thing) over the barbecue. Spread the avocado on the toast. Using a knife and fork, lift the mackerel flesh off the bones and put on top. More lemon juice, salt and pepper. Open cold beer. Admire sunset.

RULES AND REGS

If you're trying to pin down the rules and regulations for your patch of seaside, search for your local IFCA. There are ten around the country: Cornwall, Devon & Severn, Eastern, Isles of Scilly, Kent & Essex, North Eastern, North Western, Northumberland, Southern and Sussex.

HOW TO MAKE A BEACH BARBECUE

Modern conveniences are convenient, but one innovation you should have no truck with is the sad, tin-foil thing that is the *disposable barbecue*. Their low profile forces you to hunch back-breakingly over your sausages. They're a pain for the diligent beachgoer because you've got to wait for them to cool before binning them. In the hands of the lazy beachgoer, they become both litter and a scalding menace to unwary feet.

Instead, build your barbecue from scratch. The journey is more important than the destination, and whatever you can salvage from sand and flame will taste divine. Sometimes, the proof of the pudding is *not* in the eating.

THE LOCATION

You need plenty of driftwood and decent-sized stones, ideally flat. Try to build with the wind at your back, but regardless of how you go about it, the smoke will probably end up in your face. Just give yourself the best shot.

THE BARBECUE

Dig a pit in the shape of your grill (which you've remembered to borrow from your oven). The pit should be about six inches deep, lined with flat stones to stop the sides collapsing. On three sides of the pit start building up layers of flat stones until you've got a wall 6–9 inches high. Put your grill on top of the wall and weigh it down with more stones. If everything looks shipshape, remove the grill and top layer of stones until you're ready to cook.

THE FUEL

Driftwood burns brilliantly, but unfortunately it's really bad for you. Something about the chlorine ions (from the salt) causes the fire to emit dioxins and furans which are carcinogenic. So we can only strongly discourage you from using it, and direct you towards the bags of charcoal on sale at the small beach shop, while noting that we have more than occasionally treated ourselves to a driftwood barbecue. Dry *marram* or *beachgrass* works well as an authentic firelighter.

THE COOK
Light your fire and leave it to burn until it has stopped smoking. After fifteen minutes or so, rake the fire flat in the bottom of the pit, put the grill on, weigh it down and away you go. Keep it simple. No *salmon en croûte*.

PUDDING?
Toasted marshmallows. Or try a barbecued banana split: slice a banana in half lengthways, slather Nutella and mini-marshmallows between the two halves, wrap in foil and stick in the embers for a few minutes. Very hot and messy. You'll probably need a spoon.

HOW TO CATCH SAND EELS

As with seaweed, this word covers a lot of different species, but in general it means a long thin fish with a pointed nose and no pelvic fins. Crucially, they aren't eels, so we should call them *sand lances*, but sand eels they remain, burrowing into sandy seabeds from which there are three main ways to pluck them for bait.

1. **Dig:** Choose a sandbank which would be covered at high tide i.e. a spot neither too wet nor too dry. Too wet and it's impossible to turn the sand over and the eels swim/wriggle away too fast. Too dry and there won't be any eels. Somebody needs to dig with a fork, flinging up sand and hopefully eels, while nimble helpers grab the eels and chuck them in a bait box which then needs to be submerged. Tidy up after yourself.
2. **Net:** You need a *seine* net (long, hangs vertically, weighted at the bottom, buoyed at the top) and possibly a permit. One person stands on the bank holding one end. Another person, holding the other end, walks in a circle against the tide, hopefully dragging a fizzing, jumping sack of sand eels back to shore.
3. **Knife:** You need a blunt table knife and a square of rubber with a hole in it for your thumb. Or a glove. This is a rarefied skill, but it is possible to catch eels by running your knife through a sandbank about knee-deep underwater. When you feel the flick of an eel, slap it against the rubber on your left hand. It takes a *lot* of practice: expect many lost eels, and sadly a few squashed ones.

FORAGING FRIENDS

GREY HERON (a sedge or siege of ...)
A dignified bird that wades, trousers rolled up, hunting for sand eels and molluscs. Appealingly drab and lugubrious, the heron has the beleaguered air of a Victorian father who doesn't know how to relax.

LITTLE EGRET (a congregation or skewer of ...)
Recent migrants to our shores. Slight, pretty and mischievous, little egrets only started to overwinter in the UK in the late 1980s, when rising global temperatures allowed them to settle permanently.

OYSTERCATCHER (a parcel of ...)
The (lithe, sure-footed) oystercatcher is everything the (brute, ungainly) gull is not. A diminutive cheep instead of a rasping cry. Neat black-and-white plumage. Charming orange-red bill and dashing red-pink legs. Nominatively indeterminate, it eats cockles and mussels.

CORMORANT (a gulp or flight of ...)
'The common cormorant or shag / Lays eggs inside a paper bag ...' wrote Christopher Isherwood. Scientifically fishy, yes, but at least a favourable literary outing, especially compared with Milton's *Paradise Lost*, in which Satan is to be found perching 'like a cormorant' on the Tree of Life itself. Cormorants probably have their ability to out-fish the canniest fisherman to thank for their bad rap.

WHAT SHALL WE DO WITH THE DRUNKEN SAILOR?

This versatile shanty, which would have been sung while sailors, drunk or otherwise, heaved yards or weighed anchors, has endless possible verses. We've included a selection below, but feel free to invent your own as circumstances dictate.

Question

What shall we do with the drunken sailor,
What shall we do with the drunken sailor,
What shall we do with the drunken sailor,
Early* in the morning?

Chorus

Hoo-ray and up she rises,
Hoo-ray and up she rises,
Hoo-ray and up she rises,
Early in the morning.

Answer

Put him in the scuppers with a hosepipe on him,
Put him in the scuppers with a hosepipe on him,
Put him in the scuppers with a hosepipe on him,
Early in the morning.

....

* Always pronounced *er-lie* for some reason.

Other answers, to be repeated × 3, followed by 'early in the morning'.

Give him a taste of the bosun's rope-end
Tie him to the mast and then you flog him
Beat him o'er with a cat-o'-nine-tails
Shave his belly with a rusty razor
Give him hair of the dog that bit him
Put him in the bilge and make him drink it
Take him to the pub and get him drunker

SCURVY

'You scurvy dog!' That classic insult, bandied about by pirates large and small, has long been shorn of its historical gravity: namely the millions of painful, unnecessary deaths suffered during the Age of Sail.

As European ships started probing further and further offshore in the late fifteenth century, their crews were overwhelmed by a disease as unpleasant as it was easily preventable. Vasco da Gama, the Portuguese explorer who first reached India by sea from Europe, recounted how his men fell sick while rounding the Horn of Africa, their feet and hands swelling, their gums growing over their teeth.

Poignantly, he reported that matters improved after an East African ruler gifted them, among other edible delights, 'large sweet oranges, the best that had ever been seen'. Everyone, he said, was thrilled, 'especially the sick'. But it was a long road from an aside in da Gama's logbook to the sailor's daily tot of lemon juice.

Once an occupational hazard, today scurvy is a disease of extreme malnutrition, caused by a lack of vitamin C (aka ascorbic acid), which keeps much of our bodies in good working order. As we now know, citrus is both the perfect preventative and the perfect cure for scurvy, but fresh fruit and veg were hard to come by in the *doldrums*.* Without them, sailors started to experience a panoply of symptoms, listed in numerous logbooks and diaries:

- sore, swollen limbs and joints
- puffed and bleeding gums
- teeth falling out
- red or blue spots stippling the skin
- old wounds re-opening
- new wounds refusing to heal
- lassitude, irritability and (hardly surprising, given the above) depression
- convulsions, fever, death

An early account by Sir Richard Hawkins** in his memoir *Voyage into the South Sea in the Year of 1593* shares some remedies (authentic spelling retained):

> The best prevention for this disease (in my judgement) is to keepe cleane the shippe; to besprinkle her ordinarily with vineger, or to burne tarre, and some sweet savours; to feed

....

* The doldrums are a belt of light, flukey and frustrating winds found near the equator between the northeast and southeast trades.
** Son of the better-known Admiral Sir John Hawkins, whose career at sea serves as a bleak reminder that the pioneering voyages of the period were inextricably linked with the rise in the trade in enslaved Africans, in which Britain played such a significant part, enriching its major ports and so many of its citizens at the expense of the lives of millions of men, women and children. Campaigners are today asking us all to confront how deeply Britain was implicated in centuries of wrongdoing.

upon as few salt meats in the hot country as may be; and especially to shunne all kindes of salt fish, and to reserve them for the cold climates; and not to dresse any meate with salt water, nor to suffer the companie to wash their shirts nor cloathes in it, nor to sleepe in their cloaths when they are wett.

He calls scurvy the 'plague of the sea' and 'the spoyle of mariners' and wishes 'some learned man would write of it', reckoning that in his twenty years at sea he'd seen 10,000 men die of it. Little did he know, but he too had the answer already: 'That which I have seene most fruitfull for this sicknesse is sower oranges and lemmons.'

The deaths continued. In one infamous voyage, Admiral George Anson, under orders to harass the Spanish in the Pacific, lost two-thirds of his crew to the disease. In one month alone, April 1741, he reports that forty-three men died on board his flagship, *Centurion*. One man who'd broken a bone at the Battle of the Boyne, half a century previously, even found the old break 'dissolved' after scurvy hit.

Anson did what he could. He took on board fresh food but, as we now know, 'hogs, fowls, bonitos, dolphins* and albicores' won't cure scurvy. Nor would his 'uncommon pains in cleansing and sweetning the ships'. And certainly not the 'the pill and drop of Dr Ward', which produced

....

* We can't be sure, but Anson is probably referring to the dolphinfish, also known as mahi-mahi or dorado, rather than actual dolphins.

on the patient 'a gentle perspiration, an easy vomit, or a moderate purge'. Much more to the point were the 'inconceivable quantities of coco-nuts' the men received, as well as guavas, limes, sweet and sour oranges, watermelons, dandelion, creeping purslane, mint, scurvy grass and sorrel, all of which Anson says were 'most fortunately adapted to the cure of the sea scurvy'.

If it seems baffling that nobody joined the dots when sailors clearly knew what worked, we can only agree. However, the medical establishment had their own ideas about how the disease worked, blaming it on the privations of life at sea: close quarters, bad air, worse food.

These misconceptions continued even after James Lind, a naval surgeon, conducted what appeared to be a pretty conclusive experiment. In a quasi-scientific trial in 1747, he selected twelve men in a similarly scorbutic state ('all in general had putrid gums, the spots and lassitude, with weakness of their knees'), quartered them together and fed them the same food (gruel and sugar, mutton broth, puddings, boiled biscuit, barley with raisins, rice and currants, plus sago* and wine). They were divided into pairs, each of whom was given a different treatment as follows:

- a quart of cyder a day
- 25 gutts of elixir vitriol three times a day**
- two spoonfuls of vinegar three times a day
- a course of seawater
- two oranges and one lemon
- an electuary of garlic, mustard seed, radish root, balsam of Peru and gum myrrh three times a day

....

* A starch extracted from palm stems.
** An alarming concoction of sulphuric acid, alcohol, sugar, plus miscellaneous flavourings.

You can guess the results: 'the most sudden and visible good effects were perceived from the use of the oranges and lemons'. Unfortunately, the experiment, although widely quoted now, didn't catch on at the time.

Even Captain James Cook, who has been much praised for losing not one man to scurvy during his 1768–71 voyage round the world, attributed his success – erroneously – to malt. Luckily, he kept the HMS *Endeavour* well stocked with fresh food, plus he had a sound understanding of ship-board psychology, dishing up cabbage in the form of sauerkraut at the officers' table, so the ordinary seamen saw 'their superiors set a value upon it', encouraging them to decide it was 'the finest stuff in the world' and wolf it down.*

It wasn't until the French Revolutionary Wars at the end of the eighteenth century that officers demanded to be supplied with what they knew worked, especially after HMS *Suffolk*, exceptionally well provisioned with lemon juice (to be mixed with the sailors' grog) weathered a lengthy voyage to India unscathed. Come 1795, all ships were meant to carry lemon juice, and – some teething problems aside – the ravages of scurvy finally came to an end.

....

* His enthusiasm for cabbage is echoed in Patrick O'Brian's *Desolation Island*. Stephen Maturin, the ship's physician, says: 'Let them rumble till the heavens shake and resound again; let them fart fire and brimstone, the Gomorrhans, I will not have a single case of scurvy on my hands, the sea-surgeon's shame, while there is a cabbage to be culled.'

ARCTIC

In the absence of fresh fruit and vegetables, meat from animals who synthesise their own vitamin C also serves as an anti-scorbutic. Whale skin, oysters and seal liver, for example, all make excellent substitutes, which explains why indigenous Arctic peoples survived for generations without freshly squeezed OJ. Remember, though, that heat destroys the benefits: seal liver should be eaten raw or lightly steamed, at a pinch.

FLAGS, PHONETIC ALPHABET
AND MORSE CODE

Letter	Phonetic alphabet	Flag	International Code of Signals (ICS) meaning	Morse
A	Alpha		I have a diver down; keep well clear at slow speed	·−
B	Bravo		I am taking in, discharging or carrying dangerous cargo	−···
C	Charlie		Yes or affirmative	−·−·
D	Delta		I am manoeuvring with difficulty; keep clear	−··
E	Echo		I am directing my course to starboard	·
F	Foxtrot		I am disabled; communicate with me	··−·
G	Golf		I require a pilot	−−·
H	Hotel		I have a pilot on board	····
I	India		I am directing my course to port	··
J	Juliet		I am on fire and have dangerous cargo; keep clear	·−−−
K	Kilo		I wish to communicate with you	−·−

L	Lima		You should stop your vessel immediately	.-..
M	Mike		My vessel has stopped; making no way	--
N	November		No or negative	-.
O	Oscar		Man overboard	---
P	Papa		All personnel return to ship; proceeding to sea	.--.
Q	Quebec		Ship meets health regulations; request clearance into port	--.-
R	Romeo		None	.-.
S	Sierra		Moving astern	...
T	Tango		Keep clear; engaged in trawling	-
U	Uniform		You are running into danger	..-
V	Victor		I require assistance	...-
W	Whiskey		I require medical assistance	.--
X	X-ray		Stop carrying out your intentions and wait for my signal	-..-
Y	Yankee		I am dragging anchor	-.--
Z	Zulu		I require a tug	--..

PIRATES

'Pirates,' cried John, seizing his Sunday hat,
'let us go at once.'*

Over the past 400 years, pirates must have been using their ill-gotten gains to fund some exceptional reputation management. These men – bar a couple of celebrity exceptions, 99 per cent of pirates have been male – who, let's make no bones about it, made a living robbing other ships, have been transmogrified from vicious criminals into romantic heroes into a dressing-up opportunity.

Nowadays, you're most likely to spot a pirate scrapping with Elsa or Moana over the last chocolate finger, which is really *weird* if you think about it. Imagine a children's party a century hence: toddlers in Red Sea pirate outfits, brandishing replica AK-47s, ammo belts slung round their necks.

YOU SAY PIRATE; I SAY PRIVATEER

That is what is so fascinating about pirates. Not so much what they *did* (attack, kill, steal, etc.), but how their gory stories have been glamorised to immense public delight.**

Just as the internet age has created new types of criminal – hackers, phishers, trolls – so too did the massive expansion of travel and trade in the early modern era open up a new grey area between legitimate warfare and maritime

....

* From J. M. Barrie's *Peter Pan*.
** Neil Rennie's comprehensive and very readable *Treasure Neverland: Real and Imaginary Pirates* is a treasure chest brimming with jewels, which helped illuminate our understanding of all things piratical.

banditry, ushering in golden opportunities for enterprising seamen.

Elizabeth I, for example, might issue a *letter of marque*, allowing a captain so favoured to act as a freelance naval officer, harassing both enemy shipping afloat and enemy forts ashore. Spain, enemy no. 1 at the time, was busy transferring the immense wealth it had so brutally extracted from the New World back home, and its ships, laden with gold and silver, were extremely tempting prizes. Men such as Sir Francis Drake and Sir Walter Raleigh became household names: doughty buccaneers singeing the King of Spain's beard if you were English; pirates if you were Spanish.

The British state eventually moved to suppress what was a threat to trade, tightening their grip on the international seaways via, for example, the Piracy Act of 1698, but as it became harder to *be* a pirate, people's appetite for tales *about* pirates only continued to grow.

TRUE CRIME

In 1724, Captain Charles Johnson (probably a pseudonym) published *A General History of the Robberies and Murders of the Most Notorious Pyrates*, which created a canonical list of ne'er-do-wells. But even such an early work was already alive to the gap between fact and fiction:

> None of these bold Adventurers were ever so much talked of, for a while, as [Henry] Avery ... he was represented in Europe as one that had raised himself to the Dignity of a King, and was likely to be the Founder of a new Monarchy; having, as it was said, taken immense Riches, and married the Great Mogul's Daughter, who was taken in an Indian Ship, which fell into his Hands; and that he had by her many Children, living in great Royalty and State.

After listing all the things Avery was *meant* to have done, Johnson appends: 'Yet all of these were no more than false rumours, improved by the credulity of some, and the humour of others who love to tell strange things.'

Notorious Pyrates also features Captain Teach, better known as Blackbeard ('that large Quantity of Hair, which like a frightful Meteor, covered his whole Face, and frightened America, more than any Comet that has appear'd there a long Time') and introduces us to Captain Rackham, Mary Read and Anne Bonny, whose biographies, brimming with sex, violence and saucy cross-dressing, offer the salacious reader (as yet unencumbered by Victorian morality) everything they could desire.

ALL THE NICE GIRLS

Daniel Defoe, already well known as the creator of Robinson Crusoe, also wrote a fictionalised life of Henry Avery, loudly blurbed by a contemporary as 'A TALE WHICH HOLDETH CHILDREN FROM PLAY AND OLD MEN FROM THE CHIMNEY CORNER'.

The hero is abducted from the bucolic fields of Islington (while his nursemaid enjoys an assignation with her sweetheart), before being sold first to a beggar woman and then to a gypsy, encouraging us to understand it's not his fault he turned out so bad. He embarks on a series of very successful adventures, but finds no joy in his immense wealth:

> I looked upon it as a hoard of other men's goods, which I had robbed the innocent owners of, and which I ought, in a word, to be hanged for here, and damned for hereafter.

This was repentance enough for Defoe to allow him to return incognito to England, his fortune intact, to marry a friend's sister with whom, he said, 'I am much more happy than I deserve'.

The pioneering Scottish novelist Walter Scott turned his attention to what might happen when a wrongdoer tries to reform, basing *The Pirate* on the life of one John Gow, who reportedly hosted dancing parties in an Orkney village, successfully wooing a well-to-do young lady before his true identity was revealed.

This mouthwatering titbit was the inspiration for the novel's romantic plot, which as one editor put it, 'will always be among the special favourites of those who, being young, are fortunate enough not to be critical'. Love and morality collide when the heroine tells her pirate that she can only love him as a penitent, never as a hero, prompting the pirate to muse to himself:

> She startled not at the name of my perilous course of
> life, yet seems totally unprepared for the evil which must
> necessarily attend it; and so all the merit I have gained
> by my resemblance to a Norse Champion, or King of
> the Sea, is to be lost at once, because a gang of pirates do
> not prove to be a choir of saints. I would that Rackham,
> Hawkins, and the rest, had been at the bottom of the Race
> of Portland ...*

This trope – pirate as lover – is perhaps best served in Lord Byron's verse poem *The Corsair* (1814). It was a massive hit, selling out its first print run of 10,000 copies on publication day.

The corsair, Conrad, is unfeasibly Byronic: noble, mysterious, tortured, a lover of intense passion, untethered from civilisation. Inevitably, the gossips speculated (baselessly)

....

* A fiendish tidal race off Portland Bill in Dorset.

that Conrad *was* Byron, his fictional exploits Byron's own, and what exploits they were.

Conrad leaves his Mediterranean hideout to attack a Turkish pasha, leaving behind Medora, his one true love. The raid goes according to plan, but Conrad is distracted by the pitiful cries of a woman enslaved in the harem. He is captured. Gulnare, the woman he (nobly) longed to save helps him escape, cutting the pasha's throat herself after Conrad (nobly) refuses to kill him in cold blood. They return to his island, where Medora has died from grief. Conrad (nobly) doesn't settle down with Gulnare, but instead ... vanishes.

> Long mourn'd his band whom none could mourn beside;
> And fair the monument they gave his bride:
> For him they raise not the recording stone –
> His death yet dubious, deeds too widely known;
> He left a Corsair's name to other times,
> Link'd with one virtue, and a thousand crimes.

A BOY'S OWN DREAM

By the late nineteenth century, the rules of the genre were so well established that when Tom Sawyer, Mark Twain's boy hero, tires of life with his Aunt Polly, he knows the answer is to turn pirate on the Mississippi River, backed by his two friends, Joe Harper and Huckleberry Finn. Poor Huck, though, hasn't had the benefit of Tom's literary education.

> 'What does pirates have to do?'
> Tom said:
> 'Oh, they have just a bully time – take ships and burn them,
> and get the money and bury it in awful places in their
> island where there's ghosts and things to watch it, and kill

everybody in the ships – make 'em walk a plank.'

'And they carry the women to the island,' said Joe; 'they don't kill the women.'

'No,' assented Tom, 'they don't kill the women – they're too noble. And the women's always beautiful, too.'

'And don't they wear the bulliest clothes! Oh no! All gold and silver and di'monds,' said Joe, with enthusiasm.

'Who?' said Huck.

'Why, the pirates.'

Huck scanned his own clothing forlornly.

'I reckon I ain't dressed fitten for a pirate,' said he, with a regretful pathos in his voice; 'but I ain't got none but these.'

A POST-MODERN TURN

Pirate stories even start to refer to *other* pirate stories, as well as to real pirates, in a sort of fictional one-upmanship. In *Peter Pan*, which appeared both as play then novel, Captain James Hook is so scary that he is the only man whom Long John Silver – the terrifying pirate in R. L. Stevenson's *Treasure Island* – feared. Peter, in turn, boasts that *he* killed Long John Silver, or Barbecue as he nicknames him, a knowing reference to Silver's initial disguise as a sea cook.

Hook also evokes Byron's corsair in demeanour: a 'handsome countenance', eyes 'the blue of the forget-me-not', 'a profound melancholy', an air of 'the grand seigneur', and he was 'never more sinister than when he was most polite'. His hair, however, which 'looked like black candles' from a distance, is meant to remind us of Blackbeard, whose bosun Hook once was.

The final nail in the pirate's coffin – or the greatest incarnation yet – is of course Captain Jack Sparrow, as played by Johnny Depp, lording it over the *Pirates of the Caribbean* franchise. Apparently the studio bosses were so weirded out by his performance – 'Goddamnit, Johnny Depp's ruining the film!' – he thought he was going to get fired. Instead, of course, he redefined how to be a pirate for a whole new generation.

THE COD WARS

The Cod Wars, fought in the cold and stormy seas off Iceland, are emblematic of the decline of Great Britain as a global maritime power. Once the world's (self-appointed) police officer, *Pax Britannica* enforcer and all-round ruler of the waves, Britain was defeated by a remote nation with no navy to speak of and a population on a par with Cardiff's.*

Even though, thankfully, the vast majority of lives lost** were piscine, the repercussions for Britain's offshore fishing fleet were devastating. The collapse of a long-standing, respected and potentially lucrative (if undeniably risky) way of life caused immense damage to coastal communities, especially in the north and east of Britain.

At stake was this far-from-dry legal question: how far from its coast does a nation exercise its sovereignty, and therefore its exclusive right to fish? The answer, at the end of the Second World War, was *not very far*: three or four nautical miles, the distance of a cannon shot. Beyond that, it was the high seas, fair game, open to all.

....

* Cf. the Icelandic football team's 2–1 defeat of England in the 2016 UEFA European Championship for a twenty-first-century replay.
** An Icelandic engineer was killed when the coastguard vessel *Ægir* collided with a British frigate. As you'll see it's a miracle nobody else died.

For a long time, this had suited Britain, which wanted to be able to manoeuvre freely around the world without having to worry about other countries complaining the Royal Navy was in *their* waters. Indeed, when Spain and Portugal secured papal bulls giving them dominion over large chunks of the Atlantic Ocean, Elizabeth I pronounced:

> 'The use of sea and air is common to all. Neither can any title to the ocean belong to any people or private persons for as much as neither nature nor public use and custom permitteth any possession thereof.'

And indeed from the Battle of Trafalgar onwards, Britain's naval dominance was so absolute that if it said sovereignty only extended for three miles, that was that – until the Second World War uprooted many old certainties.

Iceland, for one, became a fully fledged republic in 1944, dispensing with the Danish monarch as its head of state, having first achieved independence in 1918. Enriched with serious amounts of Marshall Aid,* Iceland focused on maximising crucial fishing revenues.

Back in 1901, Britain had signed a convention with Denmark, then Iceland's colonial master, establishing a three-mile limit around the island. The Danes hadn't felt the need to argue for a wider exclusion zone: the British, after all, were great buyers of Danish butter and bacon. But come 1949, just as Britain's fishing fleet was getting back in business after the inevitable hiatus of the war, Iceland gave notice that it would only recognise the convention for two more years, after which it would seek a new four-mile limit.

....

* Post-war aid given to European countries by the US to help rebuild their economies (and stop the spread of communism).

Britain was sufficiently piqued that it slapped an import ban on Icelandic fish, but Iceland's remote geography (for once) worked in its favour.

Iceland straddles what's known in the language of international relations as the *GIUK gap,* i.e. the sea lane between Greenland, Iceland and the United Kingdom. This was the Soviet Union's (and now Russia's) key route from its Arctic ports to the Atlantic and beyond, meaning Moscow was inclined to be friendly to the young nation. It struck a barter deal with Iceland, promising to swap fish for oil and farm machinery.

That four-mile demand, however, was only a shot across the bows. Iceland unilaterally extended its exclusion zone to twelve miles in 1958, then to fifty miles in 1972 and finally to 200 miles in 1975, which is where it stands today.

The British government was in a tricky position. The waters around Iceland were the offshore fishing fleet's best hope of catching cod. Other fish were less popular. Other fishing grounds were too far away, overfished or subject to stringent quotas. If trawlers couldn't sail to Iceland from Hull, Grimsby and Fleetwood, there was nowhere else to go, threatening not just the fishing jobs themselves* but also the fabric of the port economies that revolved around the industry.

So began several rounds of an extremely risky game of high-latitude cat-and-mouse. British trawlers breached whatever limit Iceland put in place. The Icelandic coastguard advanced, informed the boats they were in territorial waters, and ordered them to leave. The British refused. The Icelanders tried to cut the wires attached to their nets. (These would have been under immense load: imagine the danger when they sprang free.) British naval ships entered the fray, trying to protect the fleet, positioning themselves between the trawlers and the coastguard.

'I can say quite definitely that the Icelanders are skilful enough to bring their gunboats – and their victims, the trawlers – within a hair's breadth of disaster. It would only take a momentary error of judgment for the two ships to collide, with all that means in heavy seas and strong winds ... So let no one think that this cod war is a polite and danger-free dispute between two NATO allies,' reported one journalist on BBC Radio 4.

The memoirs of those involved do read a little like *Boy's Own* adventures: high on adrenaline and camaraderie, tough guys facing down a worthy enemy. And certainly, ...

* The number of British fishermen has fallen from 50,000 before the Second World War, to 20,000 in 1970, to some 12,000 today. Upon joining the proto-EU in 1972, the UK (reluctantly) had to allow others equal access to its territorial waters – one of the reasons fish-rich Norway never joined.

back home, the public was hooked on tales of this macho, old-school way of life.

The wars occasionally had their lighter side. Norman Storey, a tug master and author of *What Price Cod?*, tells a lovely story about one man using the open radio channel to ask his brother to sort flowers for his wife back home in Grimsby on their wedding anniversary. His surprised wife was sent fourteen bunches of flowers by the fourteen other trawlers who were out that day.

In the end, Iceland won every round, with Britain forced to stomach increasingly meagre concessions. Why? Two main reasons:

1. Iceland was blazing the trail which international law would follow. The 1982 UN Convention on the Law of the Sea granted nations a special *economic exclusion zone* a full 200 miles offshore, including the right to 'determine the allowable catch of the living resources', i.e. to be boss of its own fish. Britain could jump up and down as much as it liked, but the world increasingly saw the cod as Iceland's.
2. It was the height of the Cold War, and Iceland hosted a US base that kept a keen eye on Soviet activity around the GIUK gap. Iceland threatened to kick the Americans out. Washington leant on Britain to back down.

Come June 1976, Britain's fishing boats had to retreat for good. In the words of a reporter, embedded on HMS *Naiad*, writing for the *Sunday Independent*:

> The nasty little war ended with four silent ships stopped on an icy and painted ocean, moodily glowering at each other like boxers between rounds. We were nine miles off

the southeast coast of Iceland and the vessel in the centre
of the little cameo was the squat, powerful gunboat *Aegir*,
her helicopter flightdeck buckled and her hull ripped and
scraped along its length from a dozen skirmishes.

Around her in perfect triangulation, stood the Royal
Naval frigates *Naiad* and *Diomede* – and the huge ocean-
going tug *Statesman*. Away to the southwest the lads from
Hull and Fleetwood lay in a bunch, steam rising from their
winches, dirty and businesslike, pulling in the cod as if there
was to be no tomorrow. And we all knew that there would
be no tomorrow for most of them.

It was silent, beautiful and menacing – the wolf, the
shepherds and the flock frozen in a pure liquid bowl of the
sea and sky where you can see forever.

PATRICK O'BRIAN, C. S. FORESTER AND NELSON'S NAVY

You'd be forgiven for thinking that a series of books about
a British naval officer during the Napoleonic Wars would
be nothing more than a gold-embossed romp. But Patrick
O'Brian's twenty novels (plus one unfinished) about
Captain Jack Aubrey and his best friend, the physician-spy
Stephen Maturin, are as perfect an evocation of square-
rigged society as Jane Austen's are of the country gentry of
the same period.

'Like Jane Austen, O'Brian is really happiest working on
two or three inches of ivory and turning to art the daily
lives of three or four families in a locality – except that the
village happens to be a wooden ship of war at the apogee

of a great Navy's world sea-power in the days of sail,' writes
A. E. Cunningham in his critical appreciation of the author.

Those ships of war were needed after the seismic upheaval
of the French Revolution pitted the heretical forces of
liberté, egalité and *fraternité* against the entrenched con-
servatism of Britain. The subsequent rise to power of the
military genius Napoleon Bonaparte meant that Britain
was not only trying to quench this unsavoury democratic
fervour but also defending itself from an ambitious foe.

As Napoleon said: '*Que nous soyons maîtres de la Manche
pendant six heures et nous serons les maîtres du monde.*' Let
us be masters of the Channel for six hours and we will be
masters of the world.

The most famous battle of the era was of course the 1805
Battle of Trafalgar, a victory for Vice-Admiral Horatio
Nelson, who looms over the period, immodest, acclaim-
hungry and indiscreet, his life a better story than even
O'Brian could write.

On the eve of another of his victories (the Battle of the
Nile, 1798), he said, 'Before this time tomorrow, I shall have
gained a peerage or Westminster Abbey.' In the end, death
and glory were both to be his: he lost an eye off Corsica
(allowing him to turn a blind eye to an order to retreat at
the Battle of Copenhagen), an arm off the Canaries, and
his life at Trafalgar.

His fame was enhanced, if possible, by his very public
affair with Emma Hamilton, blacksmith's daughter, art-
ist's muse, wife to the British envoy in Naples, hostess and
style-setter extraordinaire. Her husband, it seems, turned
his own blind eye to her passionate affair, but Nelson's wife
was less amused.

Outgunned and outmanned, the Battle of Trafalgar
pitted twenty-seven British ships against thirty-three
French. A big fleet battle would normally have involved the

enemy ships sailing past one other in two lines, cannons blazing madly, but Nelson plumped for nimbler tactics. He split his fleet into squadrons, breaking the French line, forging an anarchic melee in which the more highly skilled British ships could triumph.

His flagship, the HMS *Victory*,* became entangled with the French ship *Redoutable*. A marine fired a shot from the mizzen, catching Nelson in the shoulder. The bullet lodged in his back, killing him.

His death was the JFK assassination or the Twin Towers attacks of its day. Dorothy Wordsworth burst into tears. Samuel Coleridge, no blind patriot, wrote, 'All were made acquaintances in the rights of a common anguish.'

You can still visit the *Victory*, saved from the scrap-yard by a passionate public campaign, in its dry dock in Portsmouth, and gaze upon the spot where Nelson begged that his belongings should go to Emma, where he whispered 'Kiss me Hardy ...' to his loyal captain, where he thanked God he'd done his duty and breathed his last.

MOTLEY CREWS

Nelson's victory gave Britain control of the world's oceans, which was the basis for its unquestioned superpower status until the end of the First World War.

But, of course, he didn't do it alone. During the Napoleonic Wars, the navy needed *a lot* of manpower, but because seamen's pay hadn't risen in the whole of the eighteenth century, it wasn't a popular occupation. When volunteers were hard to come by, *press-gangs* scoured harbour towns, scooping up fishermen and merchant

....

* The crew of this most British of ships included men from Holland, Sweden, Italy, Malta, Norway, Germany, Switzerland, Portugal, Denmark, India, Russia, Brazil, Africa, the West Indies ... and even France.

sailors, dragooning them into a hard life before the mast. Unsurprisingly, mutiny was a constant threat.

Occasionally a successful captain might try to appeal to genuine adventure seekers, promising prize money in return for unrelenting risk and toil. This was what drew many sons of upper-middle-class families to sea as officers. With a following wind, it was possible for men born outside the aristocracy to become rich and feted, an opportunity few other professions provided in Britain's stratified society.

A boy might become a *midshipman* at thirteen, looking after a small group of sailors, helping the officer of the watch and learning all there was to know about the running of a ship. Next, as *lieutenant*, he had to pass a gruelling interview with grumpy senior officers, before relying on luck, talent and patronage to win a place on a good ship, and then to be promoted to captain himself.

On board, the captain lived in splendid isolation. The midshipmen *messed* together. In the *wardroom* or *gunroom* you found lieutenants, marine officers, the surgeon, the chaplain, the purser and the master, who probably wasn't a 'gentleman', but doubtless knew more about sailing than the rest of them put together. The other warrant officers, the boatswain (or bosun; *always* exacting and bad-tempered), the gunner and carpenter, not grand enough to mess in the wardroom, had their own space separate from the crew.

This cast of characters, confined for weeks or months at a time, took sightings, went aloft, practised gunnery, punished some, praised others, obsessed over food, obsessed over women, obsessed over each other, thirsted for wind, for prize money, for a kind word from the admiral, courted disaster, averted disaster – a rich feast for the writer of fiction.

BLIGHTY VS BONEY

Before the cannons fell silent, naval officers were already writing up their real adventures and imagining better ones. Captain Frederick Marryat (best avoided nowadays unless you're a naval fiction nut) created the parameters of the genre, such as the ingenue at sea, the intricate relations between shipmates, the exotic locations, the sweethearts ashore, the storms and shipwrecks, the death and glory.

The first truly great series, by C. S. Forester, stars Hornblower: shy, from a (relatively) modest background, and a great leader. Like Nelson, he is seasick. He weaves in and out of history, forging documents that make the French fleet put to sea before Trafalgar, organising Nelson's funeral, hooking up with the Duke of Wellington's sister, and surviving a death sentence thanks to the French defeat at the Battle of Waterloo.

Forester knocked up the first book en route back to Britain by sea after an unsuccessful stint in Hollywood before the Second World War. His timing meant that Hornblower's adventures couldn't help but be read as analogous to Britain's fight against Hitler.

The novels were immensely popular, and it took a writer of O'Brian's skill to even begin to rival them, using Stephen as the cerebral foil for the physical, hearty, sometimes unreflecting Jack. The physician also has a more liberal, less compliant view of naval hierarchy than the captain. He is an outsider: an Irish-Catalan Catholic. He does *not* turn a blind eye:

> 'The world in general, and even more your briny world, accepts flogging. It is this perpetual arbitrary harassing, bullying, hitting, brow-beating, starting – these capricious torments, spread-eagling, gagging – the general atmosphere of oppressions.'

Harsh worlds, however, make for gripping stories, and writers are still exploiting the field today. If all the above is old hat to you, seek out a delightful series called *Temeraire*, nine novels by Naomi Novik, who deftly inserts dragons, a biotic airforce, into the Napoleonic Wars.

WATCHKEEPING

Question: when is seven bells of the first watch?

The crew on a naval sailing ship (and on a yacht making any kind of serious passage today) was split into two groups, the port and starboard watches, who took it in turns to stand watch.

On watch: Steering the boat, trimming the sails, keeping a look-out, plus any other jobs the officer of the watch dreamt up.
Off watch: Eating, sleeping, dancing hornpipes. Of course, sometimes an enemy attack or a gale in the offing demanded *all hands on deck*.

Starting at 8p.m., the day was divided into six blocks, each four hours long, with the 4–8p.m. block further subdivided into two-hour stints known as *dog watches*.

(Why? We rather like the joke that dog watches are *cur-tailed*; the truth is doubtless more prosaic.) In practice, dog watches mean that the same half of the crew doesn't get stuck with the grisly midnight til 4a.m. shift every day, which is as welcome now as it was two hundred years ago.

The midshipman of the watch kept track of time using a half-hour sandglass: when the sand ran out, he turned the glass and struck the ship's bell, meaning it rang eight times per watch. (This obviously wasn't entirely accurate, so the sandglass was 'reset' at the noon sight.) Which gives us ...

Answer: 11.30pm

WHEN I WAS A FAIR MAID ...

Gutsy girls running away to sea in the Age of Sail were as popular as they were rare. This traditional song celebrates one such fair maid, hitting the requisite salacious notes.

> When I was a fair maid about seventeen,
> I listed in the navy, for to serve the Queen.
> I listed in the navy, a sailor lad to stand,
> For to hear the cannons rattle and the music so grand,
> And the music so grand, and the music so grand,
> For to hear the cannons rattle and the music so grand.
>
> Well, the officer that listed me was a tall and handsome man,
> He said, 'You'll make a sailor, so come along, my man'.
> My waist being tall and slender, my fingers long and thin,
> Oh the very soon they learned me, I soon exceeded them,

I soon exceeded them, I soon exceeded them.
Oh the very soon they learned me, I soon exceeded them.

Well, they sent me to bed and they sent me to bunk
To lie with a sailor, I never was afraid,
But taking off my blue coat, it oft times made me smile,
For to think I was a sailor and a maiden all the while,
And a maiden all the while, and a maiden all the while.
For to think I was a sailor and a maiden all the while.

Well, they sent me off to London for to guard the Tower,
And I'm sure I might be there till my very dying hour.
But a lady fell in love with me, I told her I was a maid.
Oh she went unto the captain and my secret she betrayed,
My secret she betrayed, my secret she betrayed.
Oh she went unto the captain and my secret she betrayed.

The captain, he came up to me and he asked was this so?
Oh I dare not, I dare not, I dare not say no
'It's a pity we should lose you, such a sailor lad you made.
It's a pity we should lose you, such a handsome young maid,
A handsome young maid, a handsome young maid.
It's a pity we should lose you, such a handsome young maid'.

So it's fare thee well, captain, you've been so kind to me,
And likewise, my shipmates, I'm sorry to part with thee.
But if ever the navy needs a lad, a sailor I'll remain,
I'll put out my hat and feathers and I'll run the rigging again,
And I'll run the rigging again, I'll run the rigging again.
I'll put out my hat and feathers and I'll run the rigging again.

MARY LACY

Square riggers were undoubtably a man's world, but if we
peer through the cracks, it is possible to spy a few women
aboard, whether a bold lady in an Empire-line dress taking
a turn about the quarterdeck or an ambiguously gendered
figure shinning up the ratlines.

'I have crossed the Atlantic four times and have been
once to the East Indies and back again,' says Mrs Croft, wife
to an admiral and one of Jane Austen's more sympathetic
characters. She admits being a little 'disordered' during the
first day at sea, and confesses that life aboard a frigate can
feel 'confined', but says it was worth every moment to be
with her husband.

The wives of warrant officers also went to sea. They
weren't official members of the crew, but nor were they

sub rosa or in any way taboo. (Apparently, captains did complain that they used too much water.) An ordinary seaman might occasionally bring his wife on board; she'd eat with his messmates and sleep in the fo'c's'le, lacking even the primitive privacy of a warrant officer's tiny cabin. You can also be sure that female sex workers were encouraged aboard when a ship was in port.

A very few women, however, went to sea disguised as boys, doing a boy's work among their unsuspecting shipmates. One of the best documented is the tale of Mary Lacy, who wrote her own memoir, *The Female Shipwright*, after her naval days were over. Her account is corroborated by the muster books of the ships on which she served, as well as in Admiralty minutes when, her disguise abandoned, she applied for a pension.

Born to a poor family in Kent, Mary Lacy couldn't settle to suitable work: she was 'of a roving disposition'. And although her memoir shows her to be much, *much* more interested in women than men, she became 'disturbed and uneasy' with unrequited love for a young man she met dancing.

'A short time after, a thought came into my head to dress myself in men's apparel, and set off by myself; but where to go, I did not know, nor what I was to do when I was gone.'

That didn't deter her. She swiped a frock coat, breeches, shoes, stockings and a hat, and off she went without a goodbye to anyone. She was nineteen.

'On the first day of May, 1759, about six o'clock in the morning, I set off; and when I had got out of town into the fields, I pulled off my cloaths and put on mens, leaving my own in a hedge, some in one place and some in another.'

After a sorry night in a pig shed in Chatham, she got talking to a gentleman who asked her whether she wanted to go to sea, the Seven Years War being then in full swing.

She listed on the *Sandwich*, giving her name as William Chandler, her father's first name and her mother's maiden name, starting out as servant to the ship's carpenter. She learnt to mix his flip (hot beer, rum and sugar), broil his beefsteak and make his bed, feigning ignorance of that simple task so as not to give herself away as a woman.

The *Sandwich* slipped Chatham to join the main fleet off Brest, where Admiral Geary came on board, bringing his own servants with him, 'stout boys, very wicked and mischievous'. One of them slapped Mary in the face, witnessed by the cook, who warned she'd have to fight back – promising her a plum pudding if she won. The toughest bit of the fight was insisting she kept her shirt on, it being the done thing to fight bare-chested. She fought hard, knowing the boy would never leave her alone if she gave in.

'[T]herefore we kept to it with great obstinacy on both sides; and I soon began to get the advantage of my antagonist, which all the people who knew me perceiving, seemed greatly pleased, especially when he declined fighting any more, and the more so, as he was looked upon as the best fighter among them.'

Soon afterwards, Mary finally wrote home, signing herself 'your undutiful daughter'. She weathered her first of many attacks of what was probably rheumatoid arthritis, faced down 'great and boisterous seas', suffered from scurvy, and missed out on a great British victory at the Battle of Quiberon Bay by two days.

Come the spring of 1763, attached to a different ship, she took a significant step up in the world, being apprenticed at the Portsmouth shipyard, her chance to learn a respected trade. It was hard work, but she still had time for lively parties back on board ship, singing lustily, boating ashore to buy more beer – and flirting copiously with young women.

Seven years after being apprenticed, she received her

shipwright's certificate, writing the good news to her parents and signing herself for the first time 'your dutiful daughter'. She had every reason to be proud.

Tragically, a spell of overwork crippled her again: 'I was seized with so bad a swelling in my thighs that I was not able to walk, and was unwilling the doctor should look at it, lest he should find me out.' She recovered, relapsed, recovered, relapsed, until worst of all, an erstwhile friend blew her secret wide open once and for all.

With no other option, Mary dressed as a woman and petitioned the Admiralty for a pension, which 'in consideration of my extraordinary sufferings and services', settled twenty pounds a year on her for life.

As for Mary's memoir, it ends with her marrying a certain Mr Slade, a man she met on the road from Portsmouth to London. He is sober and industrious, upright and exemplary. A model man for a reformed woman? In fact, no record of their marriage has ever been found. Instead, in 1777, we can trace one Mary Slade of King Street, Deptford (the name and address under which Mary's memoir was published), moving into a new house with one Elizabeth Slade.

We can only hope they lived happily ever after.

SEALAND

Sealand is a glorious tale of unintended consequences.

During the Second World War, two types of fort were built across the Thames Estuary to defend the nation against invasion. Closer inshore were three *army forts*, anti-aircraft platforms which looked like the inspiration behind AT-ST walkers.* Further out to sea were four *navy forts*, which looked more like little oil platforms. You can call both types *Maunsell forts* after their designer, the engineer Guy Maunsell.

Peace came. Soldiers and sailors happily quit their posts. The government had more on its plate than working out what to do with wartime relics. The forts might have slowly disintegrated, were it not for that 1960s phenomenon: pirate radio.

Before the sixties really started to swing, you could only listen to the new 'popular' music for a few hours a week on the BBC, which seems all but incomprehensible today. Not surprisingly, there was a huge thirst for the new sounds, but no way to hear them, until a few enterprising people had a bright idea.

If you couldn't get a broadcast licence in the UK, how about broadcasting from *outside* the UK, say on an old ferry anchored just outside territorial waters? Founded in 1964, Radio Caroline was the trailblazer, but others soon realised that the abandoned forts, lying as most of them did in international waters, would make prime bases.

David Edward Sutch (aka Screaming Lord Sutch, the founder of the Monster Raving Loony Party) set up a radio station on the Shivering Sands army fort, before selling it to music manager Reginald Calvert, who ran it until he was killed in a scuffle over whether he actually owned it.

Pirate radio was successful – and *cool*.

In 1965 'Paddy' Roy Bates, who'd served as major in the Second World War and evidently still had a taste for adventure, took his twelve-year-old boy Michael on an unusual

....

* All Terrain Scout Transport (cf. the big Ewok battle in *Star Wars VI: Return of the Jedi*).

father-son outing. They motored out to Knock John, the most westerly of the navy forts, and with the tide sucking and surging round its base, climbed ashore using a dodgy old ladder. They scoped the place out, watched over by cormorants, and Bates decided it'd be the perfect spot for his own radio ambitions.

Unfortunately for Bates, the British government didn't like what the pirate pioneers were up to, and manoeuvred successfully to argue that Knock John technically lay inside territorial waters. Bates was taken to court for operating illegally and fined £100, with another £100 to accrue every day the station didn't close. It had to shut down by the end of the year.

Bates, evidently, was not a man to give up easily: he scouted another naval fort, Fort Roughs, which at 7.5 miles off Harwich was indubitably in international waters. According to his son Michael's memoir, *Holding the Fort*,* when they arrived, two guys from Radio Caroline were perched on the fort preparing their Christmas dinner. They weren't there long. Michael writes: 'We told them to pack up their gear and we would take them ashore.'

But by this point, Bates's ambition had grown. Roughs Tower was going to be more than another radio station. He had a grander idea. On 2 September 1967 (his wife's birthday) he declared the fort to be the new Principality of Sealand. The micronation's official history states:

....

* Worth a read. You only wish it'd been turned into a film starring Michael Caine as Roy and Julie Christie as his wife, Joan. Michael admits his mother found it tough at times: 'For someone who hates heights, can't swim and has the strength of a louse, I sometimes wonder looking back how she coped. On top of all that, she couldn't deal with the cold ... Sealand was hell for her.' Nevertheless, he reports her wielding a Walther P38 in its defence.

It was not long before the British Government decided they could not have what ministers described as a possible 'Cuba off the east coast of England'. The military were promptly dispatched to destroy all other remaining forts located in international waters. The Bates family looked on as huge explosions sent the massive structures hurtling hundreds of feet in the air. Twisted and buckled debris floated past Sealand for days.

Helicopters that had carried the explosives buzzed menacingly above, and the navy tug carrying the demolition crew passed close by our fortress home and shouted 'You're next!' with an angry waving of arms. A while later a government vessel steamed to within fifty feet of Sealand, its boisterous crew shouting threatening obscenities at Michael, and his sixteen-year-old sister. Warning shots were promptly fired across the bow of the boat by Prince Michael, causing it to hastily turn and race away towards the UK, amongst a large cloud of black engine smoke.

It wasn't long before Sealand was again in peril. In 1968 Bates father and son had to appear in court on firearms charges. The possession wasn't in question: at stake was whether the fort did in fact fall inside the jurisdiction of the English court. The judge delivered his verdict: Sealand was *terra nullius* – no man's land. The law couldn't touch them.

Ten years later, they faced another existential threat. Michael was alone on Sealand while his parents were in Austria on state business, but the negotiations they were conducting, as it turned out, were a red herring, designed to lure them away and leave the fort unguarded. A helicopter landed some of Bates's erstwhile business partners on the tower, who locked Michael in the fort's living room, threatened to chuck him overboard and finally shipped him to Holland from where he somehow managed to get back into the UK without a passport.

The Sealand royal family, once again, prepared to fight back. A friend had a helicopter. They levered off its doors, rounded up rope, guns and ammo, and went in at dawn. The raid was a complete success, as witnessed by the *Sun*, which had hired a boat to report on the original coup, only to arrive and discover the Bates family were ascendant once more. The newspaper ran its scoop, complete with a photo shoot of the (pleasingly) German prisoners.

Sealand survives to this day. In the best tradition of monarchy, you can buy a Sealand title: £29.99 if you're content to be a lady; £499.99 if you won't settle for any less than duchess.

SEALAND FOOTBALL RULES

1. Don't lose ball over the side
2. Re-read rule one

FORTS

The Second World War wasn't the only time Britain decided to fortify its coasts. Back in the early nineteenth century, everyone was convinced Napoleon was going to swoop across the Channel, so the government ordered the building of dozens of *Martello towers* – round, two storeys tall, a gun platform on top – around the more vulnerable sections of the southeast coast. Since then, some have been washed away by storms or blasted to pieces during target practice; others have become interesting museums, galleries or houses.

After Napoleon met his Waterloo, everyone relaxed – until the 1850s, when his nephew became first president and then emperor of a resurgent France. Louis Napoleon said he came in peace (*'L'Empire, c'est la paix'*), but old habits die hard, and Britain watched nervously as the French navy embarked on a serious steamship-building programme.

The result was another raft of coastal forts, chunkier than the Martellos. They were named *Palmerston forts* after Lord Palmerston, the don of Victorian foreign policy, who'd vigorously supported what was a hideously expensive (and in the end, unnecessary) piece of defence spending. The most arresting examples are three huge sea forts – man-made islands, in the middle of the Solent – two of which play up to their Bond villain lair appeal and operate as luxury hotels, awash with helicopters and champagne.

DISTRESS SIGNALS

THEN: FLAGS, CQD AND SOS

Before the invention of radio, you could only tell somebody you were in trouble if they could see you – if they had *line of sight*. As well as classic waving and shouting, you could also communicate your distress by hoisting your ensign upside down or by flying a *wheft* (a flag with a knot tied in the middle).

With the arrival of radio, matters improved. The company set up by radio pioneer Guglielmo Marconi to capitalise on his invention of 'telegraphy without wires' created a series of standards, known as *General Orders*, to make sure ships could communicate as seamlessly as possible. In 1904, the first distress code was formalised.

THE MARCONI INTERNATIONAL MARINE
COMMUNICATION COMPANY, LIMITED. CIRCULAR NO. 57
It has been brought to our notice that the call 'C.Q.' (All Stations), while being satisfactory for general purposes, does not sufficiently express the urgency required in a signal of distress.

Therefore, on and after the 1st February, 1904, the call to be given by ships in distress or in any way requiring assistance shall be 'C.Q.D.'

This signal must on no account be used except by order of the Captain of the ship in distress, or other vessels or stations retransmitting the signal on account of the ship in distress.

All stations must recognise the urgency of this call and make every effort to establish satisfactory communication with the least possible delay.

Any mis-use of the call will result in the instant dismissal
of the person improperly employing it.

THE MARCONI INTERNATIONAL MARINE

COMMUNICATION COMPANY, LIMITED,

18, Finch Lane,

London, E.C.,

7th January, 1904.

Be assured that CQD is *not* an acronym of Come Quick
Danger. It derives instead from an old *all stations* signal,
which in turn derives from the French word *securité*. (Say
the first two syllables in a French accent and you'll see why.)
The D was added to signal *distress*.

CQD's life as a distress signal was short.* Two years later
the International Radiotelegraphic Convention agreed to
adopt an existing German signal:

Ships in distress shall use the following signal:

••• ‒ ‒ ‒ •••

repeated at brief intervals.

In Morse code, S is the letter equivalent of *dot-dot-dot*,
and O of *dash-dash-dash*, but (we're sorry to tell you) SOS
wasn't chosen because it spells out Save Our Souls or anything else, but purely because it was easy to recognise and
remember.**

....

* It did have something of a swansong in 1912 when the *Titanic* broadcast
both an old-fashioned CQD and a new-fangled SOS as it was sinking.
** It also works very well as a visual signal. Three rocks, three logs, three rocks,
if you're stranded on a desert island. Three pistachio shells, three matchsticks,
three pistachio shells, if you're stranded at a party.

NOW: MOBILE PHONES VS VHF

If you run into trouble, you can obviously take out your mobile phone, dial 999 and ask for the coastguard. That might do the trick, so long as a) you have signal and b) your phone hasn't got wet. But a phone call has one very significant drawback: other people nearby won't know you're in trouble.

Instead, you should put out a call on a VHF (*very high frequency*, a line-of-sight, short-range radio that works both ship-to-ship and ship-to-shore). This will alert both the coastguard *and* other boats, which might be able to get to you faster than a lifeboat, or at least stand by and offer reassurance. If you're heading out to sea, whether to sail, fish or kayak, take a VHF with you. They're – literally – lifesavers.

ISSUING A DISTRESS SIGNAL: CHANNEL 16

If you have a basic handheld VHF, you can use it to issue a *mayday call* (this *is* derived from the French *m'aidez*/help me) over *channel 16*. The coastguard will be listening 24/7, and other vessels are supposed to monitor it as well. Make sure your radio is on and the power is turned up to high. Press the transmission button and say the following:

Mayday, Mayday, Mayday
This is [say name of vessel three times]
Call sign [e.g. Mike Charlie Charlie Hotel 2]
MMSI [e.g. 924677123]*
Mayday
This is [repeat name of vessel, call sign and MMSI once]
My position is [ideally give latitude and longitude, failing
....

* Don't panic if you can't momentarily lay your hands on your call sign or MMSI (Maritime Mobile Service Identity). These will have been issued with your radio licence, and you should keep them with your radio, but the coastguard won't ignore you if you can't find them.

that a bearing and distance (e.g. three miles off Bolt Head on a bearing of 160°), failing that a rough idea of where you think you are (e.g. I'm being swept out to sea past Burgh Island)]
We [give nature of distress, e.g. taking on water, man overboard, sinking, etc.]
We have [e.g. 4] persons on board
[Then give any other useful information, including type of vessel, hull colour, injuries, etc.]
Over

Take your finger off the transmission button and hopefully, in no time at all, you'll hear the coastguard answering. Help is on its way.

ISSUING A DISTRESS SIGNAL: DSC
Nowadays, there's a more sophisticated distress system called DSC (*digital selective calling*), which you'll find on newer boat radios and more expensive handheld VHFs. Any other radio that picks up your DSC distress call will sound a (hopefully loud and annoying) alarm until the operator acknowledges it. Your call will include your position (if it's GPS-enabled) and your MMSI. Here's what you do:

1. Open the cover of the red distress button, which may be tucked into the side of a handheld VHF.
2. Press the red distress button.
3. This will bring up a preview of the distress message you're about to send, including the option to be more precise about the nature of your troubles. If you (understandably) can't think straight, you can leave the message in its default *undesignated distress* mode.
4. Press and hold the button for three to five seconds to

send it. Your radio will make it obvious if you've been successful.

5. Wait for the signal to be acknowledged. Again, your radio will make it obvious. If nothing happens after fifteen seconds, try again.

6. Whether it's acknowledged or not, issue a standard voice mayday call over channel 16, as above.

ISSUING A DISTRESS SIGNAL: EPIRB

An EPIRB (*emergency position-indicating radio beacon*) is a vital piece of kit if you're bound further offshore. Once triggered, your distress call is picked up by satellites, alerting international rescue services to come and find you, no matter where you are. Sensibly, EPIRBs can also activate automatically on immersion or impact.

WHAT COUNTS AS DISTRESS?

The coastguard is constantly having to deal with rookie errors: I didn't put the *bung* in, I left my oars in the car, I ran out of fuel, I ignored the weather forecast, and so on. But of course, however foolish you've been, to err is human, and the coastguard will organise help.

Technically, to put out a distress call, you, your crew, or your boat should be in *grave and immediate danger*, which is a pretty high bar, but as long as you're genuinely worried about your safety, nobody's going to tell you off for issuing a mayday prematurely.

If you're worried, but not *we're all going to die* worried, you do have a more low-key option.

THE PAN-PAN CALL

A *pan-pan call* (also French: *panne* = breakdown) is a step down from a mayday, perfect for when you're in trouble, but not in danger. Perhaps your engine has failed and you're approaching a busy harbour under sail and you need other boats to understand what you're up to. It has the same format as a mayday call, but you substitute pan-pan for mayday. Obviously, you don't need to go pressing your red DSC button.

HOW ELSE TO ISSUE A DISTRESS SIGNAL?

If your radio's bust, there are several other options, mostly involving *making a spectacle of yourself*.

Flares: Rocket flares, smoke flares and handheld candle flares. Useful both as a distress signal and to make it easier for rescue services to find you in bad weather. Use with care.

Noise: Sound your foghorn continuously. Fire a gun (if you have one; you might have something like a starting pistol) at one-minute intervals.

Flags: Hoist a square flag (ideally plain and dark) above a ball. Fly signalling flags C (yes) and N (no) at the same time.

Dye in the water: Very helpful (again, if you have it) if your boat's small and you want to make it easier for rescuers to find you.

CROSSING THE BAR

by Alfred, Lord Tennyson

A bar is a shoal at a river mouth, rough and dangerous to cross, leading *in* to the shelter of an estuary or *out* to the unknowable beauty of the sea. As the great folklorist James

Frazer tells us, the flood tide promises exuberance, prosperity and life, while the ebb presages failure, weakness and death.

We all end as fallen warriors, floating out to sea, whether or not we believe a wise, bearded pilot awaits us. We can all dream of being reborn on the flood.

Sunset and evening star,
    And one clear call for me!
And may there be no moaning of the bar,
    When I put out to sea,

But such a tide as moving seems asleep,
    Too full for sound and foam,
When that which drew from out the boundless deep
    Turns again home.

Twilight and evening bell,
    And after that the dark!
And may there be no sadness of farewell,
    When I embark;

For tho' from out our bourne of Time and Place
    The flood may bear me far,
I hope to see my Pilot face to face
    When I have crost the bar.

ST KILDA

Since prehistoric times, a community had existed, thrived even, on St Kilda, one of the remotest places in the British Isles. But in August 1930 the tiny archipelago's remaining thirty-six inhabitants were evacuated, at their own request, to the Scottish mainland. Hard winters, infectious disease, infant mortality, all had taken their toll; but ultimately it was increasing contact with – and reliance on – the outside world that made the islanders' old way of life impossible.

St Kilda (there is no saint; *Kilda* is probably a corruption of an old Norse or Gaelic word with *St* tacked on) lies more than 100 miles from mainland Scotland, and more than 40 miles from the Outer Hebrides. Before steamships that meant a very long day's sail with a following wind, or (more likely) a grim twenty-four hours close-hauled against a prevailing southwesterly. Today, it's a five-hour round trip in a motorboat, though still not a crossing you'd attempt in unsettled weather.

But it's worth it: thanks to its volcanic origins, St Kilda is every bit as dramatic as it is remote. 'Had it been a land of demons,' reported one yachting visitor, 'it could not have appeared more dreadful.'

That may sound fanciful, but the dark cliffs (the UK's tallest) of the main island, Hirta, rising sheer out of the sea, shrouded as often as not in mist, are an unforgettable sight. At the southeast corner of the island, the heights slope down almost hospitably to the sea, offering a fair-weather anchorage. This bay was where the islanders made their home, described here by Màrtainn MacGilleMhàrtainn (anglicised to Martin Martin) in the late seventeenth century:

> The inhabitants live together in a little village, which carries all the signs of an extreme poverty; the houses are of a low form, having all the doors to the northeast ... on purpose to secure them from the shocks of the tempest of the southwest winds ... This little village is seated in a valley surrounded with four mountains, which serve as so many ramparts of defence, and are amphitheatres, from whence a fair prospect of the ocean and isles is to be seen in a fair day.

The St Kildans' lives never were going to be luxurious, but the thousands upon thousands of seabirds (fulmars, gannets, puffins) which nested on the sea-cliffs furnished them with both meat and eggs, so long as there were men bold enough to scale the rocks to gather them. They used three enormous ropes, 24 fathoms long, made out of salted cow hide twisted round hemp, to make sure the rope didn't chafe on the rocks. Wrote MacGilleMhàrtainn:

> The inhabitants, I must tell you, run no small danger in the quest of the fowls and eggs, insomuch that I fear it would be thought an hyperbole to relate the inaccessibleness, steepness, and height, of those formidable rocks which they venture to climb.

The birds could be eaten fresh or salted down for winter. Bird fat could be used in lamps. Bird bones made good fertiliser for the scanty crops the islanders grew. Bird entrails made good bait, although fishing in the open Atlantic was less popular than chancing the cliffs.

But we shouldn't assume a hard life was necessarily miserable (although the surviving Victorian photographs do tend to show rows of stern faces). To MacGilleMhàrtainn, the islanders had 'a genius for poetry', were 'great admirers of musick' and liked to 'dance mightily'. They had good memories and were 'resolute in their undertakings, chaste and honest'. They were Christian, but he says given neither to 'enthusiasm' nor 'popery'. He makes it sound like a rocky Garden of Eden.

One flip-side of island life was a rate of infant mortality that was shockingly high even by the standards of the time. Reverend Kenneth Macaulay, a minister from Ardnamurchan, wrote in his 1764 history of the island:

> The St Kilda infants are peculiarly subject to an extraordinary kind of sickness; on the fourth, fifth or sixth night after their birth, many of them give up suckling; on the seventh day their gums are so clenched together that it is impossible to get anything down their throats; soon after this symptom appears, they are seized with convulsive fits, and after struggling against excessive torments, till their little strength is exhausted, die generally on the eighth day. I have seen two of them expire after such agonies.

More complete records from the nineteenth century show that up to two-thirds of babies died before they were a month old, many on the fateful eighth day after birth. Contemporaries suggested the deaths were the result of poor food, consanguinity or peat smoke, but we now understand that neo-natal tetanus was the culprit. Initially, the island practice of smearing the stump of the umbilical cord with fulmar oil was thought to be at fault, but in fact there were numerous other ways the bacteria responsible could have infected the newborns.

These deaths were the islanders' most acute tragedy, but the insidious creep of tourism was harmful in its own way. By the Victorian era, St Kilda no longer felt quite so remote. Yachts, their owners seeking a personal dose of the sublime, started to visit, and where smart yachts went, steamships followed.

Norman Heathcote, a painter and photographer who visited the island at the end of the nineteenth century, liked it very much: 'I believe many people would call it ugly, but personally I like desolation.' He had, however, great reservations about the effect of visitors on the St Kildans (all the time trusting himself to be on the right side of the snob-line dividing cultured traveller from yobbish grockle).*

> The advent of steamers and tourists have shown them the value of money and taught them to be discontented with their lot, and the result is that several cases of dishonesty have occurred in recent times ... I do not wonder that they dislike foreigners, so many of the tourists treat them as if they were wild animals at the Zoo. They throw sweets to them, openly mock at them, and I have seen them standing at the church door during service, laughing and talking and staring in as if at an entertainment got up for their amusement.

The islanders, necessarily, pandered to the tourists, offering them souvenirs such as eggshells or mittens knitted by the women. In return, they started to enjoy the fruits of mainland life, and who could blame them for wanting a few treats? Inevitably, though, their self-reliance was eroded,

....

* In best traveller tradition he is even brave when trying local food: 'I must say that we were agreeably surprised. We had expected something nasty, but it was not nasty. It was oleaginous, but distinctly tasty.'

and come the First World War,* a naval base on Hirta gave the young men another chance to learn about what they were missing in the outside world. Emigration escalated, until in 1930, the end came.

OFFSHORE EXPLOITS

There is a rich back catalogue of deep-sea adventure yarns. Here are five stand-outs – the very sternest stuff – from a crowded field.

WILLIAM BLIGH

When: 1789
Where: from Tonga to Indonesia
Distance: 3,600 miles
Duration: 47 days
Key sustenance: coconut, scraps of cured pork and stale bread
Story: Lieutenant Bligh (the *Bounty* was too small for its commander to be called a captain) had been charged with shipping breadfruit samples from Tahiti to the Caribbean under the auspices of the Royal Society (which wanted cheap food for enslaved Africans working on British plantations). The crew, led by master's mate Fletcher Christian, mutinied. Bligh (*not* the tyrant we meet in Hollywood movies) and eighteen men loyal to him were loaded into the *Bounty*'s 23-foot launch. They steered first for a nearby

....

* In May 1918 a German sub surfaced and – after issuing a warning – shelled the wireless station. Casualties: one lamb.

Tongan island, but after one of their number was killed by islanders, Bligh decided it was safest to head for a Dutch settlement on Timor, and so began their long voyage west. (Some mutineers remained on Tahiti; others settled on Pitcairn Island, where their descendants – they abducted eleven Tahitian women – continue to live to this day.)

A triumph because: The open launch was hopelessly over-laden, its gunwales only a few inches above the water. Bligh had no charts and no way of establishing longitude. The latter part of the journey – island-hopping through the Great Barrier Reef – would have been especially challeng-ing. Everyone survived.

Read on: *Captain Bligh's Portable Nightmare* by John Toohey

ERNEST SHACKLETON

When: 1916
Where: from Elephant Island (500 miles south of Cape Horn) to South Georgia (750 miles east-southeast of the Falklands.
Distance: 800 miles
Duration: 16 days
Key sustenance: *hoosh* (a thick stew made of pemmican, ground biscuits and water)
Story: Polar explorer Ernest Shackleton was trying to cross Antarctica for the first time, but his ship, the *Endurance*, became trapped in pack ice and sank. He and his twenty-seven-strong crew stowed what provisions they could in the ship's lifeboats, and part-paddled, part-carried them to Elephant Island, one of the South Shetland Islands, where the crew hunkered down under two up-turned boats to sit out the winter. Meanwhile, Shackleton and five others set sail for South Georgia where a whaling station was their one shot at salvation.

A triumph because: The deep Southern Ocean is no place for a ship in winter, let alone for the *James Caird*, a 23-foot open boat. Navigation was all but impossible because extreme weather – non-stop gales and storms – made sun sightings extremely rare. Shackleton was forced to land on the southern, uninhabited, side of the island and cross a snowbound mountain range to reach help. The entire crew of the *Endurance* was saved.

Read on: *Shackleton's Boat Journey* by Frank Arthur Worsley

ROBIN KNOX-JOHNSTON
When: 1968–69
Distance: 20,000+ miles
Duration: 312 days
Key sustenance: Anything in a tin
Story: Other sailors had pioneered single-handed voyages around the world. Nova Scotian-born Joshua Slocum was the first man make it round alone, taking a good three years in the 1890s. Francis Chichester, in 1966–67, first completed the more testing *clipper route* (i.e. that followed by the *Cutty Sark* and other tea clippers in their heyday: down round the Cape of Good Hope, past Australia and back via Cape Horn, riding the powerful westerlies that blow round the Southern Ocean).

The *Sunday Times* decided to cash in on public interest in gung-ho tales of high drama in the Roaring Forties, and sponsored a race, offering a trophy to the first single-hander to make it round the world *non-stop*. Robin Knox-Johnston, in the 32-foot wooden *Suhaili*, was one of nine men who started ...

A triumph because: ... he was the only one to finish.

The race took the life of one competitor: Donald Crowhurst – we assume – committed suicide after setting off in an unsuitable boat, faking his position for weeks, before going slowly mad sailing aimlessly round the Atlantic.

Bernard Moitessier, the superbly Gallic mystic-cum-sailor, could have finished *if* he'd wanted, but to him the race represented everything wrong with our commercial, fame-hungry culture. After rounding Cape Horn, he didn't turn left to return to Europe, but opted for a longer spell communing with the Southern Ocean, finishing in Tahiti after one-and-a-half circumnavigations.

Read on: *Sailing Alone Around the World* by Joshua Slocum, *A World of My Own* by Robin Knox-Johnston, *The Long Way* by Bernard Moitessier and *The Strange Last Voyage of Donald Crowhurst* by Nicholas Tomalin and Ron Hall

DOUGAL ROBERTSON AND FAMILY

When: 1972
Distance: 750 miles
Duration: 38 days
Key sustenance: Raw turtle flesh and blood
Story: Dougal Robertson, his wife, three children and a young Welshman who joined them as crew, were about 200 miles west of the Galapagos Islands when killer whales attacked and sank their 43-foot schooner, the *Lucette*. They abandoned ship for the *Lucette*'s life raft, taking a 9-foot fibreglass tender in tow. They survived for more than a month at sea before being picked up by a Japanese fishing boat.

A triumph because: Where to begin? The whole crew – Dougal in particular – showed extraordinary resourcefulness. They improvised sails and sea anchors to drag them towards the Pacific fishing lanes. They fashioned spears and hooks, catching turtles and flying fish. Some fish they ate raw, some they dried. They sucked moisture from fish bones and drank turtle blood. They weathered storms and shark attacks. Worst of all, after seventeen days they had to abandon the life raft and crowd into the tiny dinghy. By the time they were rescued, however, they'd become so adept at harvesting and husbanding food and water that they were already regaining their strength and planning to row towards the Central American coast.

Read on: *Survive the Savage Sea* by Dougal Robertson. For a slightly less varnished account read his son Douglas's account: *Last Voyage of the Lucette*.

ELLEN MACARTHUR

When: 2000–01

Distance: 24,000 miles

Duration: 94 days

Key sustenance: Champagne rounding Cape Horn

Story: The Vendeé Globe has a pretty good claim to be the toughest sporting event in the word. A single-handed, non-stop, round-the-world yacht race, it follows the same route as the Golden Globe, with competitors racing flat out in 60-foot thoroughbreds called Open 60s. The boats are infamously skittish and fragile, but that doesn't stop the men and women who race them pushing themselves to their utter limit, venturing deep into the Southern Ocean to find the strongest winds, rarely sleeping for more than twenty minutes at a stretch. The statistics tell their own story: around half of the competitors do not finish, and three people have lost their lives trying.

A triumph because: MacArthur won everything but the race. Although she'd traded the lead with the eventual winner a number of times on the final leg, her yacht *Kingfisher* hit a submerged container and she had to slow down to make repairs.

Why then did 200,000 people brave the February cold to celebrate her return? It was partly her nationality: single-handed racing had been heavily dominated by the French. It was partly her age: at twenty-four she was the youngest competitor ever to finish. It was partly her sex: only one woman before her had completed the race. Most important of all, though, was her character: she was tough, down to earth, immensely likeable – and absolutely unafraid to show her vulnerability. Millions watched her video messages, rooting for her as the non-stop pressure reduced her to tears, cheering as she ordered herself to soldier on.

Since that race, MacArthur went on to break the world record for the fastest solo circumnavigation of the globe, before retiring from professional sailing to work as an environmental campaigner.

Read on: *Taking on the World* by Ellen MacArthur

SAILING TECHNOLOGY AND THE AMERICA'S CUP

Ocean racing is like standing under a cold shower tearing up £5 notes. *

People who've made a lot of money like expensive hobbies (Wagner, Bordeaux, Young British Artists). People who've made a lot of money also like *winning*. And nothing

....

* Attributed to former prime minister, Sir Edward Heath, a keen and successful ocean racer. When he said it, a £5 note bought you a hell of a lot more than it does today.

combines conspicuous consumption and crude competitiveness better than the America's Cup. It attracts the richest owners, the most radical design, and a mother lode of prestige.

It began in 1851 when the yacht *America* saw off fifteen boats belonging to the Royal Yacht Squadron in a race around the Isle of Wight. The story goes that as the *America* passed the Royal Yacht, Queen Victoria asked who was in second place. The reply came back: 'Your Majesty, there is no second.' The winners donated the trophy to the New York Yacht Club, and it has since become an international cup, where one challenger takes on one defender, with the glory accruing to the winning boat, the boat's yacht club and the yacht club's country.

Britain lost that first race. It lost its next sixteen challenges. For more than half a century it hasn't even won the right to challenge – although in 2021 it came closer than it has in years. If Britain ever challenges, it'll be a big deal. If it ever *wins* – well, it won't quite be 4–2 in 1966, but pretty close for anyone who knows their port from their starboard.

To win, you need a syndicate with vast amounts of cash: nobody's letting on quite how much competing in the America's Cup costs, but it could be in the region of $300 million. Not surprisingly, it has long been the province of mega-rich businessmen: tea magnates have challenged railroad plutocrats, chemicals tycoons have battled chemicals tycoons, Silicon Valleyites have rivalled biotech billionaires.

Each race only lasts about half an hour, so designers don't have to fret about finding space for food, bunks, storm sails or anything that might slow the boat down: it's round-the-cans dinghy-racing on an epic scale, and has showcased many of the biggest innovations in speed sailing.

BREAKING THE HULL BARRIER

Building super-fast yachts boils down to one key challenge: overcoming *hull speed*, a notional top speed that always used to be determined by a boat's length.

A regular boat, whether powered by oars, sail or steam, traditionally travelled *through* the sea, shoving water out of the way. All that shoving – correctly called *displacement* – created a *bow wave* at the front of the boat, with a trough behind the bow wave, and a *stern wave* at the back.

As this old-fashioned boat started to speed up (bigger muscles; bigger sails; bigger engines), the bow wave got bigger and longer, effectively creating a hill the boat had to climb. Diminishing returns kicked in. The more power you applied, the bigger the bow wave grew, and the harder it became to push your boat faster. Each increment of extra power won you an ever smaller increment of extra speed, until eventually your boat got 'stuck' at its maximum speed: its hull speed.

This figure is unusually easy to calculate. Take the square root of your boat's waterline length in feet, multiply it by 1.34, and you have your hull speed in knots. For example: take an 80-foot yacht:

the square root of 80 is 8.9
8.9 × 1.34 = 11.9
which means your dream boat wouldn't go much faster than 12 knots.

For much of nautical history this held true, but over the last 150 years designers have battled with boat physics until the idea of a top speed now seems almost quaint. Defying hull speed rests on two core techniques:

1. Make the hull so narrow it slices through the water without creating much of a bow wave. No bow wave means nothing for the boat to get stuck behind.
2. Convince the boat to *plane*, i.e. create a lifting force which pushes the boat out of the water, so it skims *on top* of the water, surfing its own bow wave.

Back to the America's Cup, where we can see how this theory has been deployed in practice.

If looks could keel: In 1983, the challenger *Australia II* won the America's Cup (by a margin of forty-one seconds) thanks to the innovation of a *winged keel*, which generated more lift and less drag. There *were* rules governing how long the keel could be, but nobody had said anything about its shape. Because this wasn't any old race, but the first time the United States had lost the cup in its 132-year history, what followed was the unedifying spectacle of the (extremely) sore losers wrangling in the courts of New York about whether the keel was fair. (It was.)

The righting stuff: To sail as fast as possible, you need to stay as flat as possible, counteracting the force of the wind on the sails that makes your boat want to heel over. A New Zealand merchant banker challenged for the America's Cup in 1988 with a boat that had huge fibreglass wings sprouting on either side. The *KZ1* (nicknamed *Big Boat* with characteristic Kiwi practicality) was crewed by an army of forty sailors who sat on the edge of its wings to hold it flat.

One is the loneliest number: *Big Boat*'s opponents, the San Diego Yacht Club, didn't have long to prepare a defence. They put on their thinking caps, scrutinised the rules, fortified themselves with the opinions of expensive lawyers – and built a *catamaran*. If you tried to build a yacht with a *single* narrow hull (to pierce the water efficiently, creating a minimal bow wave), it'd be as unstable as a pirate who's lost his peg-leg. Introduce a *second* hull, and you have a totally different proposition: a boat balanced on two dainty feet.

They also realised that nowhere in the rules did it say that sails had to be bendy, so they kitted *Stars & Stripes* out with a *wingsail*, which was solid like the wing of a plane, rather than flappy like a sail. Usually made out of carbon fibre (very strong, very light and very expensive), wingsails are far more efficient aerofoils than retro canvas. *Big Boat* had no chance.

Come fly with me: The America's Cup hit a new technological apogee in 2013 when *hydrofoils* were added to wingsail catamarans, to create a new class of speed monster, capable of hitting 40 knots when the wind was scarcely stronger than a force 4.

These hydrofoils, originally invented more than a century ago, work by attaching what's essentially a set of wings beneath the twin hulls of the boat. As the boat accelerates, the hydrofoils generate so much lift that both hulls soar clean into the air. With only the hydrofoils in the water, drag becomes negligible – hence the extraordinary speeds.

For the latest edition of the cup, racing's top brass made the switch back to monohulls – only this time with giant hydrofoils poking out of each side of the boat to stave off capsize. They scream through the water at 50+ knots, perched on their leeward foil like giant break-dancing pond-skaters – and because they always appear to be milliseconds away from disaster, sailing is finally gripping to watch.

THE 1979 FASTNET RACE

The Fastnet is a supreme challenge to ocean-racing yachtsmen in British waters. In the 1979 race, the sea showed that it can be a deadly enemy and that those who go to sea for pleasure must do so in the full knowledge that they may encounter dangers of the highest order.*

The Fastnet Race is the world's most famous offshore team race: *the* one to win. Even securing a place is competitive, with spots disappearing minutes after registration opens. Organised by the Royal Ocean Racing Club (RORC), it has taken place biennially for nearly a century.

The race starts at Cowes, exiting the Solent through the Needles and tracking west down the Channel, before turning right at Land's End. From there, the yachts cross the Celtic Sea and round the Fastnet Rock, four miles off the southwest coast of Ireland. On their way back, they leave the Isles of Scilly to port and race towards Plymouth after 605 miles at sea. It's a serious undertaking at the best of times.

When the race began on Saturday 11 August 1979, there was no hint of what might be in store. Even at lunchtime on Sunday 12, the forecast was still pretty benign: southwesterly 4 or 6, increasing 6 or 7 for a time, veering westerly later. No big deal for experienced racers.

But the next day a depression crossing the Atlantic deepened dramatically, sending a sudden summer storm tearing through the fleet, killing fifteen people, and leaving

....

* The conclusion of the 1979 Fastnet Race Inquiry, carried out for the Royal Yachting Association and the Royal Ocean Racing Club.

many hardened sailors shocked and reeling. Out of the 303 boats that started, only 86 crossed the finish line. Twenty-four were abandoned.

At 1606 on Monday 13 the BBC first broadcast a force 8 gale warning. Definitely time to shorten sail; inconceivable to think about abandoning the race. The next forecast at 1750 promised more of the same. Forty minutes later, and again at 1906, the BBC did broadcast a more severe warning: force 9. Enough, perhaps, to make a less experienced skipper blench.

Most yachts, however, didn't hear it. They were out of range of VHF reports from coastal stations, nor did skippers keep Radio 4 switched on between scheduled shipping bulletins, for fear of draining their boats' batteries.

Shortly after midnight on Tuesday 14, the men and women huddled next to their radios would have heard the bad news: southwest veering westerly 7 to severe gale 9, locally storm 10 in Fastnet. But by then, it wasn't really news. The storm had already hit.

It's important not to blame the weather forecasters. With satellite technology still in its infancy, the only way they could predict wind strength was to draw atmospheric pressure charts based on ad hoc reports from ships further out in the Atlantic. As the race inquiry said:

> There is at present no method of predicting with any certainty when a depression will deepen rapidly in the Western Approaches to the British Isles; so gales which arrive with little warning are a feature of our weather, which those who sail must expect to encounter from time to time.

The reality, of course, was less clinical. Nick Ward, in his harrowing account of the race, *Left for Dead*, says that when he took the helm that night, he felt excitement – for the briefest moment.

> But this feeling swiftly turned to one of horror, then fear.
> I saw and felt the power and magnitude of these black,
> storm-ridden seas with their white-capped peaks ... Nobody
> could have prepared us for this. There were no rules, no
> boundaries to this fight, for a fight it was now – we were
> fighting for our lives.

To experience storm force winds for yourself, you could stick your head out of a car window when you're next driving down a motorway.* But there's no way to simulate the insanity of those sorts of seas.

'Many very experienced competitors stated that the wind strength was not unusual but the sea conditions were the most dangerous they had ever experienced ... Most of the damage done to the fleet appears to have been caused by waves rather than wind,' said the report.

Research by the Institute of Oceanographic Sciences estimated that the *significant wave height* (the mean height, trough to crest, of the highest third of the waves) during the storm would have reached 10–14 metres, which meant that the very biggest waves could be twice as high, with 'steep or near-vertical-sided profiles'.

What can a small boat do? Traditionally, there are three options for riding out bad weather.

1. *Heave-to*: Heave the jib to the windward side. The jib and mainsail act against each other, stalling the boat.

....

* Obviously don't actually do this.

This should allow the crew some respite, but it can be hard to maintain, nor does it allow a yacht to avoid bigger waves.

2. *Lie ahull*: Drop the sails and lash the tiller to leeward (or the wheel to windward), so the boat tries to point to windward, but never rounds up fully because of the counter-force of wind and waves. This can leave the yacht very vulnerable to breaking seas, especially when the waves are coming from two directions following a shift in wind direction, as was the case during the race.

3a. *Run off under storm sails or bare poles*: Set a storm jib and trysail, or nothing at all, and steer away from the breaking seas. Since the yacht is moving *through* the water, it still has steerage way, i.e. you have a modicum of control over where you want to go. You do, however, need a very skilled person on the helm, and the boat can *pitch-pole* (somersault) or *broach* (surf down a wave, round up, capsize) if it's going too fast.

3b. As above, but you also *stream ropes astern* (or a specialist device called a *drogue*) to reduce speed. Not a bad idea if you're careering out of control or the wind is blowing you towards a lee shore.

Different boats tried different options or some variety of all three. Some felt they coped pretty well: plaudits especially to the crew of a tiny Contessa 32 who said they 'kept sailing to windward, without particular problems'. Others reckoned there were waves that would have capsized them no matter what they did: 'Ran directly before waves successfully for several hours, but then rolled over when caught by a cross sea which appeared from nowhere.'

Here is Nick Ward again, describing the first time (of many) his boat was overwhelmed by the sea.

The wave roared under us and lifted *Grimalkin's* stern up. It wrenched the tiller from our hands and rendered the rudder useless. *Grimalkin* was out of control – the wave's mass completely overtook us. I felt the straps of my harness tighten, and a huge gaping pit seemed to open in my stomach. As we began to tip over to a 45-degree angle, my harness tether jarred under pressure at its fullest extent. My attempts to cling to something, anything failed. I was sucked from my seat and thrown through the air ... While in the air I caught sight of the foredeck and the mast toppling into the sea and staying there. I was both spectator and participant. Yes, this was it, a knockdown. Gravity then took over and I was forced downwards at speed.

Grimalkin was far from the only boat struggling through that night, and like many others, its crew hoped that dawn would bring respite, hope – something. But the light of day did nothing but reveal the full extent of what they faced.

'A grey and threatening dawn lit up the absolute fury of a full-blown storm at sea,' recalled journalist Tony Paterson, thirty years after he crewed aboard the 38-foot yacht, *Xara*. 'From the cockpit of the yacht, the spectacle was almost unbelievable, like something out of a film. It was awesome, frightening and strangely sublime. The biggest thing on earth was wild and angry. The waves towered above us, the size of blocks of flats, streaked with hundred-yard slashes of white spume and topped by boiling masses of breaking foam.'

At the time, people asked why on earth the organisers didn't call off the race. But even if they had, most of the boats wouldn't have known. Offshore communications were still basic in the 1970s, with only two-thirds of the boats carrying VHF radios, which would have had a very limited range.

John Rousmaniere, author of the compelling account *Fastnet, Force 10: The Deadliest Storm in the History of Modern Sailing*, who himself took part in the race, reckons that advance warning of the weather wouldn't have deterred many people.

> Of the two dozen or so other boats in the Fastnet fleet that lost men overboard, suffered incapacitating damage, or were abandoned by their crews, perhaps one or two – but no more – might have run for shelter if the 'Fastnet, force 10' warning had been made during the BBC Radio 4 shipping bulletin early on Monday morning. The challenge of sailing through rough weather is indisputably one of the attractions of ocean racing.

His words capture the essence of ocean sailing: the appeal of freedom and self-reliance, the desire to test yourself to your limits. Sometimes, though, the risks aren't worth it.

Fifteen people died. Six were washed overboard, often when harnesses failed. Two men were trapped underwater after their yacht turned upside down. Four were lost when life rafts capsized or broke up. Three drowned while trying to board a pilot cutter that was trying to save them. That was the hardest lesson learnt. So long as a boat is afloat, don't leave it: the vast majority of abandoned boats were later found drifting safely.

Practical changes did follow the disaster: more robust steering gear, watertight companionways, better harnesses, hacksaws to cut away rigging, storm sails that were easy to access. And, of course, yachts today have satellite phones, EPIRBs and weather forecasts on demand. But ultimately, all the technology in the world cannot save you when truly bad weather hits. As the report concluded:

The common link between all fifteen deaths was the violence of the sea, an unremitting danger faced by all who sail.

BRUTUS OF TROY

Today we often read about, or perhaps even witness, people trying to cross the Channel to Britain, fleeing the impacts of war, poverty and global heating. How we as a nation treat these men, women and children will become a defining part of this century. As we seek the right response, we could remember that Brutus,* the mythological founder of Britain, was himself descended from refugees of the great conflict of ancient times: the Trojan War.

According to the twelfth-century historian, Geoffrey of Monmouth, Brutus's great-grandfather, Aeneas, escaped the sack of Troy, carrying his father on his back, his son clinging to his hand, realising only when he reached safety beyond the city walls, that he'd lost his wife Creusa in the chaos. Grief-stricken, he raced back into the fire and slaughter. There he met her ghost, who begged him to seek a new life in the west.

Aeneas travelled the Mediterranean, a straighter, more upright Odysseus, abandoning his great love, Queen Dido, in Carthage, in order to found the city that was to become Rome.

Two generations later, the young Brutus killed his father, Aeneas's grandson, by accident, and was exiled. After many

....

* Not the Brutus of 'Et tu, Brute?' fame.

adventures, he begged the goddess Diana to tell him where he could live in safety, to which she replied, in a dream:

> Brutus, beyond the setting sun, past the realms of Gaul, there lies an island in the sea, once occupied by giants. Now it is empty and ready for your folk. Down the years this will prove an abode suited to you and to your people; and for your descendants it will be a second Troy.

That island is Britain.

DOVER BEACH

by Matthew Arnold

The sea is calm tonight.
The tide is full, the moon lies fair
Upon the straits; on the French coast the light
Gleams and is gone; the cliffs of England stand,
Glimmering and vast, out in the tranquil bay.
Come to the window, sweet is the night-air!
Only, from the long line of spray
Where the sea meets the moon-blanched land,
Listen! you hear the grating roar
Of pebbles which the waves draw back, and fling,
At their return, up the high strand,
Begin, and cease, and then again begin,
With tremulous cadence slow, and bring
The eternal note of sadness in.

Sophocles long ago
Heard it on the Ægean, and it brought
Into his mind the turbid ebb and flow
Of human misery; we
Find also in the sound a thought,
Hearing it by this distant northern sea.

The Sea of Faith
Was once, too, at the full, and round earth's shore
Lay like the folds of a bright girdle furled.
But now I only hear
Its melancholy, long, withdrawing roar,

Retreating, to the breath
Of the night-wind, down the vast edges drear
And naked shingles of the world.

Ah, love, let us be true
To one another! for the world, which seems
To lie before us like a land of dreams,
So various, so beautiful, so new,
Hath really neither joy, nor love, nor light,
Nor certitude, nor peace, nor help for pain;
And we are here as on a darkling plain
Swept with confused alarms of struggle and flight,
Where ignorant armies clash by night.

ACKNOWLEDGEMENTS

First of all, we'd like to thank the whole team at Profile Books, especially our sterling editor Cecily Gayford for taking a chance on us. We have enjoyed her unerring eye every bit as much as her deft and gracious manner. We are also indebted to Penny Daniel for her herculean efforts in turning a rag-bag of chapters into this glorious whole, to James Nunn and Lucy Devenish for their lovely illustrations, and to James Alexander for the beautiful page design.

And business or pleasure, there's nobody better to have in your corner than our agent, Victoria Hobbs. Thank you, Victoria, we count ourselves extraordinarily lucky.

Next, our mother and father – Jane and Jonny. From the moment *Sea Fever* was underway, they rolled up their sleeves, suggested sections, walked dogs, checked facts, babysat grandchildren and, crucially, stopped us writing anything *un-seamanlike*. (Blame us though, not them, if we've gone awry.) In fact, in writing *Sea Fever*, we've really been trying to distil a little of the vast ocean of knowledge with which they've been indoctrinating us since we were old enough to get up at 5 a.m. to fish the autumn spring tides. This book celebrates the terrific – and the terrifying – times we've spent at sea together.

Chris has some additional thanks of his own:

The first goes to Mary. While writing *Sea Fever*, Mary and I got divorced. Divorce is never fun, but Mary has been absolutely amazing at minimising the misery, and she is already a great partner in this next stage of our lives. Not only that, but she was generous enough to help me hit my deadlines when we both had plenty of other things on our minds.

The second goes to Meg. As the writer of the family, she's inevitably done much of the heavy lifting, breathing life into my technical prose and stopping me wandering off too far into the weeds. But more importantly, she took care of me when I needed taking care of, like the big sister that she is.

To which, Meg can only reply:

Well done Chris a) for coming up with the idea to write this book in the first place and b) for resolutely refusing to give up until I understood how tides actually work. It's been a joy – a beam reach under sunny skies, you could say, compared with the windward thrash of fiction.

And, Rupert. You keep me ship-shape. Sorry we cut the chapter about outboard engines. That one was for you.